Now or Neverland

Marie-Louise von Franz, Honorary Patron

**Studies in Jungian Psychology
by Jungian Analysts**

Daryl Sharp, General Editor

Now or Neverland
Peter Pan and the
Myth of Eternal Youth

A Psychological Perspective on a Cultural Icon

ANN YEOMAN

For Fraser and John

Canadian Cataloguing in Publication Data

Yeoman, Ann
    Now or neverland: Peter Pan and the myth of eternal youth

(Studies in Jungian psychology by Jungian analysts; 82)

Includes bibliographical references and index.

ISBN 978-0-919123-83-0

1. Barrie, J.M. (James Matthew), 1860-1937. Peter Pan.
2. Psychoanalysis and literature.
3. Mythology—Psychological aspects.
I. Title. II. Series.

PR4074.P43Y46 1999   823'.912   C98-932156-8

INNER CITY BOOKS
Box 1271, Station Q, Toronto, ON M4T 2P4, Canada
Telephone (416) 927-0355 / Fax (416) 924-1814
Web site: www.inforamp.net/~icb / E-mail: icb@inforamp.net

Honorary Patron: Marie-Louise von Franz.
Publisher and General Editor: Daryl Sharp.
Senior Editor: Victoria Cowan.

INNER CITY BOOKS was founded in 1980 to promote the
understanding and practical application of the work of C.G. Jung.

Cover: "Tinker Bell and Peter Pan," by P. Martins, s.o.f.a., © 1998.

Index by Victoria Cowan.

Printed and bound in Canada by Thistle Printing Limited

CONTENTS

Acknowledgments and Credits 6

Foreword by Marion Woodman 7

Introduction 11

1 **The Eternal Boy: From Divine Image to Pathology** 15

2 **Peter Pan's Mythological Ancestry and Types of the Puer Aeternus** 31
   Some Literary Uses of Myth 31
   Hermes/Mercury/Mercurius 36
   Pan 40
   Dionysus, Christ 46
   Icarus, Phaeton, Prometheus, Lucifer 52
   Attis, Actaeon, Narcissus, Hyacinth, Adonis 58
   Simon Peter: A Speculative Fantasy 62

3 **J.M. Barrie and the Accidental Art of Mythmaking** 69

4 ***Peter Pan,* the Novel: Twentieth-Century Image of the Eternal Boy** 81
   Some Place Else: Structures of Fantasy and Fairy Tale 81
   The Darlings: Stocks, Shares and Tidy Drawers 88
   Neverland: Where We Beach Our Coracles on Magic Shores 102
   Peter Pan and Captain Hook: "Hook or Me This time" 119
   Beyond Mother and Father: Peter Pan, Puer, Phenomenon of Spirit 144

5 **Peter Pan: Past and Present, at Home and Abroad** 157

Bibliography 180

Index 185

See final page for descriptions of other Inner City Books

Acknowledgments

Special thanks to Ian Baker, John Hill and Ursula Ulmer for their support and critical reading of my work. My appreciation and thanks to Marion Woodman for her encouragement and generous Foreword. Thanks also to Tuula Haukioja, Brian Mayo and Norma Rowen for their careful readings and helpful suggestions.

Credits

All due effort has been made to obtain permission from copyright holders for the illustrations used in this book. The author and Inner City Books are grateful for permissions granted. See the bibliography for publication details of books cited.

Pages 10, 21, 27, 71, 159, 166. From Andrew Birkin, *J.M. Barrie & the Lost Boys.*

Page 37. From *New Larousse Encyclopedia of Mythology.*

Page 41. Courtesy Vicki Cowan.

Page 47. From Joseph Campbell, *The Mythic Image.*

Page 55. Musées Royaux des Beaux-Arts, Brussels.

Pages 68, 79, 155, 179. Courtesy P. Martins, s.o.f.a.

Pages 90, 134. From J.M. Barrie, *Peter Pan and Wendy.*

Pages 100, 146. From Susan Hudson, *The Eternal Peter Pan: The Wisdom of J.M. Barrie.*

Page 105. From Timothy R. Roberts, *Myths of the World: The Celts in Myth and Legend.*

Page 113. From Gerhard Adler, *Studies in Analytical Psychology.*

Pages 162. From Bram Dijkstra, *Idols of Perversity: Fantasies of Feminine Evil in Fin-de-Siècle Culture.*

Foreword

Does fantasy lead to escape, or to the embracing of a new perspective? In other words, does it support psychic growth or impede it? That distinction is often complicated by paradox, but it helps to ask ourselves, "Is concentrating on this fantasy or daydream opening my creative possibilities, or is it sapping my ego strength in the real world?" As Ann Yeoman points out:

> Story ideally concerns an encounter between two worlds. I suggest that meaning resides in the *relation* we imagine to obtain between these two worlds: between such perceived disparities as Edwardian London and Neverland, fact and fiction, linear and holistic consciousness, intellect and intuition. . . . How we understand the order of existence and how we relate to nonexistence—the eternal, the archetypal, the Other—depend upon our sense of place, purpose and relation to the world, in other words upon our sense of identity.[1]

It is vitally important to recognize where the sense of identity is located and how it engages in soul-making in the shifting borderlands between the worlds of rational and nonrational experience.

Early in his psychiatric career, Jung was working with a seventeen-year-old schizophrenic patient who had been seduced by her older brother. She believed she lived on the moon and had to stay there to save women and children from a winged vampire that threatened an otherwise paradisiacal land. In a letter to Jung, Freud dismissed her beliefs as "nothing other than carefully cultivated daydreams," springing from fantasies built upon repressed memories.[2] Freud also rejected religion as infantile daydreaming cut off from reality, while Jung recognized the imaginal world, the world of myth, as an authentic reality. He objected to Freud's dismissal of unconscious fantasy as cultivated daydreaming that could and should be dissolved once its sexual etiology had been unveiled.

"Unconscious fantasies," he replied to Freud, "contain a whole lot of relevant material, and bring the inside to the outside as nothing else can."[3] When the patient had the strength to deal with the vampire, its wings opened and a man of unearthly beauty stood before her. Although Jung realized that he was possibly

---

[1] Below, p. 118.
[2] William McGuire, ed., *The Freud/Jung Letters,* p. 429.
[3] Ibid., pp. 430f.

"attaching too great hopes to these excavations," he declared that "fantasy is an amazing witches' cauldron," and quoted the final chorus from Goethe's *Faust II:* "Formation, transformation, / Eternal Mind's eternal recreation."[4]

Jung focused on the archetypal expression of his patient's trauma. He saw her visions not simply as an opiate to protect her from pain by maintaining her in a catatonic state (the witches' cauldron), but as healing powers that, when she again found her ego, could enlarge her consciousness and release her from the previously protective prison of her psychosis. Jung believed that the Self, the ordering center of the psyche, creates the myth and that the ego (with the help of the therapist) has to find the core of worldly reality in the myth in order to bring consciousness back into relation with the unconscious.

Jung's patient had lived totally in her own Neverland. She had left her ego and lived in the Self. So in this case fantasy was destructive. Jung helped her to recognize how her moon myth was related to this world, and how it could contribute to her healing. The woman eventually regained her sanity, married and raised a family. Her story is an example of the soul-making process that touches the whole spectrum of being, from the farther reaches of fantasy to the innermost power of metaphor.

This book, *Now or Neverland,* centering on the myth of eternal youth, guides us through J.M. Barrie's story of Peter Pan and everything he represents in the human psyche—another example of soul-making. Peter Pan's interactions with the Edwardian world do not so much shake that world as offer to enlarge the child Wendy's consciousness by making obvious the limitations of the society in which she lives. At the same time, Barrie shows us that Wendy cannot stay in Neverland without dealing with Captain Hook—the shadow side of life.

Peter Pan finds its focus in the interaction between the two worlds so that the reader cannot comfortably stay in either. That dynamic dialogue is the process of soul-making in the puer—the redemption of the narrow, established order by bringing to it a life of deeply committed symbolic action. Puer energy becomes a creative force when the archetype is released from the stereotype. We are fortunate indeed to have Ann Yeoman as our guide to a deeper understanding of this enduring tale.

In her timely study of Peter Pan as a still vibrant archetypal image in contemporary society, Ann Yeoman asks us to look at our own ego strength in coming to grips with the inherent strangeness of our world and the consequences of in-

---

[4] Ibid., p. 431.

tegrating, or not, our shadow side. She vividly illustrates the relationship between storytelling and the dynamic activity of soul-making. With her thorough knowledge of Jung's understanding of the roots of the eternal boy archetype in both male and female psychology, she puts the *puer aeternus* under a microscope that reveals many layers of both creative and destructive energies. She does not judge or blame. Rather she helps us to understand, individually and culturally, how we can relate to puer psychology and the fantasy life within us in order to enrich our lives.

Who will be interested in this book? Those who find themselves unable to commit to work, unable to commit to a relationship, unable to commit to the discipline of education, unable to carry the weight of responsibility, will find it invaluable. So, too, will those who love these eternal charmers and forever find themselves entangled in their shadows. Equally, those who respect the puer's creative dreams will recognize the importance of the eternal youth who can bring new life to a dying order.

Marion Woodman

Michael Llewelyn Davies, aged 6
(J.M. Barrie's model for Peter Pan)

Introduction

This book grew out of my life-long relationship with Peter Pan. Since his debut on the London stage shortly after the turn of the twentieth century he has become a household name, even to those who have never read the tale or seen a production of the play in which he first appeared. I think it is safe to assume that almost everyone exposed to modern Western culture knows Peter Pan, that is, is familiar with the personality traits and boyish heroism he embodies, and the compelling ideal of childhood discovered on his island kingdom of Neverland. However elusive or frustratingly irresponsible he may be, few would champion his arch-enemy, Captain Hook, over Peter Pan's magnetic figure of joy, spontaneity and youth.

Events of the past ten years have confirmed the longevity of Peter Pan in a number of ways. To name but a few, in 1987, in London, an amendment to the Copyright, Designs and Patent Bill was effected when the House of Lords ruled to restore to the Great Ormond Street Hospital for Sick Children, to which author J.M. Barrie had willed *Peter Pan,* the Hospital's expired rights to the royalties.[5] In 1990, the Disney and Mary Martin movie versions were made available for home viewing on videotape; *Peter Pan and the Pirates* appeared on American television.[6] Steven Spielberg introduced an adult Peter Pan in *Hook* in 1991; and Disney released a restored version of the original 1953 animated film on March 3, 1998. Such popular interest in Peter Pan, as well as my own fascination with Barrie's hero, led me to ask myself a number of questions.

Why did the figure of Peter Pan so surely grip the Edwardian imagination? Why did he become a household name so quickly and why does it continue to be so? What value does he represent in the twentieth-century Western psyche? Why are we experiencing a resurgence of interest in Peter Pan at this time? What manner of child, what type of eternal boy, is he?

My desire to throw some light on these questions led me again to the novel, first published in 1911 as *Peter and Wendy,* in which Barrie paints a more precise portrait of the enigmatic Peter Pan than we find in the script of the stage play of 1904.

For those who have not read Barrie's novel, and as an aid to memory for

---

[5] Jacqueline Rose, *The Case of Peter Pan or the Impossibility of Children's Fiction,* p. ix.
[6] Bruce K. Hanson, *The Peter Pan Chronicles,* p. 259.

those who read it many years ago, I offer a synopsis of the story:

Barrie's tale is set in Edwardian London. The action begins at "No. 14," the home of the Darling family. More precisely, the action begins in the nursery where the three Darling children, Wendy, John and Michael, are taken care of by Nana, the Newfoundland dog hired as nursemaid. With the sudden invasion of Peter Pan, the genteel innocence and security of the Darlings' home erupts into unprecedented adventure for the children, and chaos and grief for the parents. Mr Darling, occupied with stocks, bonds and other business matters in the city, does not believe in Peter Pan. Mrs Darling has a dim memory of Peter Pan from her own childhood. Peter Pan is most alive and well in Wendy's dream and fantasy life, although this does not explain the appearance of skeleton leaves, from a tree foreign to English soil, on the nursery floor one morning.

Peter Pan, who is habitually clad in skeleton leaves, arrives one night in the nursery only to be frightened off by Mrs Darling and Nana. Nana slams the window shut so quickly after Peter flies away that she cuts off his shadow. Peter returns on the fateful Night of Nights to search for his shadow. On this particular evening, after Mr Darling's childish tantrums over his tie that will not tie and his medicine that he refuses to take, after dancing and family fun, Mr and Mrs Darling leave for a party at "No. 27." Nana is chained outside in the garden and Liza, the maid, is busy elsewhere in the house. The children are virtually alone.

Wendy wakens to the sound of Peter Pan's sobs as he discovers he cannot stick his shadow on with bathroom soap. The fairy Tinker Bell had found it for him, neatly folded away in a drawer. Wendy sews Peter's shadow on him and listens to him describe his life in Neverland, where he is the uncontested leader of a band of "lost" boys. She learns that Peter Pan's lost boys are babies who fell from their prams when their nurses neglected them and whom Peter Pan took to his underground home in Neverland; she hears of their longing for stories and for a mother. Charmed by Peter Pan, Wendy escapes the nursery on the "mainland" with her younger brothers and heads for Neverland just as soon as Peter Pan has sprinkled the three with fairy dust that they may fly, and only precious moments before Mr and Mrs Darling return to find the nursery window open and the children gone.

In Neverland, the Darling children are caught up in a round of adventures with Peter Pan, Tinker Bell and the lost boys. They encounter the legendary Captain Hook and his pirates, the Indian braves of the Piccaninny tribe and their princess Tiger Lily, and the wolves, beasts and birds of the island. They learn of the infamous crocodile to which Peter Pan once fed Hook's right arm after severing it in combat and whose progress in pursuit of the rest of Hook may be tracked by the tick-tock of the clock she swallowed long ago. The childhood idyll of life in Neverland is eventually broken by Wendy, the eldest of the Darling children, as she remembers and tries to teach John and Michael to remember their parents, Nana and life on the mainland.

In the final battle, when the Darling children and the lost boys are preparing to return to No. 14, Hook initiates a clever tactical maneuver and surprises the Indians who are protecting Peter Pan's underground home. Most of the braves are killed and the children are taken captive by Hook. Only Peter Pan remains below ground and Hook believes he has taken care of him by slipping poison into his medicine while he sleeps. Tinker Bell, however, is aware of Hook's treachery and saves Peter Pan's life in order that he may, in turn, save the day by stealing aboard the pirate ship to free the children. In the ensuing fight, all the pirates are either killed or abandon ship, and Peter Pan forces Hook to walk his own plank and fall into the inevitable jaws of the crocodile.

The Darling children and the lost boys return to London where the lost boys are adopted by Mr and Mrs Darling. Peter, although desperately lonely, refuses to be adopted by the Darlings. He will not be made to grow up and become a man with a beard, business suit and briefcase; he wants to remain a boy forever. Mrs Darling makes Peter Pan one concession: Wendy may fly to Neverland for two weeks in the spring to take care of his spring-cleaning. Peter promises to return each spring for Wendy but after the first spring he forgets.

Time passes. By the next time that Peter alights on the nursery floor to take her to Neverland, Wendy is grown up, married and has a daughter of her own. Peter believes that no more than one year has elapsed since his last visit: he has no memory. All the children have become adults. They have forgotten about Peter and their adventures in Neverland. Peter Pan, and all he embodies, belongs, in Barrie's novel, to the island of childhood that exists apart from and invisible to the adult world.

. . . cry Bacchus! Buster! Lightningboy! the one
& only Double-mothered! Laffer! Injun!
Longhair! Good Old Winemaker!
Nightcap! Aleman! Whackus & Yahoo!
all your old Greek names, god

(youth inexhaustible, you eternal boy!
most gorgeous god in heaven! head of girl
with your horns off: you Orient-charmer!
all the way to tawny India awash in its Ganges!
venerable: got Pentheus too, for sacrilege, & Lycurgus,
that other heathen with an axe to grind! Tuscan
sailors dolphinized! you yoked lynxes,
pretty reins on necks, Bacchants & Satyrs
behind you & that shaky-leg old drunk,
Silenus, supported on staff or falling from wobbly ass
wherever you go: one noise: young men
& women voices, hands banging drums, horns
going & long boxwood flute sound)

 —Ovid, *Metamorphoses,* IV (trans. Charles Boer).

And all should cry, Beware! Beware!
His flashing eyes, his floating hair!
Weave a circle round him thrice,
And close your eyes in holy dread,
For he on honey-dew hath fed,
And drunk the milk of Paradise.

—Samuel Taylor Coleridge, "Kubla Khan."

1
The Eternal Boy
From Divine Image to Pathology

Peter Pan first appeared on the London stage in 1904; consequently he is fast approaching his hundredth birthday. Even those who have never seen either the play or the movie, or read J.M. Barrie's novel, to child and adult alike the figure of Peter Pan is as well-known as the heroes, heroines, ogres and witches of classical fairy tale, such as Cinderella, Snow White, Little Red Riding Hood, Hansel and Gretel, the Frog Prince, Jack and the Beanstalk, Bluebeard. As a familiar figure of spontaneity, adventure and play, in the common mind Peter Pan *is* "the little boy who did not want to grow up," the spirit of perpetual youth and joy associated with Neverland, Barrie's country of childhood. Yet the captivating image of Peter Pan at the nursery window, enticing Wendy and her brothers to fly away with him to Neverland, inevitably resonates differently in the child than in the adult. The majority of adults, once belief has been suspended and Barrie's Edwardian sentimentalism forgiven, may experience the gamut of emotions from nostalgia to quiet identification to envy to impatience. For the child, Peter Pan means, perhaps more than anything else, freedom.

Mythologically, Peter Pan is linked to figures of youthful excess, to the eternal boy, to the young god who dies and is reborn: to Bacchus/Dionysus, Icarus, Phaeton, Narcissus and Adonis, as well as to Mercury/Hermes, psychopomp and messenger of the gods who moves freely between the divine and human realms, and, of course, to the great goat-god Pan. In the popular imagination, following the propensity of the second half of the twentieth century to idealize the young, resist physical change and undervalue old age, Barrie's hero has been associated almost exclusively with eternal youth. He embodies childhood innocence and imaginative spontaneity, while less appealing aspects of his characterization have been downplayed or ignored. In early performances of Barrie's play, Peter Pan appeared on stage with both pipes and a live goat. Such undisguised references to the chthonic, often lascivious and far from childlike goat-god were, not surprisingly, soon excised from both play and novel.

The story-line itself encourages an uncritical and oversimplifying polarization of youth and age, good guys versus bad guys, with Peter Pan leading the forces of good and idealized youth against Captain Hook, who exemplifies all

15

that is bad and grown-up, or all that is bad *because* grown-up. This sanitized representation of Peter Pan is often found in Disney productions, in cartoons, comic books and commercial advertising. Yet Pan and Hook in fact share many characteristics. They both have difficulty relating to others; they are isolated and self-centered; each is motivated by a lust for power and control; and each fears the passage of time with the inevitable changes and transformations it occasions. When we turn to Barrie's original depictions of both eternal boy and old man, in the stage play and especially in the later novel, we find them to be rich, suggestive and problematic, presenting a more accurate picture of psychological complexity than modern media's popularizations of his characters allow.

In terms of C.G. Jung's analytical psychology, the eternal boy is understood as a form of *puer aeternus,* the old man as *senex.* Puer and senex (and to a lesser extent the supposed female equivalents of *puella aeterna* and crone) received a great deal of critical and analytical attention in the 1960s and 1970s, the era of hippies, flower children, ban-the-bomb and peace campaigns, love-ins and Woodstock (August, 1969). This interest in eternal youth was timely and welcome, as the sixties "revolution" seemed a collective manifestation of that mythological figure and archetypal dynamic.

However, critical discussion may tend toward one-sidedness when, driven by immediate concerns, it addresses the effect of a psychological phenomenon on the individual, family and social norms, without the distance and objectivity to afford due recognition to the mythological context of the image. The danger is to personalize and pathologize archetypal phenomena, and this tendency in the psychological debate of the time paralleled the establishment's often brutal repression of youth's struggle for civil liberties, racial equality and sexual freedom. Rebellious young men and women were seen by their elders as rebels without causes or, at best, rebels misguidedly backing the wrong causes. They were regarded as typical puers and puellas in their refusal both of the status quo and of maturity and responsibility as defined by the status quo.

Those who were not politically active but who retreated into a private spiritual realm of more or less passive fantasy, frequently inspired by Eastern religious practice, fared no better than the activists. They were equally in danger of being labeled as pathological and in need of a curative dose of hard work in order to become productively grounded in the same adult reality to which they conscientiously objected. In America, the shootings by the National Guard on May 4, 1970, at Kent State University, and the plight of draft dodgers opposing military service in Vietnam, are only two examples from a long list of incidents and protest in the Western world's social revolution of the 1960s and 1970s.

In her extensive study of puer psychology first published in 1970, Marie-Louise von Franz characterizes the typical puer as one who leads a "provisional life." This means the person harbors a "strange attitude and feeling" that his job, career, city, car, creative endeavor, or woman is *"not yet* what is really wanted, and there is always the fantasy that sometime in the future the real thing will come about."[7] Von Franz summarizes her view of the puer as follows:

> None of his reactions are really very personal or very special. He becomes a type, the type of the *puer aeternus*. He becomes an archetype, and if you become that, you are not at all original. . . . He is merely the archetype of the eternal-youth god, and therefore he has all the features of the god: he has a nostalgic longing for death; he thinks of himself as being something special; he is the one sensitive being among all the other tough sheep. He will have a problem with an aggressive, destructive shadow which he will not want to live and generally projects, and so on. There is nothing special whatsoever. The worse the identification with the youthful god, the less individual the person, although he himself feels so special.[8]

Although his spontaneity, creativity and joy were highly valued, the puer tended to receive a largely negative press, mainly because emphasis was placed on the inevitable pathology of one who remains unconsciously identified with the archetype of youth well into adult life, in other words, stuck in stereotypically boyish or adolescent behavior.

In much of the early literature, "puer" and "mother's son" were treated as synonyms. Puers were described as trapped in a debilitating relation to "the mother," tied to her apron strings or metaphorically devoured and kept effectively out of life by an over-possessive "death-mother." The initial instinctive bond between mother and child then develops into an emotional tie between mother and son that determines the son's path in life long after and despite his having physically flown the coop. Everything continues to turn on the approving

---

[7] *Puer Aeternus: A Psychological Study of the Adult Struggle with the Paradise of Childhood*, p. 2. Von Franz mentions "another type of *puer* that does not display the charm of eternal youth, nor does the archetype of the divine youth shine through him. On the contrary, he lives in a continual sleepy daze, and that, too, is a typical adolescent characteristic. . . . The sleepy daze is only an outer aspect, however, and if you can penetrate it, you will find that a lively fantasy life is being cherished within." (Ibid., p. 4) This other type of puer is discussed by Giles Clark in "The Transformation of 'Spiritual Image' and 'Instinctual Shadow' into 'Instinctual Spirit.' "

[8] *Puer Aeternus*, pp. 121f.

or disapproving gaze of the mother. Even in rebellion against the strictures of the personal mother, the son who strikes a seemingly heroic and independent stance frequently remains in service to the archetypal Mother through his duty to family, profession, civic and cultural life (all part of the material province of the Great Goddess), with the result that he often unwittingly "avoids his destiny."[9]

In terms of personality traits, a strong emotional attachment to what we may call the mother-realm manifests on the one hand in a certain preciousness, a sense of specialness and difference, a fictional example of which we see in James Joyce's young hero Stephen, who is always "on the fringe," a little apart from his fellows, an isolate. On the other hand, when out of the province of the mother and, metaphorically, the reach of mother's watchful eye, the mother's son experiences an incapacity to stand on his own and embrace the risks, challenges and unpredictable fullness of life, or realize the courage "to live, to err, to fall, to triumph, to recreate life out of life," to cite Joyce once again.[10] As a result, the puer remains dissociated from his feelings. In order to shield himself unconsciously from suffering, he protects himself from the possibility of abandonment, rejection and disappointment with an array of defenses which prevent his fully committing himself to life in the first place.

Jung describes the neurosis of such a "mother's boy" in terms of a "secret conspiracy between mother and son, . . . [in which] each helps the other to betray life."[11] He continues:

> There is in [the son] a desire to touch reality, to embrace the earth and fructify the field of the world. But he makes no more than a series of fitful starts, for his initiative as well as his staying power are crippled by the secret memory that the world and happiness may be had as a gift—from the mother. The fragment of world which he, like every man, must encounter again and again is never quite the right one, since it does not fall into his lap, does not meet him half way, but remains resistant, has to be conquered, and submits only to force. It makes demands on the masculinity of a man, on his ardour, above all on his courage and resolution when it comes to throwing his whole being into the scales. For this he would need a faithless Eros, one capable of forgetting his mother and undergoing the pain of relinquishing the first love of his life.[12]

---

[9] James Hillman, "The Great Mother, Her Son, Her Hero, and the Puer," in Patricia Berry, ed., *Fathers and Mothers*, p. 175.
[10] *A Portrait of the Artist as a Young Man*, p. 172.
[11] "The Syzygy: Anima and Animus," *Aion*, CW 9ii, par. 21. [CW refers throughout to *The Collected Works of C.G. Jung*]
[12] Ibid., par. 22.

This type of puer is, then, never quite *in life*. He hovers above it all in the realm of ideas and fantasy, feeling that life owes him a living because he is special. As von Franz says, "Many *puer aeterni* cannot even be quite unhappy! . . . they anticipate the disappointment in order not to suffer the blow, and that is a refusal to live."[13]

Throughout our discussion it is important to recognize the way in which such terms as "mother" and "father" are used. Behind every personal experience of mothering and fathering (which need not come to us from either our biological parents or, in the case of mothering, a woman, and in the case of fathering, a man) there stand collective, cultural images of Mother and Father, seen in our institutions, churches, religious iconography and concepts of the Godhead. Our personal experiences of mothering and fathering are necessarily partial, mediated to us through our ordinarily human, and therefore limited, primary caregivers; they are also influenced by the mystery of our own innate predispositions. Likewise cultural images of the archetypal parents, though mediating far more than the personal parents, are inevitably limited and limiting. This is why the history of civilization is marked by such cultural phenomena as the death and birth of religions, as an old idea of the Godhead dies and another, usually expanded, image of the nature of ultimate reality is realized.

We have two archetypal Mothers: Mother Nature, whose pull toward instinctuality and unconsciousness we must, as conscious human beings, resist; and Mother Culture, variously represented as Mother Church, Mother Country, the institutions and companies which take care of our various needs. The archetypal Father, following Western Christian culture's picture of God the Father inherited from the Old Testament, is represented in the laws, commandments and social norms by which we structure society and collectively govern ourselves. In the Biblical tradition, only after Job's questioning of the limitations of this ancient God-image, and later through the birth of Christ, representing a new spiritual ethic founded on love rather than obedience, do we find a new dimension or potentiality of father-spirit introduced into Western consciousness.

The daunting task of individuation, Jung's term for the lifelong quest for self-realization, involves the struggle to consciously differentiate parental and cultural manifestations of the archetypes, in order to realize one's unique and independent way of living the so-called feminine and masculine energies that together form the ground, the matter and spirit, of our psychobiological being. The

---

[13] *Puer Aeternus,* p. 118.

old forms into which archetypal energy tends habitually to flow, in personal complexes, family neuroses and cultural prerogatives, need to be tested if not broken, if one is not to live one's life in unconscious allegiance to a way of being (archetypal Mother) or way of thinking (archetypal Father) that may stifle one's own spirit and thwart one's natural destiny. Too much Mother and too much Father can be as burdensome an inheritance as too little:

> Mother becomes . . . Mother Welfare State, Mother University, the beloved Alma Mater, defended by Father who becomes Father Hierarchy, Father Law, Father Status Quo. We unconsciously introject the power inherent in these archetypal figures which, in the absence of the individuation process, remain intact at an infantile level. So long as they remain intact, uninterrupted by the consciousness that can disempower them, the inner dictators enslave more cruelly than the outer.[14]

Our comments on personal and collective parental images return us to our earlier concern with the relation of the puer to mother/matter, and raise the question of the eternal boy's relation to father/spirit or senex. In much of his commentary, Jung speaks of the "eternal youth" rather than the "mother's son." He emphasizes the archetypal and mythological significance of the figure of the young god which underlies any individual, and potentially pathological, incidence of puer psychology. As an image of a universal psychic dynamic, the *puer aeternus* again becomes numinous and paradoxical.

Jung appreciates the archetypal complexity of the image.[15] Indeed, the "divine child" is often seen as an ambiguous double figure, for example in representations of the infant Dionysus with adult beard. The divine youth is often paired with the father or with an old man, as in depictions of a youthful Bacchus in the company of an aged Silenus. Such images suggest a connection of the eternal youth with the ancient Phoenician cult of father and son, a connection which introduces a procreative masculine spirit or phallic quality of libido that is pre-Grecian, historically prior to and conspicuously missing from the later, more familiar image of the mother/son-lover dyad (Venus/Adonis, Cybele/Attis).

In his reflections on the *puer aeternus*, James Hillman takes Jung's recognition of mythology's link between youth and age, and elaborates it into a discussion of the configuration *puer-et-senex*, divine boy and old man. He argues that the puer presents primarily a spiritual phenomenon and, as such, begs a reread-

---

[14] Marion Woodman, *The Ravaged Bridegroom: Masculinity in Women*, p. 18.
[15] See "The Psychology of the Child Archetype," *The Archetypes and the Collective Unconscious*, CW 9i.

J.M. Barrie, aged 51, and Michael Llewelyn Davies, aged 12, in July, 1912

ing in terms of "father" and in relation to senex, rather than in terms of "mother" and in relation to matter. Hillman reminds us that early Jung focuses on the relation, and opposition, of son/hero to mother as the mythological paradigm of the development of consciousness: spirit/son-hero defined in opposition to matter/mother. Later, however, Jung turns to an alchemical paradigm, with its emphasis on the independence and autonomy of spirit, and the mysterious and complex relation of both spirit and matter to the functioning of psyche. Hillman proposes that we

> differentiate *puer,* hero, and son, and . . . suggest that the son who succumbs and the hero who overcomes both take their definition through the relationship with the magna mater, . . . [and] the *puer* takes its definition from the *senex-puer* polarity.[16]

Hillman holds that to treat puer and senex separately is to divorce each from its archetypal context and consequently to misunderstand and run the risk of pathologizing both. He argues that puer and senex represent two faces of the archetypal configuration *puer-et-senex* (or *senex-et-puer)* and, in support of his argument, reminds us that the

> archetype *per se* is ambivalent and paradoxical, embracing both spirit and nature, psyche and matter, consciousness and unconsciousness; . . . The inherent opposition within the archetype splits into poles when it enters ego-consciousness.[17]

It follows then that the expressions "typically puer" and "typically senex" mean, in effect, "only-puer" and "only-senex," in other words, possession through one face only of the archetype. When consciousness splits the archetype in this way, notes Hillman, "Then we have a too-familiar pattern: action that does not know [the puer] and knowledge that does not act [the senex], fanatic versus cynic, commonly formulated as youth and age."[18]

Arguing against an easy, uncritical acceptance of the inevitability of such a split, with its resulting polarization of puer and senex into fixed and unredeemable "half-roles," Hillman suggests that the ordering pattern of *puer-et-senex* is essential to a healthy and stable sense of "self-continuity and self-identity" through the stages of life. The process of life does not require the only-puer impulse to die or to be converted into the rigidity and cynicism of the only-senex

---

[16] "The Great Mother, Her Son, Her Hero, and the Puer," in Berry, *Fathers and Mothers,* p. 166.
[17] *Puer Papers,* p. 12.
[18] Ibid.

attitude. It points instead to the need for *puer-et-senex* unity, an ambiguous "two-fold truth" that more fully represents the equivocal nature of the archetype:

> By continuing true to one's past puer spirit and consciously affirming it one has already assumed the senex virtue of responsibility and order. . . . To be true to one's puer nature means to admit one's puer past —all its gambols and gestures and sunstruck aspirations. From this history we draw consequences. By standing for these consequences, we let history catch up with us and thus is our haste slowed. History is the senex shadow of the puer, giving him substance. Through our individual histories, puer merges with senex, the eternal comes back into time, the falcon returns to the falconer's arm.[19]

In his essay, "On the Necessity of Abnormal Psychology," Hillman follows Jung's contention that "the Gods have become diseases" and argues that the archetype is far from being "primordially pristine":

> The figures of myth—quarreling, cheating, sexually obsessed, revenging, vulnerable, killing, torn apart—show that the Gods are not only perfections so that all abnormalities can fall only on humans. The mythemes in which the Gods appear are replete with behavior that, from the secular standpoint, must be classified under criminal pathology, moral monstrosity, or personality disorders.[20]

Thus Hillman calls for a revaluation and acceptance of the *infirmitas,* or "unpristine ambiguity" of the archetype, for that alone can show us the patterns of, and thereby serve as nurse to, "our self-division and error, our wounds and extremities, providing a style, a justification, and a sense of significance" for our own *infirmitas.* When we consider any archetypal configuration, then, it would seem imperative to avoid the temptation to eliminate discomfiting paradox by splitting (moralistically) negative from positive, pathology from gift, and focusing on one pole to the exclusion of the other.

To return briefly to Barrie, we see from his notebooks of 1920, written in the aftermath of the First World War, that he was well aware of both the split, and the need for relationship, between puer and senex:

> Age & Youth the two great enemies. . . . Age (wisdom) failed — Now let us see what youth (audacity) can do. . . . In short, there has arisen a new morality which seeks to go its own way agst [sic] the fierce protests (or despair) of the old morality. No argument can exist between the two till this is admitted. In present controversy it isn't admitted — the Old screams at the New as . . . vile [because] not

---

[19] Ibid., pp. 32, 25.

[20] Hillman, ed., *Facing the Gods,* p. 3.

Old's way — and New despises Old as played out and false sentiment. When they admit that the other has a case to state, then . . . they can argue — not before.[21]

Although Jeffrey Satinover does not cite Hillman in his essay "Puer Aeternus: The Narcissistic Relation to the Self," he seems to appreciate and explore, more fully than do most writers on the subject, the rich *infirmitas* of the puer-senex archetypal configuration of which Hillman speaks.[22] Satinover locates the "problem" of the eternal adolescent in a missing sense of identity for which the puer compensates in his behavior. This missing sense of identity, or of oneself as a cohesive whole, results in disquieting feelings of fragmentation and worthlessness. It motivates the puer's pursuit of the ecstatic "high"—in drugs, alcohol, sex, sport and daredevil escapade—that transcends the outer conflict or inner depression which threatens fragmentation. It underlies his restless search for just that state of stability and harmony which, however fleeting, would support for a moment the desired experience of specialness, value and significance, and so grant an illusion of selfhood.

Erich Neumann emphasizes the importance to the later development of personality of the "primal relationship" of the initial mother-child dyad. If the mother is capable of mediating the positive aspects of the mother archetype, she will awaken in her child a sense of basic security, a feeling of the "continuity of being" and a positive experience of the world.[23] It is on the foundation of such a sense of security that the child's capacity to trust both himself and the world develops. "Basic trust" compensates the sense of "basic loss" which is a consequence of such inevitable events in the child's life as weaning, the gradual awareness of oneself as an individual separate from the mother, and diminishment of the mother's attention. Eric Erikson writes:

> The general state of trust . . . implies not only that one has learned to rely on the sameness and continuity of the outer providers but also that one may trust oneself and the capacity of one's own organs to cope with urges; that one is able to consider oneself trustworthy enough so that the providers will not need to be on guard or to leave.[24]

Accordingly, when speaking of the developmental stage of infancy, Satinover stresses the importance of a caregiver's healthy response to signs of a constella-

---

[21] Andrew Birkin, *J.M. Barrie and the Lost Boys*, pp. 286f.
[22] In *Quadrant*, vol. 13, no. 2, pp. 75ff.
[23] *The Child*, p. 29.
[24] *Identity: Youth and Crisis*, pp. 101f.

tion, or activation, of the Self in the infant, the "Self" being a descriptive term for the innate ordering factor in the psyche which must support any healthy unfolding of the unique personality toward psychobiological wholeness. Such a constellation is the foundation of any future sense of identity and self-esteem. It manifests in the two-to-three year old as assertiveness, grandiosity and self-importance. And while it may lead to behavior difficult to tolerate, fast to be checked and punished, and often too quickly labeled as pathologically narcissistic, it indicates, nonetheless, that under the surface "a coalescing of ego fragments [is beginning] to form a functional unity," which is experienced as a sense of selfhood.[25]

Satinover uses the term "proper narcissism" in talking about the infant's emerging sense of selfhood. His term describes the development of a capacity for healthy introversion, which is essential to the future stability of the personality because it enables one to "properly reflect oneself" and so "maintain a stable sense of identity." When this capacity is unrealized or impaired, the psychic cohesion on which the personality may depend in times of stress is missing. Any sense of selfhood remains tentative and labile, resulting in erratic mood swings, petulance or withdrawal. It often remains closely tied to the "polar states of the [cycles of the] Self: constellation and fragmentation" that characterize the pre-Oedipal stage of development, and which account, in the adult puer, for a repetitive experience of extreme highs and lows.[26] Satinover therefore dates the origin of puer psychology earlier than most other writers. He places it before the age of three to five, which is the age, we learn from Freud, when parental attachments dominate development, when mother and father complexes are compounded and patterns of relationship to external reality and external "others" are crystallized:

> Explicit or implicit in most descriptions of the *puer* is the idea that the neurosis consists largely of a failure to adapt to external reality. The idea I want to introduce is that the *puer's* failure to adapt to reality, when such is the case, is not primary. Rather, the primary feature of *puer* psychology is the failure to develop a particular sort of narcissism; it is a failure of introverted adaptation; and the failure to adapt to externals, when present, is a secondary consequence of this inner failure. Hence, treatment which . . . aims at adaptation to outer reality is at best treating a secondary symptom while the core of the neurosis remains untouched.[27]

---

[25] "Puer Aeternus: The Narcissistic Relation to the Self," p. 80.
[26] Ibid., p. 85.
[27] Ibid., p. 78.

The problem of the puer is, then, located in early infancy with the foundations of soul-making rather than in adolescence, when it manifests as a particular disturbance of adaptation.

The weight of analytical discussion of puer psychology in the 1970s fell on the eternal adolescent's debilitating attachment to the mother and his failure to relate to others and the external world. As arguably the most famous twentieth-century figure for eternal boyhood, Peter Pan may appear to fit this "classical" description of the *puer aeternus,* yet he is neither the typical "son" nor the typical "hero." He concerns himself with senex (Captain Hook) and proclaims a fierce independence of spirit as much as he opposes "mothers" (Mrs Darling) and resists development and convention in his refusal to grow up to be a man. It therefore seems timely to reconsider the *puer aeternus* by first considering his image as presented to us in the figure of Peter Pan, and to do so in light of Jung's mythological and alchemical commentary, Hillman's archetypal emphasis on the puer as spiritual imperative, and Satinover's insights on the resolution of the "puer problem" in a healthy rather than pathological narcissism.

Recently, and most usefully, interest has centered on psychology's concern with the narcissistically wounded.[28] However, so far there is little sustained discussion of the puer in the current literature. This is unfortunate, as the problem has certainly not disappeared, nor do I believe that it can be adequately subsumed under the umbrella of "narcissistic wounding" unless, as Nathan Schwartz-Salant argues, the archetypal dimension of the problem is addressed:

> Unless the introverted dimension is dealt with and the creative function of imagination appropriated by the ego, the healing of narcissistic disorders is incomplete and unstable. The inner domain to which introversion addresses itself is that which has traditionally been called the soul. This is why the narcissistic problem, though it appears so superficial, actually runs very deep. For the issues raised by the narcissistic character disorder are those of the suffering and depths of the soul.[29]

Mario Jacoby also argues for the careful differentiation of narcissistic personality disorders from the problem of a "dominance of the negative mother complex" (the complex assumed to underlie puer psychology), for "even though every narcissistic disturbance has its roots in a negative mother complex, the

---

[28] See especially works by Heinz Kohut, Nathan Schwartz-Salant, Mario Jacoby, Kathrin Asper (noted in the Bibliography).
[29] *Narcissism and Character Transformation: The Psychology of Narcissistic Character Disorders,* p. 28.

Michael Llewelyn Davies: *left,* in fancy dress; *right,* with house cricket cup

same complex may be found in other types of psychic illness (e.g. in borderline disorders or in psychosis)."[30] I would add to this the importance of the father to the development of selfhood and the individual coloring of the "father" complex, on which rests the positive activation—or not—of conscious creative masculine libido. Patrix, as an image of the original source of maleness, needs to be valued as essential and co-existent with matrix. The creativity and procreativity of each is realized only in and through the other: mother *and* father.[31]

To return to our novel, the longevity of J.M. Barrie's *puer aeternus,* Peter Pan, as a vital figure in popular culture, supports Satinover's contention that in the latter part of the twentieth century we are, in fact, continuing to experience

> a striking increase in the incidence of this kind of personality: a personality characterized on the one hand by a poor adjustment to quotidian demands, a failure to set stable goals and to make lasting achievements in accord with these goals, and a proclivity for intense but short-lived romantic attachments, yet, on the other hand, it is also characterized by noble idealism, a fertile imagination, spiritual insight and frequently, too, by remarkable talent.[32]

The sustained strength of Peter Pan's magnetic appeal to both adult and child audiences throughout the first quarter of this century also suggests that his contagious "magic" reflects as much the "creative function of imagination . . . [and] the suffering and depths of the soul," to cite Schwartz-Salant once again, as the shape of a personal complex or collective pathology.

Analytical psychology enjoys a history of attention to mythology and the images of popular culture as reflections of the conscious and unconscious, individual and collective psychological configurations that determine the color and tenor of a particular period or society. We will therefore begin at the beginning, with mythology, and a review of the characteristics of some of the gods, those eternal youths of antiquity, who may be considered mythological ancestors to

---

[30] *Individuation and Narcissism: The Psychology of Self in Jung and Kohut,* p. 182.
[31] See Peter Tatham, *The Makings of Maleness: Men, Women, and the Flight of Daedalus,* for a discussion of fathering; and Marion Woodman, *The Pregnant Virgin: A Process of Psychological Transformation,* for a discussion of paternal "patrix" as original source, complementary to and co-equal with maternal "matrix." See also Eugene Monick, *Phallos: Sacred Image of the Masculine,* in which Monick argues the paternal origins of the psyche, distinguishes masculinity from "the fashionable disease of patriarchy," and calls for a postpatriarchal and postmatriarchal appreciation of masculine and feminine which gives equal weight to each.
[32] "Puer Aeternus: The Narcissistic Relation to the Self," p. 75.

Peter Pan. We will then embark on a psychological reading of Barrie's novel for what light his artistic treatment of the eternal boy may shed on our understanding of puer psychology. A particular concern will be to evaluate Barrie's puer as a figure descriptive of a more general psychic dynamic, linked to the phenomenon of autonomous creativity, and active in both men and women.

To cite only a few of the authors mentioned above, Jung emphasizes the androgyny of the human psyche; Hillman reminds us of the universality of archetypal imperatives and the essential *infirmitas* of the archetype; Schwartz-Salant writes of the "proper goal" of energy invested in narcissistic activity being "the discovery of individuality guided by the central archetype, the Self"; von Franz alludes, if only in passing, to the puer problem in the psychology of women; and Satinover points out that although a sexual character (the son's early attachment to the mother) has been attributed to the origin of puer psychology which, as a result, naturally "lends itself more readily to masculine psychology, . . . puers are to be found no less commonly amongst women than men."[33]

If puer and senex, as they appear in myth, tale, literature, and the daily lives and dreams of individuals, are indeed images of universal, archetypal energies, they must each, by definition, serve as descriptive terms for dynamics at play in the psychology of men and women alike. As Peter Tatham writes, the *puer aeternus* is, after all,

> that youth which is related to eternity: the age of our universe. And he is the god of this aeon as well as of the aeon to come, ever renewed and renewing. He is both a youth and, when appearing hornless, looks like a young girl. So we have confirmed for us here the image of *puer* as the non-mature of either gender. He is the loveliest god, who dissolves the old and brings in the new, who intoxicates, sending people out of their conscious minds with his enthusiasms, only to hang over them while they recover those faculties, to await their acknowledgement. The *puer aeternus* is therefore not just what is new and to come, but the very process itself by means of which the present transforms itself into something fresh—the non-mature, the chrysalis and imago itself, all within the same whole.
>
> . . . It is important to reiterate that what has been called *puer* does not truly *possess a gender* and does not therefore need to be matched by the feminine *puella*. Similarly, *puer* is not just to do with boys but is an image of the dynamics of change itself.[34]

---

[33] Ibid., pp. 81f.
[34] Tatham, *The Makings of Maleness*, p. 25; my italics.

Our mythology has lost all too many stories concerning just those deities who are best known to us. The gist of the tales was contained in the figure of the deity itself, but no single tale could present the whole figure in all its aspects. The gods lived in the souls of our ancestors, and did not enter completely into any one story. Nevertheless each story—now as then—contains some living part of them, a contribution to their entirety.

—Karl Kerényi, *The Gods of the Greeks.*

2
Peter Pan's Mythological Ancestry
and Types of the Puer Aeternus

Some Literary Uses of Myth

> Anything, seen without prejudice, is enormous.
> —Mervyn Peake.

William Blake, in one of his Proverbs in "The Marriage of Heaven and Hell," writes: "What is now proved was once only imagin'd . . . . / Every thing possible to be believ'd is an image of truth."[35]

In the first Proverb Blake affirms the archetypal, mythological ground of our experience, as well as the infinite variety of that ground or truth, and the power of the image to evoke (and perhaps invoke) its enigmatic presence. In the second, he reminds us how we give shape and meaning to human existence through the reach of the autonomous imagination toward the unknown and unimaginable, and in the ideas, actions and works of art that result. Image and imagination may be seen, then, as the agencies which enable us to create our worlds in the first place, and to recreate them continually in new and endless possibility. To this end, and to call once again on Blake's poetic language, it is essential that the "doors of perception" of the perceiving ego are "cleansed" and open to the mystery of both inner and outer reality; and so to "Formation, transformation, / Eternal Mind's eternal recreation."[36] In the terms of British artist and fantasist Mervyn Peake, quoted above, we must learn to see and to hear without prejudice in order fully to meet the enormousness of the world.

Although the movement of imagination may appear to be outward, to probe and "give a face to" the previously unexplored, to dissolve and metamorphose old forms into new, imagination's impulse remains equally one of mediation and synthesis. Imagination is both provocative and synthetic, diabolic and symbolic, with the power to differentiate as well as to join. Above all, through the faculty of imagination we attempt to concretize and give expression to archetypal and psychic reality in an image, figure or tale. Such vehicles of expression are in-

---

[35] *Complete Writings,* p. 151 (Plate 8).
[36] Goethe, *Faust II,* final chorus.

evitably insufficient and at best fantastical in the attempt to trace the elusive strangeness of immediate psychic experience. In the process of their creation, however, we struggle to link unknown to known, inner to outer, and to make the invisible visible. In this way unconscious material is "delivered" to consciousness by means of the mediating image, which is why Jung likened the nascent work of art to an unborn child in the womb, with the role of midwife falling to the creative artist.[37]

When confronted with archetypal material and in search of images by which to represent intrapsychic dynamics, the artist needs, according to Jung, to turn to myth and mythological figures in order to give adequate expression to his or her experience:

> Since the expression can never match the richness of the vision and can never exhaust its possibilities, the poet must have at his disposal a huge store of material if he is to communicate even a fraction of what he has glimpsed, and must make use of difficult and contradictory images in order to express the strange paradoxes of his vision.[38]

Jung's reference to the images of myth as difficult and contradictory brings to mind Hillman's insistence on the inherent *infirmitas* of the gods as revealed through their stories. Yet it is important to stick to the image, Jung tells us, however problematic. The original, cryptic image in a fantasy, dream or vision presents an immediate manifestation of archetypal content. It is thereby more individual and naive, more provocative and disturbing, and at the same time less understandable than a collective symbol belonging to a known cultural or religious tradition. This latter point is particularly evident when a collective cultural symbol loses its archetypal resonance because it has atrophied, over time, as a result of excessive conscious elaboration and interpretation.

In terms of Peter Pan, we might say this has happened as a result of the machinations of Hollywood. A still vital symbol, according to Jung, is the best possible expression of "an as yet unknown and incomprehensible fact of a mystical or transcendent, i.e. psychological, nature."[39] Otherwise a symbol functions as a sign, empty of archetypal suggestion. When symbol and metaphor are reduced to commonplace labels for what is known, they lose their original

---

[37] "On the Relation of Analytical Psychology to Poetry," *The Spirit in Man, Art and Literature,* CW 15.

[38] "Psychology and Literature," ibid., par. 151.

[39] "Definitions," *Psychological Types,* CW 6, par. 815.

strangeness and fascination. They cease to connect us to that which is other than commonplace (the unconscious, the archetypal, the mythological, the transcendent), and so fail to shock, surprise, move and inspire us by evoking the ineluctable mystery of the world. This again returns us to the need to "stick to" the often contradictory and ambiguous content of an initial image or original tale.

The tendency of our modern rational, scientific conscious attitude is to become one-sided and to ignore, dismiss or find a logical explanation for the extraordinary, nonrational *un*realities of our world. The counterpole and unconscious shadow of the laudable pursuit of scientific truth is the tendency to espouse an often crippling literalism. Such a perspective will strip world and symbol alike of richness and depth, ambiguity and paradox, stifling the numinosity of the archetypal image. So Hillman writes:

> Literalism prevents mystery by narrowing the multiple ambiguity of meanings into one definition . . . [It] demands singleness of meaning . . . [and] literal meanings become new idols, fixed images that dominate our vision, and are inherently false because single.[40]

The pantheon of gods in antique mythology, on the other hand, provides a counterbalance to such a literalism. It presents a polytheism: myriad gods and goddesses which afford a picture of infinite diversity and so reflect the irreducible polyvalence of psyche and world. This the Romantic poets understood, as we see from a comment in a letter of John Keats to his brother, George:

> A Man's life of any worth is a continual allegory—and very few eyes can see the Mystery of his life—a life like the scriptures, figurative—which such people can no more make out than they can the hebrew Bible. Lord Byron cuts a figure—but he is not figurative—Shakespeare led a life of Allegory: his works are the comments on it.[41]

Keats and other Romantic poets turned to mythology because the virtually limitless number of myths provided a vast precedent from which the imagination might draw for its poetic images of human truth and experience. For Keats, the task of the poet was to reimagine a mythological figure or tale in accord with the tenor of the times and the sensibility of the individual. Poetic process serves, in this way, as a kind of crucible in which the poet may differentiate, reshape and extend the implications of mythology, rendering the antique topical and at the

---

[40] *Revisioning Psychology,* p. 19.
[41] Robert Gittings, ed., *Letters of John Keats,* p. 218.

same time clarifying his or her personal sense of things. Such an undertaking is essentially allegorical, as Keats recognizes in his remark about Shakespeare's life having been a life of allegory.

A more recent literary use of myth is described by T.S Eliot in his commentary on James Joyce's *Ulysses,* a novel in which the peregrinations through the Dublin streets of Joyce's protagonist, Leopold Bloom, owe much of their shape and significance to the far earlier wanderings of Homer's Odysseus. Eliot praises Joyce's "mythical method" of composition. He argues that the only way a modern writer may impose form and meaning on the anarchic, fragmented and spiritually barren post-First World War experience is to turn to ancient mythology.[42] There one discovers, from a twentieth-century perspective, an incomparably rich and ambiguous but cohesive world-view and set of values, the *re*-collection and *re*-membering of which may serve, if only by way of contrast, to "shore against [the] ruins" of that "heap of broken images" that is the European psyche.[43] Eliot's own work, "The Waste Land," provides perhaps the most highly acclaimed poetic use of myth by a writer of that post-war period.

For our purposes, it is important to reflect that both Joyce's and Eliot's works were published, widely read and hotly disputed in London circles at the time J.M. Barrie was working and reworking his portrait of Peter Pan, and we may expect that Barrie was to some extent caught up in and affected by the on-going literary debate of the times.

Although Barrie does not use myth as an overt structural device, as do Eliot and Joyce, his addition of Pan-pipes and a live goat to the first stage production of *Peter Pan,* and his adoption of the refrain "Come away, come away!" from a poem by W.B. Yeats for a chapter title in the novel, are only two of many indications that he was consciously working within the same mythological paradigm. Given his keen appreciation of literary tradition, Barrie doubtless considered his children's story in much the same way as Lewis Carroll viewed the Alice books: ostensibly works created for a child readership, they serve their authors equally well as vehicles for commentary on contemporary mores and values, and for exploration of the intricacies of the human psyche, imaginative fantasy and creative process.

Barrie's narrative has been narrowed, and his image of eternal youth fixed by the popular media: abridgments, comic books, film and television. While comic books and abridged versions of the tale commit the sins of omission and over-

---

[42] *Selected Prose of T.S. Eliot*, pp. 175-178.
[43] T.S. Eliot, "The Waste Land," in *Collected Poems, 1909-1962*, pp. 53, 69.

simplification, film and television make the imaginative present and concrete in our living-rooms and theaters for the duration of the show. Their sin is that of appropriation: they take something timeless and eternal and bring it into profane time, "fixing" an image in the popular imagination in only one of its myriad shapes and possibilities. So the tale and its hero grow thin and pale as each is robbed of imaginative depth by being diminished, for example, to the two-dimensional outline of a Disney cartoon, sentimentalized and emptied of mythological and psychological resonance in the process.

While it may be argued that contemporary film, and the seemingly naive animated cartoon in particular, mirror back to us the archetypal life of the collective as folktales did in former times, we must recognize the profound difference between a consciously crafted product (Disney), which meets us as culturally-determined artifact from *without,* and the more or less spontaneous tale of immediate experience (folktale) that is motivated from *within.* In order to redeem the many figures and tales of the imagination that have suffered reduction at the hands of the popular media, we must return to the original works to read and reread them with an ear to the literary and mythological antecedents of both the protagonists and the narrative for, if Italo Calvino is correct, "It is not the voice that commands the story: it is the ear."[44]

In order, then, to *hear* the mythological and psychological nuances of a tale, we need to re-educate and re-attune the inner ear by returning to the stories of the gods, for the pagan pantheon "offers the psyche manifold fantasies for reflecting its many possibilities."[45] As Hillman argues,

> We are trying to understand both what is this "Greece" that so draws the psyche and what the psyche finds there. . . . We return to Greece in order to rediscover the archetypes of our mind and of our culture. Fantasy returns there to become archetypal. By stepping back into the mythic, into what is non-factual and non-historical, the psyche can reimagine its factual, historical predicaments from another vantage point. Greece becomes the multiple magnifying mirror in which the psyche can recognize its persons and processes in configurations which are larger than life but which bear on the life of our secondary personalities.[46]

Consequently, I find it useful to highlight a few of the often contradictory and enigmatic qualities of Peter Pan's most significant precursors in order that we

---

[44] *Invisible Cities,* p. 106.
[45] *Revisioning Psychology,* p. 29.
[46] Ibid., p. 30.

may sound the depths of Barrie's tale. Such a mythological way of hearing allows a reading of the text as essentially equivocal, harboring multiple possibilities of meaning. It invites an openness to the ghosts of psyche, myth and imagination that haunt our literature and the very interior of our language.

Hermes/Mercury/Mercurius

> If we are to have success in reviving [a] God's image in its fullness, we must be prepared not only for what is immediately intelligible, but also for what is strangely uncanny. Indeed, the images of the Greek Gods can be so resistant to conceptualization and logic that one can be tempted . . . to quote the famous lines that were spoken to describe human beings:
>
> > I am not a cleverly worked-out book,
> > I am a [God] with his self-contradiction.
>
> > —Karl Kerényi, *Hermes: Guide of Souls.*

I begin with the Greek Hermes (Roman Mercury) not only because his attributes throw light on many characteristics of Peter Pan but also because I wish my reading of Barrie's narrative to be guided by him. In a sense I invoke the god in the hope of "seeing" or understanding in the spirit of Hermes, which means attempting, however provisionally, to read, tell, retell and hear the story hermetically, hence unconventionally, in depth, psychologically and, as far as is possible, "without prejudice":

> For wherever one goes, hermetically, one is led into prolixity. . . . And Hermes goes all the way down—into Hades, if you will, certainly into the depths of sleep and psychic movement—before he returns leading the soul-messages (Persephone, Eurydice) back where they can lend insight into the daylight tedium and entrapments. That course of movement-downwards can, if we heed the tradition's iconography, be a winged, swift flight across the usual boundaries and limits.[47]

The figure of Hermes is perhaps most familiar to us as a beautiful youth with magical, golden, winged sandals and the power to cross "the usual boundaries and limits" between the divine and human realms, between the unconscious and consciousness. Such a deceptively simple picture is belied by Greek and Roman mythology which points to the irreducible contrarieties that characterize this god who is the prototypical shapeshifter. The way of being whose image is Hermes is consequently audacious, innocent, cunning, wise, chthonic, phallic, magical, dark, light, shameless, delightful, provocative, protecting. . . . It is impossible to

---

[47] William G. Doty, "Hermes," in James Hillman, ed., *Facing the Gods,* p. 130.

Hermes resting
(Greek bronze; National Museum, Naples)

exhaust the *idea* of Hermes because by his very nature he is equivocal, slippery, elusive, dual, playful, surprising, with the power to grant wishes and make one invisible.

Hermes is trickster, deceiver and master thief, having stolen the sacred cattle of his brother Apollo hours after his birth. He is psychopomp, guide of souls to the Realm of the Dead, and so is linked to Hades and to night: with his magical staff he induces drowsiness and awakens sleepers—he is the dream-maker and ruler of dreams.[48] Yet Hermes also stands as guardian of the hearth and *inspirateur* of family life in the form of the stone herm at doorways and windows, those places "where souls break in."[49] In the service of Athena, he teaches Odysseus what is phantasmal and what should be feared and avoided, so the hero may protect himself against the seductive Circe and journey safely to Hades and back. On the day of his birth he crafts a lyre from a tortoise shell as a gift to Apollo, for which exploit he is associated as much with creativity and light as with darkness. As the inventor of language, Hermes embodies clarity, mediation and communication as well as deception, confusion and guile.

Stories of the birth of Hermes, like stories of the births of all gods and heroes, afford intimations of his elusive essence. According to Kerényi, one ancient tradition claims Hermes to be the son of Heaven (Uranus) and Bright Day (Hemera) but all stories reveal his primal and primordial character: his birth is invariably associated with the original Goddess in one or other of her many forms and so with what Goethe describes as the Eternal Feminine (a state approached, we must not forget, by way of the Realm of the Mothers). Seen in this light, Hermes may be understood as "the first evocation of the purely masculine principle through the feminine."[50]

Kerényi further comments:

Hermes, the source of his own world, was traced back to a masculine kind of life-source that remains very close to the feminine, yet only so close that it, being the more active, can still manage to bless the other more constant one with two new things: with itself, and with the continuance of its active nature, the child. This "continuance" can also be called Eros.[51]

---

[48] In literature, we find Shakespeare making use of the spirit of Hermes in figures such as Puck and Ariel in *A Mid-Summer's Night's Dream* and *The Tempest,* respectively.
[49] Karl Kerényi, *Hermes: Guide of Souls,* p. 84.
[50] Ibid., p. 62.
[51] Ibid., p. 66.

One "child" of Hermes is indeed Eros, or Hermes himself in infant form, representing the perpetuation of the god's active, creative nature. Hermes' connection to the feminine is emphasized also in his relation to his sister, Aphrodite. The Cyprian cult of Aphrodite describes the first androgynous being (Hermaphro-dite) as a manifestation of the goddess's masculine aspect, born of the incestuous love between Hermes and Aphrodite. Conversely, Aphrodite may be seen as Hermes' feminine attributes, in Kerényi's view perhaps the most prominent feature of the god until his masculinity is "born" and more clearly separated from the primal matrix of the Great Goddess. (In one story this occurs when Hermes catches sight of a beautiful goddess, a metaphor for the birth of eros, of sexual, erotic desire.)

All of these qualities point to the god's being an *agency* or active element of the life source itself, that imagined undifferentiated primal chaos in which everything persists *in potentia*. If this is so, the chthonic, phallic, procreative Hermes manifests the masculine principle, or maleness, per se. Hence we have depictions of the god as dual, as at once young and old, infant and bearded youth, son and father, begetter and begotten, for all these are qualities and potentialities of the generative, transformative imperative in the life source (or patrix, to use Marion Woodman's term). This imperative we designate generally as masculine, more particularly as hermetic or mercurial, and we attribute to it the active realization *in the world* of the Promethean spark of human consciousness.

The medieval form of Hermes/Mercury was Mercurius. As a personification of the spirit of transformation, Mercurius was equally a patron of the alchemical arts, a figure for the alchemist's essential ingredient, and a symbol for both the goal and the process of the alchemist's *opus*. Outwardly, as quicksilver, Mercurius played a crucial role in the alchemist's attempt to transmute chemical substances and to turn base metal into gold. Inwardly, as spirit, Mercurius embodied the mysteries of the human psyche.

Jung identifies the spiritual Mercurius with the winged youth who "stands for everything that is winged in the psyche or that would like to sprout wings,"[52] at once a representation of autonomous creativity and of the impulse to evade the restrictions and confinement of laws, circumstances, responsibilities and destiny. Singly, the winged youth "is the best, the highest, the most precious *in potentia*,"[53] yet he is volatile and in danger of going up in smoke, as does the hapless Euphorion, Goethe's puer in *Faust II*. Mythologically, if somewhat paradoxi-

---

[52] *Mysterium Coniunctionis,* CW 14, par. 197.

[53] Ibid., par. 200.

cally, Hermes/Mercurius is also linked to Silenus, who serves as mentor and senex to Hermes as puer, as he does to the boy-god Dionysus. This pairing points to the basic harmony of Hermes' and Silenus' phallic natures, showing "two sides of the same reality. . . . the Hermetic-spiritual aspect exists in friendly union with the animal-divine aspect."[54]

So we are back with Hillman's configuration, *puer-et-senex.* Kerényi has only to add that in some depictions of the two gods Silenus and Hermes exchange roles, an indication that at bottom they share "one and the same function: the conjuring of luminous life out of the dark abyss that each in his own way is."[55] Understood as the generative imperative of the life source itself, in one form or another, Hermes stands behind (and therefore prior to) everything. So mythology, in many genealogies of the gods, names him the father of Pan, goat-god of all nature.

Pan

The origins of the god Pan are obscure and uncertain. In various accounts he is cited as fathered by Hermes, and in others by Zeus, Kronos, Dionysus or a Titan. These possible "fathers" of Pan are of different generations, so it would seem, as Kerényi argues, that each generation of gods had its own Pan.[56] We find a Great Pan in the retinue of Dionysus but also numerous little Pans, or Paniskoi, that are like satyrs and are scattered throughout the stories of the gods.

The birth of Pan, as retold by Kerényi, follows the Homeric account of the god as the son of Hermes and a nymph. The story tells how Hermes, while pasturing sheep for a mortal master (in all probability Dryops), pursues and couples with the "Nymph of Dryops." The child born of Hermes' passion for Dryope is both magical and monstrous: he has a goat's feet and horns, a wild and bearded face, and crows and laughs so that his mother panics on sight of him and takes flight, abandoning her newborn baby. Hermes wraps the babe in the pelt of a hare (an animal sacred to both Aphrodite and Artemis) and takes him to Olympus where he is named Pan—from *pandemos,* "of all the people"—because all the immortals, in particular Dionysus, take delight in him.

A large number of Pan's ambiguous characteristics may be deduced from the Homeric version of his birth. Dryope, Pan's mother, was a nymph associated with the oak, a tree sacred to the Great Goddess. This links Pan to the woods and

---

[54] Kerényi, *Hermes,* p. 89.
[55] Ibid., p. 91.
[56] *The Gods of the Greeks,* p. 174.

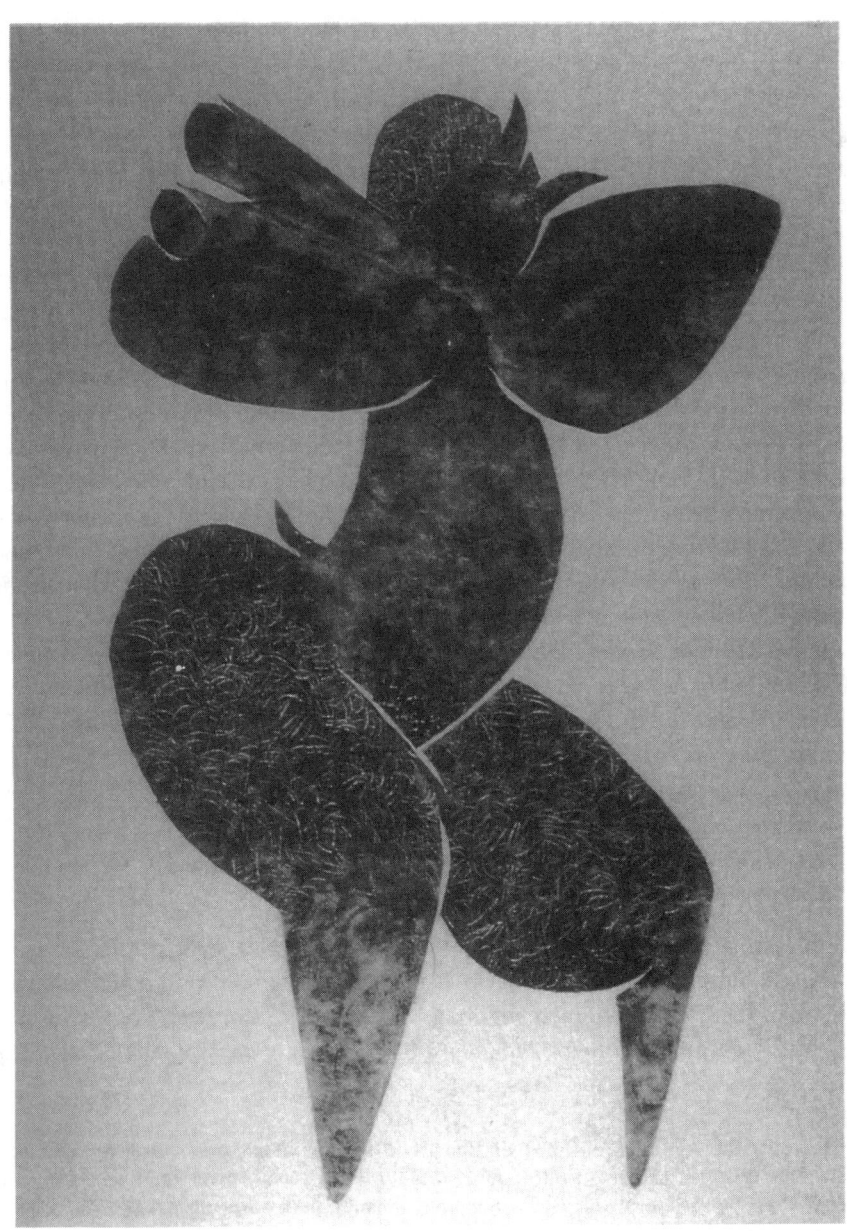

Pan the goat-god

to the physical universe in general. His cloven hooves, horns and goatish form, for which characteristics Christian imagery equated Pan with the Devil, attest to his being a god of instinct, a god of nature both *within* and *without*. Half-god, half-goat, at home in the woods and craggy mountainsides, often malignant and destructive, sometimes benign and protective, he acquires a dual aspect, combining qualities found elsewhere, in Teutonic and Celtic mythology, of the Wild Man and the Green Man of Nature, respectively.

The terror instilled in Pan's mother by the babe's monstrous appearance points to the god's dark, phallic, compulsive side and, in particular, to his capacity to awaken panic in animals and humans alike. Yet Pan "usher[s] in the morning and . . . [keeps] watch from mountain summits."[57] At night he leads in dance the nymphs that during the daytime he pursues endlessly yet fails to catch, except for one. Selene, the Moon Goddess and Pan's greatest passion, is seduced by the goat-god only after he has cloaked his dark hairiness in white sheepskins, a deception which points to two attributes of his father Hermes, as shepherd and trickster, and which likens Pan to the wolf-in-sheep's-clothing of proverb and folklore.[58] Pan must disguise his dark and wild midnight aspect when he is abroad at midday, although noon, paradoxically, is his sacred hour.

James Hillman, in his "Essay on Pan," argues that the archetypal dynamism of which Pan is a figure "expresses itself as a pattern of behaviour (panic and nightmare) and as a pattern of imagery (Ephialtes, Pan and his entourage)."[59] In the terrifying grip of the nightmare, which belongs to Pan,

> repressed nature returns, so close, so real that we cannot but react to it naturally, that is, we become wholly physical, possessed by Pan, screaming out asking for light, comfort, contact. The immediate reaction is demonic emotion. We are returned by instinct to instinct.[60]

So Hillman sees the figure of Pan as representing both ends of the spectrum on which Jung places instinctual behavior: the compulsive archaic behavior pattern of the god (panic, rape, nightmare) at one pole, and mythology's various images of Pan at the other (Dionysian Pan, Priapic Pan, Ephialtes Pan). The

---

[57] Ibid., p. 175.

[58] Several nymphs elude Pan but their successful escape of his goaty embrace exacts a high price: Pitys turns herself into a pine tree; Syrinx is transformed into a reed (the origin of seven-reed Pan pipes); Echo becomes disembodied, with the result that as pure voice, refracted sound, she is at once everywhere and nowhere in nature.

[59] *Pan and the Nightmare*, p. xiv.

[60] Ibid., p. xxiii.

mythological images constitute the form or "medium by which the compulsion can be modified through imagination . . . [so that by] . . . working on imagination, we are taking part in nature *in here.*"[61] We may add that our working imaginally on archetypal images must invariably return us to nature "in here," that is, to active reflection on psyche and in particular the instinctual ground of psyche. However, Hillman convincingly argues that Pan illustrates more directly than most mythological figures Jung's hypothesis that "images belong to the same continuum as instinct (and are not sublimations of it)."[62] Consequently, in a psychological approach to mythology and literature, our work on image, be it that of a god or literary character, will focus less on matters of concrete identity (*who* the god or protagonist might be) than, in the manner of Hermes, on the imaginal (*what* psychic phenomenon, instinct or quality is revealed in and through the figure in question).

Pan was first worshipped in Arcadia as the god of woods and shepherds. This early picture of him, as a pastoral deity concerned with the protection of shepherds, with making music and dancing, is perhaps simpler and less dark than later versions which tend to emphasize his grotesque rather than comic attributes. Yet the qualities of shock, surprise and spontaneity seem to have been part of his paradoxical half-goat, half-god nature from the beginning:

> It is not right, good shepherd, it is not right for us to pipe at mid-day: we are afraid
> of Pan; for in truth it is then he reposes wearied from the chase: and he is crabbed,
> and sharp anger ever rests upon his nostril.[63]

The story of Pan and Syrinx, as told by Ovid, gives us the origin of Pan pipes, and Arthur Golding's translation is too beautiful not to quote in full. Pursued by Pan, Syrinx comes to the river Ladon, where she discovers the water is too deep to cross. She beseeches the water nymphs to save her by changing her shape.

> And . . . when Pan betweene his armes, to catch y
>   Nymph had thought,
> In steade of hir he caught the Reedes newe growne

---

[61] Ibid., p. xxv.

[62] As possible representations of this hypothesis in art we might consider Goya's etching, "The Sleep of Reason," which depicts monstrous birds and animals crowding the sleeping thinker, and Fuselli's "The Nightmare," in which a primeval monkey crouches on the breast of a sleeping maiden while the head of a horse (for centuries symbolic of sexual, instinctual libido) watches from behind partially-drawn curtains.

[63] Theocritus, *Greek Anthology,* quoted in Patricia Merivale, *Pan the Goat-God: His Myth in Modern Times,* pp. 2f.

> upon the brooke,
> And as he sighed, with his breath the Reedes he
>   softly shooke,
> Which made a still and mourning noyse, with
>   straungnesse of which
> And sweetenesse of the feeble sounde the God
>   delighted mich,
> Saide certesse Syrinx for thy sake it is my full
>   intent
> To make my comfort of these Reedes wherein thou
>   doest lament:
> And how that there of sundrie Reedes with wax
>   together knit,
> He made the Pipe which of hir name the Greekes call
>   Syrinx yet. [64]

Here is the familiar picture of the goat-god engaged in his favourite pastime of chasing nymphs, but Ovid also alludes to his creativity and his capacity for reflection. In Ovid's depiction there is also something of the gentleness which Apuleius depicts in "Amor and Psyche" when Pan dissuades Psyche from a suicidal death by drowning. Yet Ovid's story of Pan and Syrinx is also a tale of *becoming* rather than of *being,* as it is equally one of tragedy: Pan remains alone, his passion unconsummated, and Syrinx is transformed utterly and irredeemably. The tale presents a tableau in which desire and anxiety (for Hillman the twin nuclei of the Pan archetype), the tenderness of love and the violence of rape, are as though frozen. Consequently, we are left with an image which holds, as though *in potentia,* the paradoxical quality of Pan's (and therefore our own) instinctual nature, an image which both invites and at the same time enables our conscious reflection.

The tale of Midas's judgment of the musicianship of Pan and Apollo clearly opposes the goat-god's "barbaric notes" to the "more than heavenly art" of the Olympian (without, however, suggesting an unambiguous opinion on Ovid's part). Midas alone prefers Pan's rustic pipes to Apollo's lyre and Apollo curses him with asses' ears for his pains. This tale represents a tendency in Western literature for the image of Pan to become less paradoxical and more differentiated over time until we encounter a bewildering proliferation of Pans: Pan as Devil, Pan as Christ; phallic Pan, pastoral Pan, grotesque Pan, horrific Pan and the Pan of burlesque; Pan as fat, jolly, old man and chubby cherub, Pan the Elfin

---

[64] Cited in ibid., p. 6.

Piper . . . Pan romanticized, sentimentalized, demonized, Christianized.

For our purposes, one of the most useful pictures of Pan developed in the Renaissance, giving us a more symbolic and philosophical Pan. Renaissance philosophers often paired Pan, as a figure for the Universal and the One, with Proteus, a god symbolic of the Particular and the Many, as seen in the following parable of Italian neo-Platonist Pico della Mirandola: "He who cannot attract Pan, approaches Proteus in vain." In Pico's view "mutability . . . is the secret gate through which the universal invades the particular. Proteus persistently transforms himself because Pan is inherent in him."[65] Conversely, we may understand Pico's parable to suggest that the endless possibility inherent in Pan is realizable only through the discriminating, individualizing shapeshifting of Proteus: the All of Pan, though everything, is in effect nothing unless given form as something. So Pico returns us to a more richly paradoxical Pan:

> In the ever-changing *balance des dieux* the gods reveal their Protean nature: but the very fact that each god contains his opposite in himself, and can change into it when occasion demands, makes him shadow forth the nature of Pan in whom all opposites are one.[66]

We are also back again with Hillman's notion of the *infirmitas* of the archetype and the fruitfulness of our thinking in terms of archetypal configurations *(puer-et-senex)* rather than in terms of discreet archetypal images (puer or senex). The Pan-Proteus configuration is rich indeed. It suggests the possibility of innumerable images (and therefore great psychological subtlety), depending on the relationship of Pan to Proteus imaged at any given moment (that is, what point on the Pan-Proteus spectrum or continuum is captured in a particular image). If we follow this line of reasoning it becomes clear how fitting a figure is this god whom we call Pan for imagination, for the movement of psyche, and so for life itself.

---

[65] See Edgar Wind, *Pagan Mysteries in the Renaissance,* p. 161.

[66] Ibid., p. 164. Jung has little to say about Pan but what he writes supports the idea of the god's representing the universal All, the One-in-the-Many, and instinctual nature and the body, those customarily debased repositories of perhaps the most profound wisdom. In *Mysterium Coniunctionis,* CW 14, par. 510n., Jung places the origin of the philosophical, symbolic image of Pan earlier than the Renaissance: "In late antiquity Pan was no longer a grotesque pastoral deity but had taken on a philosophical significance. The Naassenes regarded him as one of the forms of the 'many-formed Attis' and as synonymous with Osiris, Sophia, Adam, Korybas, Papa, Bakcheus, etc."

Dionysus, Christ

It is Dionysus/Bacchus to whom Ovid first applies his description of *puer aeternus:*

> He is young, this god,
> A boy forever, fairest in the Heaven,
> Virginal, when he comes before the people
> With the horns laid off his forehead.[67]

Dionysus is a type of the young, dying and reborn god. As an unborn child of Zeus in the womb of Semele, his mortal mother, Dionysus is threatened by Zeus's consort, the goddess Hera. Jealous of Zeus's love for Semele, Hera persuades Semele to ask her divine lover to appear in his true form. Knowing the girl will be destroyed when he appears to her in his full power, Zeus takes the unborn Dionysus from Semele's womb and hides him in his thigh, from which the infant god is delivered in due course. In a further attempt to annihilate Dionysus, Hera urges the Titans to dismember and devour the god's youthful body. This the Titans do. All is eaten except for the heart, and from this vital organ Dionysus is reconstituted and so born once again.

Dionysus shares many characteristics of Pan, who is frequently found in his retinue. He is a wanderer in lonely places; his domain is uncivilized nature and his rituals usually take place in the woods. Like Pan, he is born with horns, carries a staff (the phallic thyrsis, a fennel stalk wound round with ivy and topped with a fir cone). Both gods are associated with music and dance. Both gods are nature gods and vegetation deities, Dionysus presiding over the culture of grapes and the vine in particular. Each embodies the tendency to shock and surprise, to induce states of ecstasy and terror, to appear suddenly and to effect change. Dionysian excess and intoxication, comparable to Pan's lasciviousness and "barbaric notes,"[68] stand in opposition to Apollonian order and proportion, although Apollo also has his darker side. Pan's lower body is that of a goat, and Dionysus takes the form of a bull or goat during the enactment of his rites. In the shape of the animal, the god is ritualistically dismembered and his flesh consumed by celebrants in a symbolic appropriation of his divinity.

While Pan is associated with the pursuit of nymphs, Dionysus enjoys an entourage of ecstatic women, the Maenads. Neither god, however, knew a natural mother, Pan having first been cared for by Hermes and Dionysus by Zeus. As

---

[67] *Metamorphoses*, p. 81.
[68] William G. Doty, *Myths of Masculinity*, p. 182.

Head of the young Dionysus
(Late Hellenistic carving, found near Rome; British Museum)

Hillman points out, maternal abandonment, whatever form it takes, separates son from mother,[69] placing the infant in special relationship to the father and hence to the masculine principle. In such a case, the lens through which we view the genealogy and familial configuration of the god shifts subtly to focus on the young deity's spiritual connection to the father rather than his potentially incestuous and debilitating attachment to the mother. In this regard, Jung tells us of depictions of different aspects of Dionysus (as bearded man, as boy, as associated with phallus and semen) which appear on a Theban vase-painting and are believed to correspond to cult-images in the god's sanctuary, a conjecture "supported by what we know of the history of the cult, which is supposed to have been originally a Phoenician cult of father and son, an old and a young Cabir who were more or less assimilated to the Greek gods."[70]

Evidently Dionysus, like Pan, inherits from his father a powerful phallic character and so, with Pan and Hermes, is often understood as a figure for an instinctual, primordial dynamism, the "creative divinity" for which the phallus frequently stands.[71] This pattern of a strong early connection to the father suggests the persistence of a phallic power in and of itself, passed from father to son. Its continuity is independent of the mother although, instinctual and initially unconscious, it originates in the body, traditionally the symbolic domain of the Mother Goddess. The essential autonomy of this creative and procreative libido, or phallos, finds expression in Hermes' wand, the staffs of Dionysus and Pan, and the mercurial "life spark," that signal trait of the puer as spirit of renewal with which all three gods, together with Prometheus and Lucifer, are identified.

Euripides' play, *The Bacchae,* explores with great subtlety the relationship of Dionysus to the so-called feminine and masculine principles and so, by extension, the relationship of the puer to mother/mater and to senex. In the play, puer and senex personify conscious attitudes to self, world and the unconscious, as opposed to their usual role as indicators of gender or chronological age. It is the young ruler, Pentheus, who resists Dionysus's entry into Thebes, while the patriarchs, Tiresias and Cadmus, recognize the power of the god and participate, however reservedly, in his rites:

> *Tiresias:* We do not trifle with divinity.
> No, we are the heirs of customs and traditions

[69] "The Great Mother, Her Son, Her Hero, and the Puer," in Berry, *Fathers and Mothers,* pp. 182f.
[70] *Symbols of Transformation,* CW 5, par. 184.
[71] Ibid., par. 183.

hallowed by age and handed down to us
by our fathers. . . .
Did the god declare
that just the young or just the old should dance?
No, he desires his honor from all mankind.
He wants no one excluded from his worship.[72]

Old age (Cadmus, Tiresias) understands Dionysus's significance and knows how to approach him, while youth (Pentheus) is blinded by arrogance. Unconscious of his own instinctual nature, Pentheus projects the image of his divided self onto the world and sees the beast in Dionysus alone:

Pentheus: I seem to see two suns blazing in the heavens.
And now two Thebes, two cities, and each
with seven gates. And you—you are a bull
who walks before me there. Horns have sprouted
from your head. Have you always been a beast?
But now I see a bull.[73]

Unwittingly placing himself in the hands of the god when he succumbs to his own prurient curiosity, Pentheus allows Dionysus to disguise him as a woman so that he may spy on the Maenads. Once his voyeurism is discovered, Pentheus is torn apart by the deranged women of Thebes, led by his own mother. In this way, he becomes the sacrificial victim in place of Dionysus whose reality he denies, yet enacts, to his tragic end. While puer (Pentheus) and mother/matter (Pentheus's personal mother and the Maenads) remain totally under the god's power, there is clearly an active, if uncertain, relationship between puer (Dionysus) and senex/father-spirit (Cadmus/Tiresias) which is frequently represented by mythology's pairing of the boy-god Dionysus with the aged Silenus. In Hillman's terms, we see in these relationships a differentiation of puer as son, defined in relation to mother, and puer as embodiment of spirit, aligned with father or senex figures.

As a dismembered, dying and reborn god, Dionysus anticipates Christ. In both the pagan and Christian paradigms, the incarnation of the god symbolizes the realization of the divine spark, or spirit, in matter, the descent of the divinity into the material realm. In psychological terms, incarnation signifies a growth in consciousness which necessitates suffering at the divine as well as human level.

---

[72] *The Bacchae*, lines 200-209.
[73] Ibid., lines 918-923.

Both god and participant are changed. The original unity of the godhead (or unconscious) suffers division in order that the celebrant (or conscious ego) may assimilate something of the god's essence—through the ritualistic eating of the god's flesh in the case of Dionysus and the rite of the Eucharist in the Christian tradition. Again, as in the example of Pan and Proteus, the One, the godhead, becomes manifest by submitting to multiplicity. There occurs a differentiation of archetypal reality as, in the image of the dying and reborn god, a previously unrealized value enters life and consciousness. On the personal human level, the potential for renewal inherent in the godhead is experienced by celebrants of the god's ritual sacrifice as an enhancement of spirit, libido, creativity, love.

Despite the androgynous attributes of both Dionysus and Christ, the process of incarnation exemplified in their respective myths emphasizes the relation of puer to senex and the passage of spirit from father to son. We are reminded of Kerényi's description of Hermes' generative power as "a masculine kind of life-source that remains very close to the feminine, yet only so close that it, being the more active, can still manage to bless the other . . . with the continuance of its active nature."[74] This often appears in the form of a child as symbol of futurity, spirit, creative impulse, renewal, and the enlargement of consciousness, in man and woman alike. However strong the association of Dionysus with the body, the earth, seasonal cycles and hence the Great Goddess, and however prominent the traditionally feminine qualities of love, forgiveness, healing and mercy in Christ, each god is primarily a carrier of spirit. So Dionysus returns to Thebes to prove he is the son not only of the mortal Semele but of Zeus, the greatest of the Olympian gods; and Christ rebukes his personal parents in the temple, "Wist ye not that I must be about my father's business?"[75]

What is important in these examples is the recognition of the divine or archetypal dimension of spirit and of the individual as its vessel and vehicle. Both Dionysus and Christ, as culture heroes and carriers or renewers of spirit, point beyond the personal realm, beyond even the realm of the cultural manifestations of the archetypal Mother and Father to the province of spirit. The renewer of spirit must, by definition, push beyond established form, practice, idea and icon to discover a new direction that flies in the face of collective mores and an outmoded image of the godhead. So Christ's path is one of suffering as, inspired by a previously unconscious prerogative, He is spurned by the collective, whom His message redeems, and deserted by the Heavenly Father whose image He

---

[74] See above, p. 38.
[75] Luke 2:49, King James Bible.

transforms through His passion. Christ's suffering on the cross, and the dismemberment of Dionysus, speak to the ecstasy and horror that attend the birth of a new dispensation.

When we encounter the "mother's son," on the other hand, we meet the puer who either refuses to sacrifice his infantile attachments or, in heroically opposing the personal mother, buries the prerogative of his own fate in service to the collective or the Great Mother. This mother-son configuration affords no creative connection to spirit, and so the son fails to be about his "father's business," that of fulfilling his unique destiny, independent of filial obligations to the personal parents or civic responsibility to collective norms. Mythological examples are given in the next section of this chapter but examples from life might appear as the refusal of a long-desired opportunity for fear of failure, the avoidance of commitment for fear of disappointment, or lack of self-assertion for fear of social or parental disapproval and recrimination. The fundamentally insecure and ungrounded mother's son or only-puer remains focused on personal, narcissistic fulfillment, often preferring, like Walter Mitty, the incontestable realm of fantasy ideation to the inevitable risks and pitfalls of ordinary life. The fear of flying is great because the fear of falling is greater.

The only-puer has little or no connection with senex wisdom and father-spirit. He understands the father principle in its negative manifestation as law, as he understands the mother principle in terms of service or duty. As service needs to be transmuted into love, law needs to be transformed into spirit in the sense of a new ethic which, if consciously realized, would afford the courage and conviction necessary to the pursuit of an independent, and therefore individual, path. A dynamic relation of *puer-et-senex* inspires the mature adult to realize personal destiny through creative action in the world.

This process is best visualized as a continuum rather than as a dyadic, and potentially static, structure. On the continuum we must also place *vir*, the mature male, so that we may see the relation of the four ages or stages of masculine development which serve equally as metaphors for essential qualities of masculine energy in the female psyche: *puer-juvens-vir-senex*/boyhood-youth-maturity-old age. Ideally, as a perpetually vibrant continuum, the configuration puer-juvens-vir-senex holds the promise of repeated encounters of puer vitality with senex wisdom: encounters essential to the transition from sonhood to manhood (puer to vir) in the male, from maiden to woman in the female, and which shape and sustain the conscious choices of the mature adult.

While any continuum may be read as a linear progression, it is important, when describing psychic phenomena, to appreciate that in the timeless realm of psyche events overlap, fold back on themselves, occur synchronically and simultaneously. So we may understand puer-juvens-vir-senex as four qualities of libido that are always present, if not always conscious; four qualities of libido which color our perceptions, values and actions.

Icarus, Phaeton, Prometheus, Lucifer

Epithets applied to these youthful gods usually include reckless, irresponsible, defiant, rebellious, idealistic, proud, hubristic. Each figure may be seen as a type of the overreacher, one who is unconscious of, scoffs at or refuses to heed limitations. In the myths of all four, the connection to the father—its lack, insufficiency or failure—emerges as a central metaphor. Another important motif is the role of the mother. She is either missing—and so we may say that the values she typically embodies are missing and therefore "negative" (Icarus, Lucifer)—or, alternatively, she fails to carry that mature and positive aspect of the feminine principle which would promote her son's movement into adult life and relatedness and support his transition from boyhood to manhood. In any case, she fails to instill a realistic and firm sense of selfhood in the son and so to mediate a productive *puer-et-senex* alliance. The son remains forever a son.

Ovid tells us that Phaeton is full of pride as a boy, "boasting about his parentage" as supposed son of Helios.[76] However, we also learn that Phaeton only knows of his father by report, having spent his entire life in the care of his mother, the nymph Clymene. Phaeton has no relation to the senex pole of the father-son dyad and his puerile fanaticism, uncompensated by the wisdom of experience, seals his tragic fate. Finally granted his desire to drive the Sun-chariot of his father across the skies, he proves too weak and unskilled for the task and falls from the heavens to his death below.

Ovid makes two points that are of particular interest to our reflections on the relationship of puer to senex. The first is that Phaeton has been told nothing by his mother of his own limitations or of how to relate to his father's power. As "only-puer," he sets out to meet the Sun-God,

> Already imagining himself in Heaven,
> Crosses beyond his own frontiers to India,
> The nearest land to the starry fires of Heaven,
> And comes, exulting, to his father's palace.[77]

---

[76] *Metamorphoses*, p. 26.
[77] Ibid., p. 27.

Secondly, Ovid suggests that rashness is a quality common to father and son. Despite, and perhaps because of, the fact that father and son do not know each other, there is a reciprocal, compensatory connection between the two, with negative consequences because of its having remained unconscious and so unrealized: the son constellates rashness and inflated spirit in the father, which he then lives out in his fateful journey. Unthinkingly, Helios grants his son a wish. When Phaeton asks for "Control, for one day, over the winged horses" of the Sun-God's chariot,

> He [Helios] shook his shining head. "Your words,"
>   he said,
> "Have made mine rash: could I take back the
>   promise,
> This is the only thing I would deny you."[78]

There is a longer, stronger alliance between father and son in the case of Daedalus and Icarus yet it is not sufficiently strong to preclude disaster. The artisan Daedalus fashions wings that he and his son may escape from Minos's island of Crete and return to Athens. Icarus, however, fails to heed his father's warning to take the "middle way" between sun and sea. He is intoxicated with his power to fly, flies so high that the wax on his wings melts from the heat of the sun, and falls to his death in the ocean.

Although it seems that the fault lies with Icarus's youthful curiosity and impetuosity, Ovid reminds us of Daedalus's own impulsive behavior when earlier he murdered his nephew because he resented the boy's superior powers of invention. We must also remember that Daedalus, intoxicated with his ingenuity, fashioned the hollow cow which enabled Minos's Queen Pasiphae to mate with Poseidon's bull, a coupling that resulted in the birth of the Minotaur, its concealment in the labyrinth and Daedalus's imprisonment in the same labyrinth of his own making in the first place. So, in the story of Daedalus and Icarus the indication is of a regressive femininity, rather than a positive and conscious feminine principle sufficiently flexible and comprehensive to support a mature, independent malehood. There is, however, considerable evidence of a ruling masculine consciousness, both in Daedalus and the tyrant Minos who holds him prisoner, that is violent, jealous of youth and envious of youth's creative spirit. Without the support of a positive feminine influence, the failure of this *puer-et-senex* dyad might lie with Daedalus's early inability to respect limitations and so

---

[78] Ibid., p. 30.

to understand his own and therefore his son's nature. In Ovid's poetry, Daedalus's hubris is evident from the beginning:

> . . . He [Daedalus] turned his thinking
> Toward unknown arts, changing the laws of nature.[79]

Revisionings of the myth in art and literature are instructive of a tendency to undervalue the masculine configuration of father and son. Breughel's *Landscape with the Fall of Icarus* depicts Icarus's legs, small and pale, disappearing beneath the waves of the Icarian Sea in the background of the painting. In the foreground, a ploughman and a shepherd go about their business unaware of the mythological drama being played out a short distance away. W.H. Auden's poem, "Musée des Beaux Arts," written about the painting, emphasizes that while the Old Masters, such as Breughel, understood the archetypal background to life, ordinary men and women, busy with the material concerns of everyday existence, generally do not. Given our concern with the father-son dyad, we might add that while the ploughman and shepherd of Breughel's painting are engrossed in their work and so enmeshed in their relation to the earth and nature (that is, to mother/*mater/materia*), they remain unconscious of the archetypal backdrop of the masculine. The myth suggests that neglect of the masculine, and in particular the *puer-et-senex* relation, results in an unwitting sacrifice of the spirit of renewal signified by the puer.

The tragic loss of connection between father and son is taken up by James Joyce in his novels, *A Portrait of the Artist as a Young Man* and *Ulysses*. In the former, the hero Stephen Daedalus, having lost touch with and respect for his personal father, turns to his mythological father, Daedalus the Artificer, in order to find his own voice as a writer. In *Ulysses*, echoing Telemachus's search for his personal father, the wandering Odysseus of Homer's epic, a more mature Stephen continues his search for a "father" to fill the role of personal, spiritual and artistic mentor or "priest of the imagination." While it seems that separation and exile from Mother Ireland is essential to Stephen if he is to attain the objectivity necessary to the artist, Joyce's work suggests that in the end both Stephen's exile and his art are unrealizable without a living inner connection to the spirit, a viable *puer-et-senex* configuration symbolized, in this case, in the son's relation to a mythical father, Daedalus the Artificer.

Prometheus and Lucifer are figures that, with Cain, represent unrepentant defiance and rebellion against authority and so were traditionally regarded as

---

[79] Ibid., p. 187.

Landscape with the Fall of Icarus, by Pieter Brueghel, circa 1558

About suffering they were never wrong,
The Old Masters: how well they understood
Its human position; how it takes place
While someone else is eating or opening a window or just
    walking dully along;

. . . .

In Breughel's *Icarus,* for instance: how everything turns away
Quite leisurely from the disaster; the ploughman may
Have heard the splash, the forsaken cry,
But for him it was not an important failure; the sun shone
As it had to on the white legs disappearing into the green
Water; and the expensive delicate ship that must have seen
Something amazing, a boy falling out of the sky,
Had somewhere to get to and sailed calmly on.

    —W.H. Auden, "Musée des Beaux Arts."

dark and devilish until they enjoyed a form of redemption in the Romantic period. Prometheus tricks the gods and then steals fire from Zeus by hiding it in a fennel stalk in order to bring it as a gift to humankind, a gift which symbolizes the birth of consciousness, technology and the arts. For his championing of humanity he is chained to the Caucasus where a vulture devours his liver each day, the organ being replenished during the night. Finally he is rescued by Heracles and there is a reconciliation with Zeus, although Prometheus never repents his initial impulsive and creative act.

So for the Greeks Prometheus was very much a culture hero, a bringer of consciousness, and in this way his myth parallels that of Adam and Eve as well as that of Christ. In all three cases, as Edward Edinger points out, the gaining of consciousness or "egohood" is seen to be accompanied by inevitable suffering but suffering not only on the part of the ego:

> There is an archetypal advocate or benefactor that supports and assists the ego. Whether we call him the suffering servant of Isaiah or Prometheus or Christ, there is an advocate in the archetypal realm. Prometheus is perhaps the first and one of the finest expressions of this archetypal fact.[80]

The Romantic poets understood the rebellious energy that would defy authority and upset the status quo in the cause of consciousness as at worst a "necessary evil" and at best an heroic act. Such inspired rebellion is essential to the furthering of spirit even though, as Jung writes, "Since the better is always the enemy of the good, every drastic innovation is an infringement of what is traditionally right, and may sometimes even be a crime punishable by death."[81]

Thus Percy Bysshe Shelley, in *Prometheus Unbound,* his reworking of the Prometheus myth, makes the final reconciliation between father and rebel son reflect a marked change of attitude in both, a change that is mediated and supported by a strong, new feminine consciousness arising from the East in the figure of Asia.

In the case of Lucifer there is no mediating feminine influence to support a reconciliation of father and son. Rather than steal from God as Prometheus steals from Zeus, Lucifer plots to usurp the throne of God, no longer satisfied to sit at His left hand. Thrown out of Heaven as a result of his rebellion, yet unrepentant, Lucifer becomes the prototypical rebel, always in opposition to the father. There is, then, no movement, no possibility of change in the archetypal

---

[80] *The Eternal Drama: The Inner Meaning of Greek Mythology,* p. 17.
[81] *Symbols of Transformation,* CW 5, par. 396.

dynamics between this father and son who must remain, for all eternity, in a state of mutual enmity. This paralysis of psychic energy is well represented in literature in Dante's picture of a rigid, frigid Hell with Satan a giant, hairy-legged monster standing in ice to his waist.

Yet Satan/Lucifer is an angel, albeit a fallen one, and Lucifer means "bringer of light" as much as Satan signifies the Evil One. In this regard, the Romantic poets are instructive once again. They remind us that energy which pushes toward change, transgresses accepted limits and is traditionally regarded as evil, may, in fact, be good if it effects the necessary first step toward an expansion of consciousness—assuming, of course, with Jung, that consciousness is the greatest good.

Without contraries (that is, without a tension of opposites) there is no progression, or life, Blake tells us, as though anticipating Jung's model of psychic dynamics and, in particular, his concept of the psyche's transcendent function.[82] Understanding reason and inspiration as polar opposites, Blake argues that the right role of reason is not to shackle inspiration but to serve it as the limiter and shaper of that essential energy, which he understood as intuitive, transformative, poetical, prophetic and of the body. The nature of the marriage, *coniunctio* or meeting of creative libido and reason, determines the moral tone of the resulting product or action in human terms. In and of itself this vital energy of the body is amoral but, as the fire or motivating spirit of the life force, it exerts a powerful and seductive influence on the intellect, challenging the constructs of ego-consciousness in the process. This is why Blake argues that Milton is "of the Devil's party without knowing it,"[83] fascinated by the Devil's energy despite his Puritanical self, for the poetry of Lucifer's story in *Paradise Lost* has a strength and passion that is lacking when Milton writes of God and the angels.

Dual aspects of the mother (as terrible or devouring, good or good-enough), and the multifaceted face of the feminine have perhaps attracted more psychological attention than the masculine, with the result, until the publication of fairly recent studies on masculinity and the father, that an extensive differentiation of the subtleties and complexities of the masculine has been lacking. We have noted that the multifarious nature of gods such as Hermes and Dionysus, who are at the same time youths and bearded men, instinctual and reflective, returns us to an image of masculine spirit that is ambiguous and fraught with

---

[82] See "The Transcendent Function," *The Structure and Dynamics of the Psyche,* CW 8, and chap. three below.
[83] "The Marriage of Heaven and Hell," in *Complete Writings,* p. 150.

paradox. As Jung remarks, "the father apparently lives a life of unbridled instinct and yet is the living embodiment of the law that thwarts instinct."[84]

Fortunately, too, the legacy of the Romantic Movement's preoccupation with Lucifer, Prometheus and Cain provides rich and heterodox portraits of these traditional rebels in works of art which suggest, if often by default, the importance to psychological well-being and human experience of the complex relation of father to son, of senex reason to puer passion.

Attis, Actaeon, Narcissus, Hyacinth, Adonis

With these youths we come to what we might term analytical psychology's "classic" depiction of the puer, the beautiful boy who suffers a tragic and untimely death. Jung writes: "The lovely apparition of the *puer aeternus* is, alas, a form of illusion. In reality he is a parasite on the mother, a creature of her imagination, who only lives when rooted in the maternal body."[85]

The stories of all five of the youthful figures selected as examples of this type of puer show that there is in each case no saving connection to the father, no "weight" to the senex pole of the *puer-et-senex* configuration which would pull the youth into conscious maturity and out of a condition of infantile dependence, symbolized in his bond with the Mother Goddess and his early death.

Adonis, the child of Cinyras and Myrrha, a father/daughter incest deceitfully engineered by the daughter, is so adored by Aphrodite/Venus that he is unfit to fend for himself outside the cocoon of her protective embrace. His masculinity undifferentiated and his hunting skills untried, he is gored by the tusk of one of Artemis' animals, the boar. Likewise Narcissus, the child of the nymph Liriope's rape by the river god Cephisus, has no connection to either his father or to Tiresias, the blind seer to whom Liriope turns for advice but whose prophecy concerning her son's destiny (that Narcissus will live to a ripe old age "if he never knows himself") she seems neither to understand nor to consider.

In Ovid's version of the myth, even the mother disappears from the scene and Narcissus is left, an isolated youth, unable to enter into relationship with the world, unable to acquire the objective distance and consciousness of differences on which an I/Thou relationship depends. So he refuses Echo's love and is punished by Nemesis as a result, falling in love with his own image and pining away because his passion must remain unrequited: "The boy I love must die: we die

---

[84] *Symbols of Transformation*, CW 5, par. 396.
[85] Ibid., par. 393.

together."[86] Ovid suggests that the thirst Narcissus seeks to quench by the pool is an inner thirst. However, with no "father" to teach him the difference between substance and phantasm, as Hermes teaches Odysseus, he mistakes the phantasm for the substance, so his longing remains "unbodied" and the direction of his libido introverted and regressive unto death.

Narcissus is the type of Shelley's poet-hero of the poem "Alastor; or, The Spirit of Solitude," which tells of an inexperienced youth who leaves home to seek fulfillment. Shelley's hapless youth falls asleep in a lonely dell of a far country, and

> . . . A vision on his sleep
> There came, a dream of hopes that never yet
> Had flushed his cheek.[87]

The young poet dreams of a beautiful "veiled maid" whose embrace he cannot forget. Unable to distinguish the concrete from the imaginal, he believes his dream maiden to exist in the world rather than in the imagination, and seeks her single-mindedly, eschewing all offers of love and human companionship in the pursuit. Needless to add, Shelley's poet-hero dies lonely and tragically early:

---

[86] *Metamorphoses,* p. 72.

[87] Lines 149-151, in *Shelley: Poetical Works.* A note to the *Norton Anthology of English Literature* edition of the poem cites Thomas Love Peacock's statement: "The Greek word Alastor is an evil genius. . . . I mention the true meaning of the word because many have supposed Alastor to be the name of the hero." (Vol. 2, p. 665) Shelley writes in his Preface: "The poem entitled Alastor may be considered as allegorical of one of the most interesting situations of the human mind. It represents a youth of uncorrupted feelings and adventurous genius led forth by an imagination inflamed and purified through familiarity with all that is excellent and majestic, to the contemplation of the universe. He drinks deep of the fountains of knowledge, and is still insatiate. The magnificence and beauty of the external world sinks profoundly into the frame of his conceptions . . . So long as it is possible for his desires to point towards objects thus infinite and unmeasured, he is joyous, and tranquil, and self-possessed. But the period arrives when these objects cease to suffice. His mind is at length suddenly awakened and thirsts for intercourse with an intelligence similar to itself. He images to himself the Being whom he loves. Conversant with speculations of the sublimest and most perfect natures, the vision in which he embodies his own imaginations unites all of wonderful, or wise, or beautiful, which the poet, the philosopher, or the lover could depicture. The intellectual faculties, the imagination, the functions of sense, have their respective requisitions on the sympathy of corresponding powers in other human beings. The Poet is represented as uniting these requisitions, and attaching them to a single image. He seeks in vain for a prototype of his conception. Blasted by his disappointment, he descends to an untimely grave."

> . . . He did place
> His pale lean hand upon the rugged trunk
> Of the old pine. Upon an ivied stone
> Reclined his languid head, his limbs did rest,
> Diffused and motionless, on the smooth brink
> Of that obscurest chasm;—and thus he lay,
> Surrendering to their final impulses
> The hovering powers of life. Hope and despair,
> The torturers, slept; . . .
>
> . . . .
>
> . . . a bright stream
> Once fed with many-voicèd waves—a dream
> Of youth, which night and time have quenched for ever,
> Still, dark, and dry, and unremembered now.[88]

Shelley's youthful poet stands, then, as a figure for poetic inspiration itself which, if it is to live in the world, must appropriate the phallic energy represented by the father in order to resist the regressive pull toward unconscious instinctuality, represented in the paralyzing embrace of the negative mother, an embrace which signals the death of independent creative endeavor and autonomous spirit.

From Adonis's blood the anemone grows, and Aphrodite/Venus entreats Persephone, as Goddess of the Underworld, to allow Adonis to live on earth for a portion of the year. Accordingly, Adonis represents the cycle of dying and reviving nature, as does Hyacinth, a youth loved and accidentally killed by Apollo. Hyacinth's death and transformation into the flower of the same name suggest that he also originated as a vegetation god. While not associated with the cycles of nature, Actaeon, like Hyacinth, is seen only in the company of young men and, although taught to hunt by Chiron, he is shown in Ovid's account to lack the ego-strength and directedness normally associated with the phallic power of the father. Consequently Actaeon has left the hunt and is "wandering, far from certain, / Through unfamiliar woodland" when he offends Diana/Artemis by surprising her while she is bathing.[89] Impelled by instinct, Actaeon is reduced to instinct; the goddess turns him into a stag and he is torn apart by the very hounds of which he once considered himself master.

In *Symbols of Transformation* Jung discusses exhaustively the idea of the

---

[88] Lines 632-640, 668-671, in *Poetical Works*.
[89] *Metamorphoses*, p. 62.

dying and resurgent god in ancient Near Eastern sun-worshipping cults such as those centered on Osiris, Tammuz, Attis, Christ, Mithras, the phoenix. While Hyacinth, Adonis and Narcissus are linked to vegetation cults through the way in which they die and the flowers into which they are transformed, Osiris, Attis and Christ are linked to the tree. The dead Osiris is encased in the cedar tree, Christ is crucified on the rood, and Attis, the son-lover of Cybele, mutilates himself under the pine tree, symbol of the Great Goddess, because he is driven mad by his mother's jealousy.

Jung's commentary on the puer as "child of the tree" (that is, of the mother) is useful to quote at length as it summarizes our concern with the mother's son:

> As the tree signifies the origin in the sense of the mother, it represents the source of life, of that magical life-force whose yearly renewal was celebrated in primitive times by the homage paid to a divine son, a *puer aeternus*. The graceful [Norse god] Baldur [who dies by being wounded with a branch of mistletoe] is such a figure. This type is granted only a fleeting existence, because he is never anything but an anticipation of something desired and hoped for. This is so literally true that a certain type of "mother's son" actually exhibits all the characteristics of the flower-like, youthful god, and even dies an early death. The reason is that he only lives on and through the mother and can strike no roots in the world, so that he finds himself in a state of permanent incest. He is, as it were, only a dream of the mother, an ideal which she soon takes back into herself, as we can see from the Near Eastern "son-gods" like Tammuz, Attis, Adonis and Christ. The mistletoe [a parasite], like Baldur, represents the "child of the mother," the longed-for, revivified life-force that flows from her. But, separated from its host, the mistletoe dies. Therefore, when the Druid cuts it [ceremonially], he kills it and by this act symbolically repeats the fatal self-castration of Attis and the wounding of Adonis by the boar's tusk. This is the dream of the mother in matriarchal times, when there was as yet no father to stand by the side of the son.[90]

The puer who remains a mother's son fails to engage the senex pole of the *puer-et-senex* archetype. If we imagine a continuum, with Father and Mother at opposite poles, the mother's son would remain identified solely with the Mother end. The son evolves into hero only if he succeeds in opposing the maternal matrix, both inwardly and outwardly, in the forms of her cultural manifestations. Even then, as Hillman argues, he remains in the realm of the Goddess.

A youth who represents the puer as spiritual phenomenon, would, perhaps, succeed in realizing, consciously and independently, while not identifying with,

---

[90] *Symbols of Transformation*, CW 5, par. 392.

the attitudes and attributes represented by both parental poles. On a personal level, this would require the son/ego to attain sufficient consciousness to negotiate and maintain an individual stance vis-à-vis the personal parents and the parental complexes. In this way of painstaking differentiation one builds a strong and flexible ego, even as one risks being seen as an irredeemable rebel in the parental and collective eye. Such ego strength, in man or woman, would in turn support a powerful individuality, as well as enable one to mediate consciously the enigmatic movement of archetypal processes and psychic dynamics which pulls the weaker ego now toward the symbolic pole of the Mother, now toward that of the Father.

A possible fairy tale example of this is the heroine of "The Girl Without Hands."[91] Unwittingly sold to the Devil by her father and emotionally abandoned by her mother, she makes her own way in the world sustained by her faith in God, her connection to spirit and the Self. In myth we think of Perseus. Aided by Athena, a martial goddess with a highly differentiated masculine aspect, Perseus succeeds in slaying Medusa, image of the petrifying negative mother. His victory occasions the release of masculine spirit (the winged horse Pegasus is freed from imprisonment in the mountainside), which symbolizes his successful resistance to unconscious identification with the only-feminine.

Similarly Odysseus, championed by both Athena and Hermes, retains his independence of spirit and so learns to relate to but not be seduced by the numerous faces of the feminine that he encounters in the form of nymphs, sirens and goddesses on his long journey home from Troy to Ithaca.

Simon Peter: A Speculative Fantasy

Many of the attributes of the gods we have discussed are readily identifiable as character traits of Peter Pan. His habit of crowing like a cock links him to Pan and Dionysus, as does his piping. His impetuosity, magic, sudden appearances and ability to move between two worlds (Neverland and Edwardian London) are qualities of Pan, Hermes and Dionysus; spring is the season when we may expect Peter Pan to alight on our windowsill, and his association with springtime, renewal, youth, joy and spontaneity connects him to the dying and resurgent young gods of fertility and vegetation cults, as does Barrie's description of him as a type of the Green Man of Nature: "a lovely boy, clad in skeleton leaves and

---

[91] Grimm Brothers, *The Complete Grimm's Fairy Tales,* p. 160. Marie-Louise von Franz gives a psychological interpretation of this tale in *The Feminine in Fairy Tales,* pp. 80ff.

the juices that ooze out of trees."[92]

In many ways similar to father/son dyads and puer-et-senex configurations we have considered, Peter Pan's relation to Captain Hook is as necessary as it is problematic. There appears to be perpetual enmity between the two, yet the game of war in which they engage calls for "good form," an unwritten code of ethics to which both parties subscribe; and although Hook hates Peter Pan for his youth and cockiness, he is bored when Peter is not around, for all of Neverland is sleepy and lethargic until the boy returns. Mythological accounts of the son's rebellion against the father also find an analogue in Peter Pan's resentment of grown-ups and responsibility, and in his refusal to grow up to become a man.

Given the popular media's association of Peter Pan with all that is light, bright and joyful, it would seem almost sacrilegious to suggest that our children's hero harbors a dark and devilish side to his nature, reminiscent of the arch-rebel and fallen angel, Lucifer. However, when Mrs Darling looks out of the nursery window after the elusive boy she can "see nothing but what she thought was a shooting star," and we learn "there was a commotion in the firmament" on the night Peter Pan steals away her children.[93] We also have Barrie's own disappointment in the statue of Peter Pan in Kensington Gardens. Barrie commissioned sculptor Sir George Frampton to use for inspiration a 1906 photograph of his most treasured "lost boy," Michael Llewelyn Davies. Sir Frampton used another model and when the sculpture was erected (as only Barrie knew how, in secret during the night of April 30, 1912), Barrie bemoaned the fact that "it doesn't show the Devil in Peter."[94]

Neverland is certainly far from being an Edenic paradise. It has more than its share of intrigue, violence and brutality, and Peter Pan is seldom slow to mete out unmerciful retribution to enemies and erring disciples alike. Barrie's portrait of Neverland as a far from innocent and peaceable kingdom raises two further issues: the author's ambivalent treatment of the supposed idyll of childhood, and the quality of what Wendy describes as Peter Pan's "tragedy," which is perhaps the boy's refusal to sacrifice and endure the loss of Neverland, where he rules supreme, in order to enter fully into life in *this* world.

In other words, Peter Pan remains a quality of imagination, refusing incarnation into the human life cycle. This raises the possibility that he represents an autonomous creative impulse and spirit, with traits symbolic of other mythologi-

---

[92] *Peter Pan,* p. 37.

[93] Ibid., pp. 39, 49.

[94] Birkin, *J.M. Barrie and the Lost Boys,* p. 202.

cal harbingers of new consciousness (Prometheus, Christ, Dionysus).

To pursue this line of argument, and to turn to Peter Pan's Biblical namesake, Simon Peter, may at first seem beside the point or unconscionably frivolous, given that Barrie's tale is a children's fantasy. However, Peter Pan's last name was no accident, so we have no reason to suppose that Barrie's choice of the first was made without awareness of its Biblical connotations. Peter Pan shares several characteristics with Simon Peter. An amplification of the Biblical story may deepen our appreciation of Barrie's fantasy as well as shed some light on the issues introduced above: the shadow aspect of Peter Pan; Peter Pan as creative imperative and spiritual phenomenon; as "tragedy"; and as boy-god of a seeming paradise which yet thrives on conflict and is fraught with ambiguity.

Simon, later to be renamed Peter, was the first of the disciples called to follow Jesus and so to assist Him about His "Father's business." We learn from the Gospels that Simon Peter is an extremist; he is impetuous, quick to anger and capable of impulsive violence as when, for example, in his bid to save Jesus from arrest in the Garden of Gethsemane, he cuts off the left ear of the High Priest.[95] Of all the disciples, Simon Peter is perhaps the one most passionate in the profession of his faith. Jesus accordingly asks him to feed and tend His sheep, stops calling him Simon and names him Peter instead, founder of the Church and leader of the Christian fellowship on earth:

> You are Peter, the Rock; and on this rock I will build my church, and the powers of death shall never conquer it. I will give you the keys of the kingdom of Heaven; what you forbid on earth shall be forbidden in heaven, and what you allow on earth shall be allowed in heaven.[96]

Nevertheless, it is Peter who denies his relationship to Jesus three times "before the cock crows"; and it is Peter whose faith fails when he walks toward Jesus on the water and finds himself in danger of drowning.[97] Biblical legend also tells of Jesus appearing to Peter when Peter is fleeing persecution: Jesus asks him where he is going, which causes Peter to return to Rome to suffer his own death by inverted crucifixion.

While accounts of Peter point to his being too passionate to be ambivalent, his character is profoundly ambiguous: he is at different times fearless and fearful, faithful and lacking in faith, impetuous and steadfast, anxious to follow

---

[95] John 18:10.
[96] Matt. 16:18-19, New English Bible.
[97] Matt. 14:29-33.

wherever Jesus leads yet often reluctant to accept that Jesus must fulfill the prophecy of His sacrifice. Certainly Simon Peter experiences the shadow-side of faith, knowing fear, denial, anger and the failure of belief. This may be one reason why Jesus chooses him to head His Church. Given his knowledge of his own nature, Peter, of all the apostles, is perhaps most conscious of the vagaries and contradictions of human nature in general, and so more acutely aware of the particular dangers and human foibles on which the Church might founder.

The incarnation of spirit, as we have seen in our discussion of Dionysus and Christ, is a transformation often symbolized by dismemberment, sacrifice and suffering, a process which affects both the divinity and the human celebrant. In terms of personal psychology, the unconscious and ego-consciousness each undergo change. On the one hand, something of the divinity is appropriated by the believer; on the other, formerly unconscious energy is made available to consciousness, in the form, perhaps, of an insight, feeling, idea, new attitude or activity. An analogy may be drawn to the creation of many works of art. The visionary artist, that is, the artist who confronts impersonal, archetypal material, adopts a sacrificial and humble stance vis-à-vis his or her vision and so serves as the crucible in which raw inspiration becomes incarnate as artifact. The ego undergoes a form of sacrifice: it both submits to and collaborates in the autonomous creative process.

Yet sacrifice, if it is truly to be sacrifice, requires that the thing to be given up is the thing most highly valued. There is also no guarantee of the outcome, or if indeed there will be an outcome at all, for better or worse.[98] Consequently, there is often an understandable reluctance on the part of the sacrificial victim or martyr to embrace his or her fate, as there is often a corresponding reluctance on the part of the artist to relinquish the immediacy of visionary experience in order to engage in the arduous work of writing, sculpting, painting, composing. So with Simon Peter. In the Gospels, we read how on several occasions he begs Jesus to spare Himself from suffering, as later he tries to save himself by fleeing Rome. In this way, Simon Peter resists fate in a bid to forestall or deny the inevitable, even though his Christian faith promises that through sacrifice and suffering one gains rather than loses life.

Outrageous as it may at first sound, it seems that in very different ways the Biblical story of Simon Peter and J.M. Barrie's story of Peter Pan address the enigmatic qualities of faith and imagination, respectively. Both stories also

---

[98] I am reminded of Jesus' moment of total darkness on the cross when He feels utterly forsaken by God.

question the paradoxical relation of sacrifice and suffering to life, and of this world to a possible other world where new life or redemption may be attained (whether in the kingdom of heaven, the imagination or Neverland). For the believer, faith is primary, and for the poet, the prophetic imagination (hence Blake's proverb quoted earlier: "What is now proved was once only imagin'd").

Despite their differences, both faith and imagination move us away from what is ordinary toward something other, absent, missing. They open us to possibility, to the *extra*-ordinary, and in so doing enable an encounter with the transpersonal and numinous. Consequently, they connect us to our desire and, inevitably, to our lack, for we desire that which we assume to be lacking and so are pushed by our desire to unravel mysteries, fill gaps, restore order where chaos persists, become storytellers and prophets. "To imagine is to absent oneself; it is a leap toward a new life."[99]

Yet imagination, like faith, has the power to re-deem (re-value), for it allows us to re-member and, by re-membering and re-collecting, to restore life to lost possibilities. In the activity of re-membering, through religious observance, music, art, literature or life, we imagine and make present that which is lost or forgotten, as well as that which has not yet been. In this way both faith and imagination bind together past, present and future, out of which synthesis we make a cohesive story and so imbue life with meaning. However, if imagination and faith connect us to desire, they also concern us with movement and change, impelling us toward the new while at the same time compelling us to sacrifice the old. Consequently, as we learn from the Gospels, Simon Peter's faith is continually put to the test, to be proven, made incarnate, lived. First Jesus asks him to leave his work as a fisherman to become a fisher of men by spreading the gospel, and finally he is required to fulfill the prophecy of a death that, as Jesus tells him, will "carry you where you have no wish to go."[100]

In the figure of Peter Pan we have an example of one who resists change and refuses sacrifice, and in this we are reminded that imagination, like faith, must undergo constant renewal, otherwise it may become petrified and petrifying, keeping us out of life. Unlike faith, however, imagination does not only connect and sustain but also can disconnect, dissolve, loosen, deform, distort. Just as faith cannot be fully lived without being tested, imagination too must face conflict and pain. The question which follows, and which I think Barrie is asking in

---

[99] Gaston Bachelard, *On Poetic Imagination and Reverie: Selections from the Works of Gaston Bachelard*, p. 21.
[100] John 21:19, New English Bible.

Peter Pan, is: What brings us to a sense of vitality and meaning?

For Simon Peter, new life and profound meaning are attained through Christ, through self-sacrifice, through the struggle to emulate Jesus in his ministry and to live his faith *in the world.* Barrie, however, seems to be questioning where life may be found: in the world, in the imagination, or in artistic process and the work of art; in this case, in story? Peter Pan cannot make the sacrifice necessary to enter fully into the world. He draws Wendy and her brothers into *his* realm for a short while but he cannot, or chooses not, to live in theirs; as we said of the puer, he is never quite *in life.* At one point Peter Pan declares, "To die will be an awfully big adventure,"[101] and another time, in the play, he tries to say, "To live will be an awfully big adventure."[102] Each statement remains in the future tense and he does neither, trapped forever, from the perspective of ego, in a world of make-believe.

Barrie's fascination with his children's hero and his tinkering with the novel for over twenty-five years suggest that life and meaning may be found in and through the *activity* of story, an activity which primarily concerns our relationship to imagination.[103] When we think of Simon Peter, we realize that his life is embedded in story: his ministry concerned the spreading of Jesus' message, the Gospel, but he lived in *this* world and, in realizing his faith in this way, he wove his own enigmatic story. On the other hand, we learn that Peter Pan has no memory: he knows no stories, cannot remember his mother and is in danger of forgetting who Wendy is from one moment to the next.

Without memories, Peter Pan has no history, no story, no meaning. He appears to be trapped in a static, cyclical round of arbitrary adventure which he refuses to sacrifice and, in human terms, this refusal is his tragedy. It is Barrie who gives Peter Pan substance, incarnating in story something of the spirit for which he stands. Indeed, early on Barrie tells us that "there will be no story" if Mr and Mrs Darling return to the nursery before the children have flown off with Peter to Neverland.[104]

---

[101] *Peter Pan,* p. 129.

[102] *Peter Pan and Other Plays,* p. 153.

[103] I cannot help ask the question: "But how is this enough?" when I recall references to Barrie as "that odd, morbid little genius" (Lord Boothby) and as having an "overwhelming desire to end his own life—a life rendered utterly pointless without Michael," perhaps the dearest of his "boys," who drowned while bathing in Sandford Pool, Oxford, at the age of twenty. (See Birkin, *J.M. Barrie and the Lost Boys,* pp. 283, 194)

[104] *Peter Pan,* p. 65.

We may argue that Simon Peter's suffering lay in his difficulty in differentiating the historical, material person of Jesus from Jesus as the Christ, the essential new ethic or quality of spirit realized through His passion: the story of Peter's ministry becomes, then, the story of his realization that Jesus is vehicle and vessel for Christ. The equivocal, illusory nature of Barrie's hero may also lie in his problematic relation to matter: he both desires and refuses to be caught and brought into life; he both craves and resists sacrifice and transformation.

As a figure for the autonomy of spirit and creative fantasy, Peter Pan belongs to the archetypal realm of possibility. As harbinger and agent of new experience, he must suffer the pain of transformation repeatedly but never finally; yet the conscious ego may undergo finite transformation as a result of his agency. Nor can Peter Pan be brought fully into life. His story, if it is to be told at all, must be our story, a tale of the continual struggle to realize and so incarnate something of our experience of transcendent reality that by its nature can initially be "only imagin'd."

3
J.M. Barrie and the
Accidental Art of Mythmaking

It is not that we personify, but that the epiphanies come as persons.
—James Hillman, *Pan and the Nightmare.*

Italo Calvino, in his essay, "Cybernetics and Ghosts," discusses the relation of storytelling to mythical meaning, proposing a dynamic theory of myth in which narrative art and poesis play a primary and creative role:

> Mythic significance is something one comes across only if one insists on playing around with narrative functions. . . . The storyteller [or tribal poet] goes on . . . inventing new developments in composition, until in the course of this methodical and objective labour he suddenly gets another flash of enlightenment from the unconscious and the forbidden.[105]

Calvino emphasizes chance, accident, risk and play, factors which more subtly describe the unpredictable way of psyche than, perhaps, Northrop Frye's understanding that the basic structures of mythic narrative reflect, because originally derived from, the cycles of nature. For Frye, as for Joseph Campbell, the cyclical pattern of the quest or journey of the "solar" hero follows the circular passage of the sun's path and the rhythm of seasonal change.[106]

Campbell argues that the cyclical direction of the heroic quest determines the fundamental shape of Western and possibly of all mythology. And Frye affirms the relation of mythology to literary art by arguing that there are only two types of story, each structured, at base, on the same cyclical quest motif: the sacred stories of, for example, the Koran and the Bible; and secular stories. Frye describes secular stories as "displaced myth," because the indelible patterns of mythic narrative on which the writer more or less consciously structures a work, though often faint and difficult to discriminate, are nevertheless detectable beneath the contemporary cultural dress of the modern novel, drama or poem. A useful metaphor for Frye's image of literature might be that it functions as a

---

[105] *The Uses of Literature*, p. 23.
[106] See Frye's *Anatomy of Criticism, The Secular Scripture* and *Fables of Identity,* and Campbell's *The Hero with a Thousand Faces.*

palimpsest: beneath the tale and the author's consciously crafted layers of allusion may be discerned traces of the myth which confers meaning and form to the work as a whole.

Calvino's fantasy of the discovery of mythic significance through the accidental art (or art of accident) that he attributes to the storytelling of the tribal poet may well have found an analogue in J.M. Barrie's idiosyncratic method of literary composition. It seems that play, particularly the play of a youthful imagination, was of great importance to Barrie. Physically small, he appeared boyish even as a man and continued to value the wild imaginings, stories and games of boyhood all his life. So Michael Hearn quotes Barrie as having once confessed:

> The horror of my boyhood was that I knew a time would come when I also must give up the games. . . . (this agony still returns to me in dreams, when I catch myself playing marbles, and look on with cold displeasure); I felt that I must continue playing in secret.[107]

Barrie evolved the character of Peter Pan through the spontaneous play of imagination. He enjoyed many happy hours engaged in storytelling with the Llewelyn Davies boys, a family of eventually five children he befriended in Kensington Gardens, where he often walked his Newfoundland dog, Porthos. The boys were fascinated by Barrie, the strange little Scotsman who "could lift one eyebrow while he dropped the other, and . . . knew a lot of stories."[108] The childless Barrie soon came to consider them "his boys," and virtually adopted the entire family as his own, although not without some resentment on the part of Arthur Llewelyn Davies, the boys' father. In *The Little White Bird* (1902) Barrie describes the way in which he and George, the oldest of the Llewelyn Davies boys, would start with the merest snippet of a tale and then embroider it together into something quite other than the original:

> First I tell it to him and then he tells it to me, the understanding being that it is quite a different story; and then I retell it with his additions, and so we go on until no one could say whether it is more his story or mine.[109]

Finally, as Barrie describes him, Peter Pan was born of the love his author bore for all five of the Llewelyn Davies boys: "I made Peter by rubbing the five

---

[107] "Introduction," *Peter Pan*, p. 5.
[108] Janet Dunbar, *J.M. Barrie: The Man Behind the Image*, p. 138.
[109] Hearn, "Introduction," *Peter Pan*, p. 8.

The Llewelyn Davies boys in a locket.
Left, top to bottom: Michael, Peter, George.
Above, top to bottom: Jack, Nico.

of you violently together, as savages with two sticks produce a flame. That is all he is, the spark I got from you."[110] In Calvino's words, Peter Pan may be considered a gift or flash of enlightenment from the unconscious and the forbidden.

D.W. Winnicott's writings on the importance of play are useful to our understanding of the possible connection between Barrie's predilection for verbal puns, fantasy and whimsy, on the one hand, and his creation of that bright imaginative spark of life, Peter Pan, on the other. "It is in playing and only in playing," Winnicott tells us, "that the individual child or adult is able to be creative and to use the whole personality, and it is only in being creative that the individual discovers the self."[111]

---

[110] Ibid., p. 15.
[111] *Playing and Reality,* p. 54.

In play, according to Winnicott, we substitute "non-purposive being" for "purposive activity." Non-purposive being, or play, involves the free movement of fantasy. It leads to a state of "near-withdrawal" and a mood of intense preoccupation, both of which enable freedom of association and allow the child to "invest external phenomena with dream meaning and feeling." While totally absorbed in play, the child or adult feels wholly himself. Inner and outer fuse into inseparable parts of an event that is experienced as a seamless whole, for the one so engrossed unconsciously shapes and colors external phenomena according to an undeniable inner prerogative. The tattered teddy-bear discarded in the corner now begins to look like Winnie-the-Pooh, is Pooh and then, as Pooh, remains vital and present, a boon companion for a moment, an hour, a day.

Winnicott understands creativity released through play as the capacity to feel fully alive and committed to the moment, a capacity which promotes both a sense of trust in the world and a sense of oneself "as a unit . . . as an expression of I AM, I am alive, I am myself." However, he warns against the equation of creative play with creative endeavor. The search for self is not necessarily to be satisfied in the creation of a work of art, no matter how successful that work may be. If the potential for creative living is seriously impaired or thwarted, rather than realize a sense of self through an outer object or product, the individual is more likely to develop a false personality, a hidden secret life "that is satisfactory because of its being creative or original to that human being."[112]

As a young boy Barrie sought the protection of just such a hidden inner sanctuary, for his outer life, from the age of six, was continually shadowed by sadness and loss. The first and greatest tragedy was the accidental death of his brother David, whose place as the mother's favorite Barrie struggled but failed to fill. So desperate was the young Barrie for his mother's affection that "he learned his brother's special whistle from the dead boy's friends, put on a suit of David's clothes, went into his mother's room, cried 'Listen!' and began to whistle."[113] While Barrie grew older, memory enshrined and idealized David as the thirteen-year-old boy he had been when he died: in the Barrie family imagination David was the boy who never grew up.

Barrie's own memories of childhood therefore account less for his later love of youth and play than those of his mother, Margaret Ogilvy:

Barrie's lifelong quest for the Land of Lost Content, which so often seemed to

---

[112] Ibid., p. 68.

[113] Dunbar, *J.M. Barrie*, p. 13.

manifest itself in his affinity with children, was no nostalgic desire to return to his own boyhood. It was, rather, a craving to experience a childhood he had never personally known: the childhood of Margaret Ogilvy.[114]

As an adult disappointed by a childless, failed marriage which ended in divorce, and seldom fully at ease in the world, Barrie found that his irrepressible love of play ensured him freedom of access to the fantasy worlds of his boyhood reading, first discovered in Stevenson's *Treasure Island, Coral Island* by R.M. Ballantyne and the *Leather-Stocking Tales* of James Fennimore Cooper. There, and in the Neverland he was to create, Barrie could escape the pain of both life and death in a secret, timeless realm of adventure and make-believe. The need and ability to retreat into and recreate his own childhood fantasy, or that of his mother's youth gleaned from her stories of the past, does not, however, account for the fact that Barrie's best-known hero has become a household familiar and children's favorite. Nor is Peter Pan's compelling image fully explained or captured in popular psychology's diagnosis of all "men who have never grown up" as suffering from the Peter Pan syndrome.[115]

"The most powerful writers," Harry Levin argues, "gain much of their power by being mythmakers, gifted—although they sometimes do not know it—at catching and crystallizing popular fantasies."[116] The impact on the collective imagination of the figure of Peter Pan, apart from either the play or novel in which he features, points to Barrie's having created a children's hero of mythic dimension. At the same time, it would seem that Barrie's "lost boy" served to mirror something of the existential concerns of many living in the first quarter of the twentieth century, at the time of his creation, and that Peter Pan continues to reflect an aspect of the modern psyche on the individual and collective levels.[117]

---

[114] Birkin, *J.M. Barrie and the Lost Boys,* p. 38.

[115] See Dan Kiley, *The Peter Pan Syndrome.* On the cover of Dr. Kiley's book is the statement: "Every woman has known one, loved one, married one, left one, or survived one . . . but no woman can resist one." Kiley highlights six key symptoms which he argues constitute the syndrome: anxiety, loneliness, irresponsibility, sex role conflict, narcissism, and chauvinism. Together these symptoms add up to what Kiley describes as the crisis of social impotence.

[116] "Some Meanings of Myth," in H.A. Murray, ed., *Myth and Mythmaking,* p. 112.

[117] *Peter Pan,* the play, was first performed in London on December 27, 1904. The novel first appeared in 1911 under the title *Peter and Wendy. Peter Pan in Kensington Gardens* (1906) was a reprinting of *The Little White Bird* (1902), stories which Barrie had composed during the storytelling play he enjoyed with George Llewelyn Davies, and which contains only some of the events that appear in the play and the novel. Barrie continually

Peter Pan's popularity indicates that Barrie's hero carries archetypal significance, providing a fantasy figure to satisfy the child's thirst for freedom and adventure, and at the same time a twentieth-century image of mythology's *puer aeternus* or eternal boy. In terms of Winnicott's theory of creativity, we may argue that Peter Pan presents a timely "accident of play." When we turn to Jung, however, we may begin to understand Barrie's eternal boy as both the product of his author's fantasy-thinking and a symbol for spirit and the spark of autonomous creative fantasy discoverable in the matter of the individual psyche.

Jung contrasts fantasy-thinking, which brings the whole soul into play, with directed-thinking. Directed-thinking tends, as an instrument of culture, to be a linear, utilitarian thinking in words, adapted to communication and activity in the outer world. Fantasy-thinking comes to the fore as soon as consciously directed thinking and attention to external phenomena recede, and through fantasy-thinking we access "the unconscious bases of dreams and fantasies" which present a picture of archaic or mythological thought-forms. These thought-forms are, according to Jung, "based on instinct, [and] naturally emerge more clearly in childhood than they do later."[118]

Jung also talks of different levels or degrees of fantasy-thinking:

> Much of [fantasy-thinking] belongs to the conscious sphere, but at least as much goes on in the half-shadow, or entirely in the unconscious, and can therefore be inferred only indirectly. . . . The fantasy-products directly engaging the conscious mind are, first of all, waking dreams or daydreams . . . then ordinary dreams, which present to the conscious mind a baffling exterior and only make sense on the basis of indirectly inferred unconscious contents. Finally, in split-off complexes there are completely unconscious fantasy-systems that have a marked tendency to constitute themselves as separate personalities.[119]

Such "separate personalities" may be projected into the creation of literary figures as well as onto external phenomena, actual persons, concrete objects and institutions. The image of the spectrum yet again becomes useful. If we place fantasy-thinking and directed-thinking at either extreme (as Jung locates instinct and archetype at the infrared and ultraviolet ends of the spectrum, respectively),

---

reworked the play, which was not published until 1928, only nine years before his death in 1937. It is interesting to note that British and American expatriates in Paris during the 1920s were dubbed "The Lost Generation," and T.S. Eliot's "The Waste Land," depicting the spiritually bankrupt and fragmented world of that generation, was published in 1922.

[118] "Two Kinds of Thinking," *Symbols of Transformation,* CW 5, par. 38.

[119] Ibid., par. 39.

we move away from a dualistic model to one which allows a finer differentiation of thinking. Whereas ego-consciousness may ordinarily slide, often involuntarily, from the directed-thinking end of the scale toward fantasy-thinking, the artist perhaps has the capacity to work the spectrum to artistic advantage more consciously than most, stimulating creative process as a result. Jung describes what transpires when one plays both ends of the spectrum as I picture it: "Through fantasy-thinking, directed-thinking is brought into contact with the oldest layers of the human mind, long buried beneath the threshold of consciousness"—a movement of psyche essential to the artist as mythmaker.

"Two Kinds of Thinking" was an early essay (1911) and Jung was soon to replace "archaic thought-forms" with the hypothesis of the archetypes as humankind's inherited and, at base, instinctual disposition, always and everywhere, to express the experience of self and world in similar forms, stories and figures. For examples of archetypal reality at work in the world, we have only to look at the striking parallels in tales of the gods and heroes of disparate cultures and belief systems, brought to our attention by scholars of comparative mythology and religion. The archetypal basis of life is also recognized, in disciplines ranging from the pure and applied sciences to the humanities and social sciences, in the eternal return of patterns of history, cross-cultural similarities in structures of ritual and social order, correspondences between physical and psychical reality, and in the essentially unchanging face of human need and human nature reflected both in the individual and in the collective arena of social behavior, politics, religion and the arts.

Although images arising spontaneously from the *archetypal field*[120] of the

---

[120] It is useful to use the adjective *archetypal,* wherever appropriate, as opposed to the noun *archetype.* This makes one less susceptible to the error of conceptualizing archetypal reality as something ultimately knowable and representable, as a "thing" of which one may take hold. Jung emphasizes that the archetype *an sich* remains an hypothesis and cannot be known in itself and in its entirety. We surmise something of the nature of the underlying archetype from the character of its manifestations in mythological, artistic and religious symbolism, and in patterns of human behavior and thought. The word *field* is useful in discussing the realm of the collective unconscious and archetypal substratum of the psyche, especially as it meets ego. Rather than tempt one to place the unconscious concretely above, below, east or west, the term suggests a magnetic field which, by definition, is invisible, is nowhere and everywhere, whose powers of attraction and repulsion shift as external conditions change (and vice versa), and whose nature may be deduced solely from its effect on phenomena. This seems to afford a workable metaphor for the shifting, unconscious archetypal dynamism upon which ego-consciousness rests.

collective unconscious "emerge more clearly in childhood" and in the thinking of so-called primitives, Jung cites a certain type of artist as experiencing often involuntary access to this substratum of the psyche through the eruption of the creative process as an autonomous complex. Such a complex of psychic energy may invade and completely override the conscious orientation of the artist. This phenomenon often manifests in the form of an authoritative voice which dictates the material (as Milton claimed of *Paradise Lost*), or as a dream-vision, in which case we are reminded of Coleridge's "Kubla Khan," and Stevenson's *Dr. Jekyll and Mr. Hyde,* both works, according to their respective authors, having presented themselves in their entirety in dreams. We are reminded that Mary Shelley, at the tender age of eighteen, received her original inspiration for *Frankenstein* in a nightmare image of the monster that has now assumed, in the popular imagination, the name of its fictional creator, Dr. Frankenstein.

Distinguishing between the *psychological* artist who holds himself to be in conscious control of material and intent, and the *visionary* artist who becomes the vehicle of the creative process moving within, Jung writes:

> The unborn work in the psyche of the artist is a force of nature that achieves its end either with tyrannical might or with the subtle cunning of nature herself, quite regardless of the personal fate of the man who is its vehicle. The creative urge lives and grows in him like a tree in the earth from which it draws its nourishment. We would do well, therefore, to think of the creative process as a living thing implanted in the human psyche. . . . this living thing is an *autonomous complex*. It is a split-off portion of the psyche, which leads a life of its own outside the hierarchy of consciousness.[121]

We can hardly assume that Peter Pan represents a split-off portion of Barrie's psyche. Such a line of questioning amounts to speculation about the author's personal psychology that may never be verified and that is in any case not germane to our later consideration of Peter Pan as *image*. Nor is it productive to compare Barrie to those writers universally acclaimed as visionary "greats," for example Dante, Shakespeare and Goethe. An intrusion of content from the archetypal psyche, since time immemorial seen by the artist as curse as much as gift, does not necessarily result in a work of enduring aesthetic value. Aesthetic merit is dependent upon the craftsman's skill in shaping, consciously, the raw

---

[121] "On the Relation of Analytical Psychology to Poetry," *The Spirit in Man, Art and Literature,* CW 15, par. 115.

material of his art.[122] Its recognition is also subject to the vagaries of prevailing taste. Works which tap the archetypal dimension of the psyche often lack the formal cohesion of the well-made psychological (that is, psychologically coherent and rational) artifact. They may appear difficult, uneven and in places incomprehensible, evidence that the accomplished artist is struggling to discover a form that in some way approximates unfamiliar, sometimes bizarre, terrifying and unholy images.

We find several indications that Peter Pan may well be described as a gift "from the unconscious and forbidden" (Calvino). Barrie claimed that he "had no recollection of having written" the play,[123] and although such a statement is easily attributable to Barrie's whimsical nature, it may also point to the figure of his boy hero having been *presented* to consciousness by the archetypal psyche. The unevenness of the text would suggest as much, lending support to Michael Hearn's contention that *Peter Pan* "is Barrie at his best and Barrie at his worst."[124] At times Barrie indulges in extreme sentimentality (the Newfoundland dog as nurse to the children; Peter as "very like Mrs Darling's kiss"). At others he appears heartless ("Mrs Darling was now dead and forgotten"); and the tone of voice in which he occasionally directly addresses the reader is now empathetic, now a little condescending, now revealing his complex and ambivalent feelings toward childhood ("Tedious talk this . . . ," Barrie's authorial voice interjects after his description of the origin of fairies).

Inconsistencies in tone throughout, and examples of "slippage" such as that found on the opening page from "all" to "they" to "you" (*"All* children grow up, except one . . . ;" *"They* soon know that they will grow up . . . ;" *"You* always know after you are two . . .") indicate an uncertain authorial voice, and disclose a relationship of Barrie to his characters that places Barrie himself in the position of the only boy who does not grow up, namely Peter Pan.[125] These artistic "faults" also indicate that the objective distance of the craftsman is, on occasion, missing and that Barrie is consequently not always in full control of his material. Indeed, it would seem that a work bearing archetypal significance is often rec-

---

[122] This is evident from Jung's interest in minor works, for example Rider Haggard's *She*, as well as the works of thinkers and poets such as Goethe and Nietzsche. Focus is placed on figures, symbols, and images as carriers of archetypal significance within a work rather than on the work as aesthetic object in its own right.

[123] Hearn, "Introduction," *Peter Pan*, p. 3.

[124] Ibid., p. 18.

[125] Jacqueline Rose, *The Case of Peter Pan*, p. 68.

ognizable by the character of its flaws, however minor.

We have so far considered two roads, apart from night dreams and visions, by which we gain access to the mythological stratum of the unconscious: the play of fantasy-thinking and the eruption of an autonomous creative complex. There is one other psychic dynamic which we need to bear in mind when considering the accidental art of mythmaking: the transcendent function.

In his essay, "The Transcendent Function," Jung speaks of the compensatory and complementary relation of the unconscious to consciousness, and of the intensity which psychic material needs to attain in order to remain above the threshold of consciousness. Contents lacking the necessary "threshold intensity" fall into or have always belonged to the unconscious,

> [which] contains not only all the forgotten material of the individual's own past [personal unconscious], but all the inherited behaviour traces constituting the structure of the mind [collective unconscious]. . . . [Also] the unconscious contains all the fantasy combinations which have not yet attained the threshold intensity, but which in the course of time and under suitable conditions will enter the light of consciousness.[126]

The transcendent function "arises from the union of conscious and unconscious contents."[127] This inevitably results in a tension between the old ego attitude and the new, disturbing content from the unconscious which may present itself in the form of dreams, fantasies, doubts, neurotic behavior and external accident. This tension needs to be held (that is, suffered) and consciously explored until an alternate attitude presents itself. The desired change in attitude means neither a fundamental lessening in value of the two poles of the former tension, nor the assimilation of one by the other. As Jung explains,

> The confrontation of the two positions [i.e., consciousness and previously unconscious material] generates a tension charged with energy and creates a living, third thing—not a logical still-birth in accordance with the principle *tertium non datur* ["the third not given"] but a movement out of the suspension between opposites, a living birth that leads to a new level of being, a new situation.[128]

The "third [hence transcendent] thing" born of a tension between consciousness and the unconscious may present itself as a new understanding (we recognize the "ah-ha" experience that attends such moments) or as a "creative formu-

---

[126] *The Structure and Dynamics of the Psyche,* CW 8, par. 132.
[127] Ibid., par. 131.
[128] Ibid., par. 189.

lation." In the latter case, when the transcendent function of the psyche leads to the production of a work of art or of a significant motif or figure within a work of art, we are almost certainly considering a symbol, that "best possible expression of an as yet unknown and incomprehensible fact."[129]

Jung's words are suggestive in light of the fact that Barrie tinkered with *Peter Pan* for over twenty-five years, as though the meaning of Peter Pan, that "complex fact" of his own creation, continued to elude him. Equally instructive, and important to bear in mind when reading *Peter Pan,* are Barrie's ambivalent feelings toward the childhood he so envied, and which are evident in his troubled authorial stance, as he now identifies with, now distances himself from, his characters. Of comparable importance are the tensions, both inner and outer, that plagued his life. These conflicts surfaced with his mother after his brother David's death; with his wife, former actress Mary Ansell, because of their childless, unhappy marriage; with Arthur and Sylvia Llewelyn Davies over his "adoption" of their children, to whom, it should be remembered, he gave unstinting moral and financial support, proving a faithful guardian after the tragically early deaths of the parents. Finally, there is the lifelong tension between the adult Barrie, who felt he "must give up the games," and Barrie the eternal boy, who escaped into the fantasy world of Neverland to "continue playing in secret"[130] in the hope, perhaps, of eventually discovering and understanding the profundity of his own myth.

---

[129] "Definitions," *Psychological Types,* CW 6, par. 815.
[130] Hearn, "Introduction," *Peter Pan,* p. 5.

Our birth is but a sleep and a forgetting:
The soul that rises with us, our life's star,
Hath had elsewhere its setting,
And cometh from afar:
Not in entire forgetfulness,
And not in utter nakedness,
But trailing clouds of glory do we come
From God, who is our home:
Heaven lies about us in our infancy!

. . . .

Hence in a season of calm weather
Though inland far we be,
Our souls have sight of that immortal sea
Which brought us hither,
Can in a moment travel thither,
And see the children sport upon the shore,
And hear the mighty waters rolling evermore.

—William Wordsworth,
"Ode: Intimations of Immortality from
Recollections of Early Childhood."

4

Peter Pan, the Novel
J.M. Barrie's Twentieth-Century Image
of the Eternal Boy

Some Place Else: Structures of Fantasy and Fairy Tale

In the sparse page and a quarter John Rowe Townsend devotes to *Peter Pan* in his outline of literature for children, he makes three points which, despite their decidedly critical and dismissive tone, are instructive in our study of Peter Pan: 1) "Peter Pan, as everyone knows, is the boy who wouldn't grow up"; 2) "It is doubtful whether the idea of a boy who never grows up is as appealing to children as it is to parents"; and 3) "All in all, *Peter and Wendy* is not a very good book; I am sure it benefits unduly from the fame of the play."[131]

Townsend's comments return us to our earlier remarks about the artistic faults of Barrie's work and introduce the question of literary genre. How are we to classify *Peter Pan?* Why bother? How might an attempt at classification further our hermeneutic quest for possibilities of meaning in the text? Seamless, faultless and genre-specific Barrie's tale is not. Yet the more seamless and reassuringly coherent the narrative, the less provocative or rich it may prove to the searcher for new meaning. The sudden, disquieting, cryptic images of tale and dream narrative are those that open our perception to the previously unknown as they disturb our complacency and explode our preconceptions.

His elusive character makes Peter Pan impossible to fix. His tale remains equally elusive to literary definition, as Barrie draws from myth, and from the forms of fairy tale, Romance, adventure tale and fantasy, for the structure of his novel. As a result, the novel presents a collage of styles and genres, as it introduces a confusion of voices and points of view. Barrie now sides with his characters ("Some like Peter best and some like Wendy best, but I like [Mrs Darling] best"), now observes from the distance of a cynical adult ("You see, the woman [Mrs Darling] had no proper spirit"); he is now inside, now outside, of the action; he contradicts later what he, or the narrative, affirms earlier, changes his authorial mind in mid-paragraph, and then writes as though he, with the reader, is discovering the narrative as he proceeds:

---

[131] *Written for Children,* pp. 106f..

Now I understand what had hitherto puzzled me, why when Peter had extermi-
nated the pirates he did not return to the island and leave Tink to escort the children back to the mainland. This trick [of closing the nursery window so the children would not be able to return home] had been in his head all the time.[132]

This veritable Babel of authorial voice and point of view introduces the possibility of Barrie's uncertain relationship with his material and is indicative of his
profound ambivalence toward children and childhood as much as toward mothers, fathers and adulthood.

Townsend is right when he states that everyone knows Peter Pan and that the
1911 novel benefits from the 1904 play. In writing the novel, Barrie was not
creating a character but writing about a figure already six and a half years old
with a vibrant life of its own in the imagination of the theater-going public. Barrie was faced with the extraordinary task of capturing the ever-deepening popular "myth" of Peter Pan *as fiction,* as well as the essence of the immortal and
eternal boy of classical myth embodied by Peter Pan *as figure.*

No wonder he resisted requests to write the novel for so many years and finally published the play only in 1928. No wonder Barrie's repeated changes to
the script, particularly the ending, from production to production, and the mystery about the outcome of the plot during the first 1904 production, when cast
members were not given copies of the entire script or informed of the fates of
the characters they were playing. After all, the theater seems far more Peter
Pan's element than the printed word. In the theater, he makes his sudden appearances and disappearances, and may never be exactly the same from year to year.
It is, perhaps, the Peter Pan in Barrie, as much as the irreducible quality of Peter
Pan's own mythic resonance, that refuses easy containment in print and genre.

Drawing from fairy tale as well as from myth, Barrie does not, however, lo-
cate the action of his novel in mythic time, the "Once upon a time" of traditional
fairy tale. We are introduced to a specific time, place and family (the Darlings),
and to a sense of normalcy ("All children grow up . . .") in what might appear
the beginning of a domestic "nursery" story. The disturbing anomaly is the ex-
ception of the first line: All children, except one, grow up. It raises the question
of whose tale is to be told: the opening pages indicate this to be Wendy's story
but it is Peter Pan who is the one who does not grow up, and he soon commands
center stage. An extension of this question of the relative centrality of Peter or

---

[132] *Peter Pan,* p. 207. [Quoted passages, sentences and phrases from Barrie's novel are
ubiquitous in this chapter. In order not to overburden the reader, footnote references to
these are hereafter given only for lengthy or significant extracts.—Ed.]

Wendy to the tale is seen in the problematic relation of Edwardian London to Neverland, "this" or Wendy's world to that "other" world of Peter Pan. Barrie seems to struggle throughout the novel to decide whether his story has a hero or a heroine, or both, and on which side of the dividing line between London and Neverland, the real and the imaginal, he wants to position himself.

Although it lacks the flatness of characterization and description, and the objective starkness of the fairy story, in many ways the structure of Barrie's novel is similar to that of the traditional tale. Neverland and Edwardian London present two different realities; the plot involves the relation of one to the other and an exploration of the values implicit in each. In traditional tales also, two worlds are usually presented: the conscious, familiar, mundane world, in which a problem or missing value is evident, and the magical world indicative of the unfamiliar and unconscious, which nonetheless harbors the means to resolve the initial problem and restore the lost value. Movement from the mundane to the magical realm is often abrupt at the opening of the tale, for the hero or heroine is generally unaware of the existence and certainly of the potency of the unconscious, and so falls unwittingly into its power. We see this in the sudden appearance of the Beast's castle to Beauty's father in "Beauty and the Beast," and in how Hansel and Gretel stumble unexpectedly on the witch's gingerbread house in the forest. Typically, the protagonist from *this* world falls into the realm of the *other* world. In the case of Peter Pan, however, it happens the other way around, with Peter's sudden appearance in the nursery.

In the course of the traditional tale, the unfamiliar becomes increasingly familiar as the hero/heroine learns to cope, aided by magical animals and helpers, with the strangeness of the other world, until a bridge, or connection, is established between the disparate realms. The fairy tale, in its customary flatness, offers no interpretive clues to its possible meaning through the insights of characters or the intrusion of the narrator's opinion: there is no self-conscious narration and the narrative is not self-reflexive. The tale serves as a blank canvas, inviting the audience's projections and interpretations alike, and speaking to each listener insofar as it reflects his or her psychological truth.

Analytical psychology usually understands the bridge which develops between conscious and unconscious, as each is portrayed in the tale, to signify the development of a dialogue or flow of energy between the two levels (consciousness and the unconscious) of the psyche. This dialogue results from the ego's increased awareness of the reality of the unconscious or objective psyche, an awareness represented in the developing consciousness and strength of the hero/heroine. On the one hand, the boundary separating the two worlds becomes more clearly defined as an enhancement of ego-consciousness develops, and, on the other, the hero/heroine learns more readily to differentiate the two realms. With every expansion of consciousness, symbolized by such things as a royal wedding or success in finding the lost treasure, the ego is strengthened and so becomes less liable to fall into a strange world or psychic state of which it has no prior inkling and against which it is consequently unprotected.

The metaphorical bridge or psychological awareness of which we are talking is represented symbolically in "Hansel and Gretel" by the white duck who ferries the children back across the lake to their father's cottage. In "Beauty and the Beast" the link between the two worlds is effected through the mirror; in "Cinderella" through the slipper. In Barrie's children's fantasy the two worlds are linked through Peter Pan, his fairy dust and magical power of flight, although the inclusion of fairies and fairy dust in the tale arguably has more to do with Barrie's debt to Celtic mythology, as we shall see in our later discussion of Neverland, than with the fairy tale genre.

Modern literary fantasy's concern with alternate realities links it structurally to the fairy story. Often the alternate reality is explicitly represented in the creation of a secondary world (as in utopian- and science-fiction). In many cases the alternate realm is implicit, appearing as the other, inner world of a dissociated psyche (for example, in the figure of Golyadkin in Dostoyevsky's narrative of a descent into madness in *The Double),* or in the form of an inner prerogative or state of mind (as in the case of Kafka's protagonist K. in *The Trial* and *The Castle).* So J.R.R. Tolkien, author of the popular fantasies *The Hobbit* and *Lord of the Rings,* argues that the fantasist becomes the sub-creator of a world which stands in opposition to the primary world of consensus reality. This secondary creation of self-contained fantasy realms serves as a means to awaken desire in the reader for a different reality, for what is missing from the primary but promised in the secondary world. The implication is that ultimate value lies elsewhere, in the spiritual fantasy world of which this world is a poor reflection. If the work is successful, in Tolkien's view, desire for this other world must remain unsatisfied, for according to Tolkien fantasy should continually direct the reader toward the type of spiritual consolation and joy afforded by, in the Christian context, the greatest fairy story of all time, the Gospels.[133]

The type of fantasy tale of which Tolkien speaks is far removed from the

---

[133] "On Fairy-Stories," in Tolkien, *Tree and Leaf,* pp. 64ff.

noncommittal flatness of the traditional tale. On the one hand, it is overtly mor-
alistic and, on the other, serves as a Christian allegory, offering a fictional Great
Escape from the primary world, and consequently, for the duration of the story,
from our fear of death. Tolkien's successful tale securely locates the longed-for
grace intimated by the happy-ever-after resolution of the typical fairy story in a
transcendent realm "beyond the walls of the world."

At first glance, Barrie's secondary world of Neverland may seem to belong in
the tradition of Christian fantasists such as George MacDonald, Tolkien and
C.S. Lewis, and we are tempted to draw comparisons between Neverland, Middle Earth and Narnia. Neverland presents a childhood paradise filled with adventure, joy and youth, promising the Great Escape from a primary world of
grown-up consensus reality. It does not, however, afford a satisfactory allegory
of the Christian message. As well as Barrie's more or less overt pagan references, we discover in Neverland a continuous round of violence and intrigue, the
only moral ingredient of which is the somewhat ambiguous "good form" or "fair
play" insisted upon by Hook and Pan. When the cycle of action is seemingly
broken in Pan's defeat of Hook at the end, there is no symbolic resolution or
expectation of redemption through the final victory of a Christian ethic: Hook is
devoured by the crocodile; the pirates are dead or have fled the scene; the Indians have been brutally massacred; the lost boys return with Wendy to the
grown-up world; and Peter Pan is left alone, trapped in an endless web of make-
believe, which confirms Wendy's sense when she first encounters him that she
is "in the presence of a tragedy."[134]

Perhaps, then, more than may be immediately apparent, Barrie uses his children's fantasy as a vehicle to challenge collective mores and traditional concepts
of what is real by proposing Neverland as an imaginative alternative to the consensus reality of Edwardian England. Certainly, the opposition of two worlds in
fantasy provides a structure which may be exploited by the author to social, political or moral ends. This mode of fantasy enjoys a long tradition and we know
that Barrie acknowledged the influence of many such fantasists and satirists.[135]

However, while we may read Barrie's tale for his commentary on Empire,

---

[134] *Peter Pan*, p. 53.
[135] Michael Hearn notes in his Introduction to *Peter Pan* that "The names of other writers
[besides Defoe, Ballantyne and Cooper] whom Barrie aligned himself to through his play,
if in spirit only, were included on the curtain the author himself designed for the 1908
revival, supposedly a sampler stitched by Wendy, nine years old: Hans Christian Ander-
sen, Charles Lamb, Robert Louis Stevenson and Lewis Carroll." (p. 13)

and on contemporary political, military and social matters, the satirical strain in the narrative is faint indeed compared to the author's questioning of the nature of the actual and the imaginal, imagination and dream, conscious experience and the reality of the unconscious psyche. Hence the story's ambiguities and equivocations: If Peter is part of Wendy's dream, how may Mrs Darling explain the leaves left behind on the nursery floor, leaves which do not come "from any tree that grew in England"? The children are missing from their beds, yet the Neverland to which they fly is something that "you play at . . . by day with the chairs and table-cloth . . . but [which] in the two minutes before you go to sleep . . . becomes very nearly real."[136]

By questioning the boundary between the real and the imaginal in this way, Barrie aligns his narrative with the Romance genre, and modern literary fantasy may be seen as the successor to Medieval Romance, thematically as well as structurally. We have only to recall those most familiar Romances which focus on the quest of King Arthur's knights for the Holy Grail, the tragedy of Tristan and Isolde, and Sir Gawain's encounter with the Green Knight, to realize that Medieval Romance exemplifies the pattern of the hero's journey, in which the protagonist is challenged, among other things, to differentiate worldly from spiritual values.

The Romance genre addresses the hero's search for identity and meaning, both on an outer and an inner level. Two worlds are usually posited, representing the known and the unknown, in which opposition we discover Romance's structural similarity to myth and fairy tale. The quester must journey into the night world in search of knowledge or a value missing from the daytime world. Above all, Romance concerns "man's vision of his own life as quest,"[137] the outer journey standing as a metaphor for the inner. Consequently Romance, and fantasy as its modern equivalent, have as much to do with individual identity and the protagonist's achieving a secure sense of being in the world as with the desire, more explicit in science-fiction and allegorical or didactic fantasy, to change givens and alter reality, whether out of boredom, play, moral or political vision, or the longing for something lacking.

We can, then, make an argument for two principal modes of fantasy: The focus of one involves the conscious creation of imaginative alternatives to the everyday world (science-fiction, moral and Christian allegory, fantasy with a didactic or satirical intent) and brings to mind Jung's commentary on "psycho-

---

[136] *Peter Pan*, pp. 35, 33.

[137] Northrop Frye, *The Secular Scripture: A Study of the Structure of Romance*, p. 15.

logical" literature as writing ostensibly directed and controlled by the intent of the author. The other addresses the eruption of the unfamiliar within the context of familiar, apparently logical, rational experience (magic realism, fantastic, grotesque and horror fiction), and is closer to Jung's description of "visionary" writing, where the author becomes the vehicle of an autonomous complex.

The fairy tale would seem to demand a category of its own: In the "pure" folk tale there is usually little or no evidence of allegorical intent, and in analytical psychology's approach to the tale, the primary world is understood as already serving as a metaphor for the dynamics of psyche represented in and through the characters and objects, while the appearance of a secondary world in the images of forest, magical castle, ocean, cave, etc., symbolizes psychic activity at a deeper archetypal substratum of the unconscious. Consequently, Marie-Louise von Franz and others attribute the origin of folk and fairy tales to their being a symbolic expression of a direct, and otherwise irrepresentable and unintelligible, experience of the autonomous psyche.[138]

The first mode of fantasy described above may be seen as subversive in that it questions, challenges and inverts the real. The chief characteristic of the second is disjuncture: it focuses on the uncanny and our struggle to understand and relate to the unreal; it explores the anomalous and fantastic event as it erupts into everyday life, and in this way is a "form of writing which is about opening up subversive spaces within the mainstream rather than ghettoizing fantasy by encasing it within genres."[139] There is, of course, no literary law that precludes the coexistence of both strains of fantasy in a single work, and this is what I believe we find in *Peter Pan*. On the one hand, Barrie's depiction of life in Neverland enables a critique of Edwardian institutions—childhood, the family, motherhood, fatherhood, social and sexual mores: it is subversive.[140] However, the very title of Barrie's first chapter, "Peter Breaks Through," suggests something of the nonrational has indeed broken through the veil of rational experience in the figure of Peter Pan: it is disjunctive and concerns the fantastic.

Certainly Barrie did not manage, and probably did not even try, to make a

---

[138] *An Introduction to the Psychology of Fairy Tales,* chap. 1.

[139] Lucie Armitt, *Theorising the Fantastic,* p. 3.

[140] Jonathan Rutherford argues that Peter Pan was "the culminating adventure story of the Victorian era and revealed what had been repressed and denied in the imperial fantasy of manly racial supremacy—the domestic world of mothers, sexuality and emotional need. It was an act of acute, if unconscious, reflexivity." (*Forever England: Reflections on Masculinity and Empire,* p. 25)

"good" piece of children's literature, as that was conceived in his day. This is evident in the number of abridgments and versions of *Peter and Wendy* written by others to make the tale more "suitable for children" than Barrie's original. All the usual distinctions between fairy story, fantasy, domestic story and boys' adventure tale are violated: Neverland and Peter Pan are as inappropriate to the domestic tale as is Wendy's domesticating presence in Neverland to the boys' adventure story. So in the novel it seems that Barrie was less concerned with elaborating the tale and profile of his 1904 dramatic hero than with finding a way to describe his experience of an autonomous force, with a life of its own, that cannot be contained within the boundaries of genre or the collective norms of Edwardian culture.

To return to a remark of Townsend's we have not yet addressed, namely, that the idea of a boy who never grows up is more appealing to parents than to children, we may certainly agree that Peter Pan presents an enigma of considerable concern to parents, but also argue that such an enigma must surely *engage* adults in general and one in particular: J.M. Barrie.

The Darlings: Stocks, Shares and Tidy Drawers

In order better to appreciate Barrie's eternal boy from a psychological and symbolical perspective, we will engage the novel through an interpretative lens similar to that applied by analytical psychology to the study of fairy tales. We will read *Peter Pan* for what its symbology and symbolic action may reveal about the dynamics of puer psychology in general, and about the psychodynamics represented in Barrie's compelling hero in particular. This approach is not the stretch it might at first appear to be. As Jung reminds us:

> Since it is a characteristic of the psyche not only to be the source of all productivity but, more especially, to express itself in all the activities and achievements of the human mind, we can nowhere grasp the nature of the psyche *per se* but can meet it only in its various manifestations. [141]

We find an artistic recognition of this truth in the literary term *psychomachia* ("battle for the soul"), and in the many pieces of literature where authors explicitly refer to their works as dramas of the psyche, for example Christopher Marlowe's *Dr. Faustus*, Lord Byron's "Manfred," Shelley's *Prometheus Unbound* and "Alastor," to name but a few.

Barrie tells us, "Of course [the Darling family] lived at 14." No. 14 therefore

---

[141] "Psychology and Literature," *The Spirit in Man, Art and Literature*, CW 15, p. 85.

represents the primary world of consensus reality (Tolkien), and certainly the conscious, everyday world of middle-class Edwardian family and social life. The somewhat off-hand expression, "Of course," asks the reader to assume the portrait of the family which follows to be a portrait of the social norm. We know that Barrie looked on the Llewelyn Davies as the embodiment of a family ideal of which he could never fully be a part, and that this family formed the basis of his characterization of the Darlings. However, we can assume, from Barrie's ambivalence toward Mrs Darling and his sometimes gentle, sometimes more cruelly satirical portrayal of Mr Darling, that he only loosely based his characterization of the Darling parents on Arthur and Sylvia Llewelyn Davies, the parents of his "boys." Sylvia had, on the one hand, an "innate and underlying tendency towards melancholy," as described by her son, Peter Llewelyn Davies, and on the other an "appetite for luxury that [her husband] neither shared nor could hope to satisfy," while Arthur was "in no sense the typical Edwardian father of the Mr Darling variety . . . [being] so tender and gentle with children . . . [and with] a more parental instinct than Sylvia."[142]

Nevertheless, the predominant values of the Darlings' world, as summarized and satirized by Barrie, present us with a family dynamic that promotes the early development of mother's son psychology, as well as its perpetuation in adult life. Mr and Mrs Darling provide a parental background and environment which encourages that quality of psyche represented in the puer as carrier of spirit to be "split off" and relegated to a Neverland of the unconscious. As we shall see, Mr and Mrs Darling seem to represent everything the puer most fears: routine, groundedness, the dull round of adult responsibility. Theirs is the "buttoned up" conscious attitude that produces in the Neverland of the unconscious a Peter Pan and a Captain Hook, fairies, pirates and redskins, mermaids, sirens, wild beasts and a devouring crocodile, all of which add up to the inventory of a child's odyssey that has been domesticated, neither recognized nor valued, but discarded in a dusty corner of the nursery.

What ego-consciousness rejects falls into shadow in the unconscious. We must bear this in mind in our discussion of the Darlings which follows: collective values, in the guise of perceptions of gender roles and the norms of social interaction, change, and often quite rapidly. What was considered acceptable behavior in Victorian and Edwardian England may appear as neurotic or perhaps even pathological to an observer from a different era or culture. In comparison,

---

[142] Birkin, *J.M. Barrie and the Lost Boys,* chap. 9.

The Darling family

psychological dynamics remain constant. While the psychology of the typical Edwardian family may today be far more subtly differentiated than at the time of Barrie's novel, we regularly encounter Mr Darling's intransigence and need for control, Mrs Darling's tendency to smother her children, and Peter Pan's challenge to adventure, in various forms of generalized anxiety, "over-parenting," and the current popular phenomenon of the business executive who rides his Harley-Davidson to a bikers' convention.

We will first consider Mr Darling. He is depicted as a businessman who knows "about stocks and shares" but has "no real mastery of his tie." Barrie's picture of Mr Darling is of one whose main psychological function and values are identified with persona, with the opinion of neighbors and colleagues, to the point where his excessive attention to the rational and to social and professional propriety leads him to absurd, inappropriate behavior. He says:

> I warn you of this, mother, that unless this tie is around my neck we don't go out to dinner tonight, and if I don't go out to dinner tonight, I never go to the office again, and if I don't go to the office again, you and I starve, and our children will be flung into the streets.[143]

The image of Mr Darling's having difficulty with his tie and his feeling that his world will collapse unless it is securely around his neck introduces a marked tendency to paranoid thinking that points to an overdefended because weak ego, a tendency that increasingly dominates Mr Darling's personality in the course of the novel. It points also to his obsession with appearances and to his psychology and world-view as a whole. The tie identifies Mr Darling as a prestigious member of the business community; however, it also suggests that he is confined—as later he confines Nana to her kennel by placing a leash around her neck—by an allegiance to the status quo and an attitude to the world that over-values success and materialism at the expense of spirit and intuition.

Mr Darling's adherence to the rational is so exaggerated that it pushes him to the inhuman extreme of looking upon his children primarily in terms of economics: his being "very honourable" entails a hardening of the heart that allows him coldly and carefully to calculate the cost of raising a child in order to decide whether or not to keep Wendy "as she was another mouth to feed." This presents a picture of frozen feeling that is often the consequence of a fragile ego's tendency to overadaptation in a characteristic attempt to compensate a deep fear of falling apart. So Mr Darling exhibits many of the behavior traits of a person suf-

---

[143] *Peter Pan*, p. 43.

fering profound emotional abandonment and which include, according to Kathrin Asper, overadaptation, an almost robotic conformity and identification with collective values, a reliance on intellect, a tendency to withdraw and an effort "to lead a shadowless existence," among others.[144]

In many ways Barrie's portrait of Mr Darling suggests such a case of arrested development and deep emotional abandonment or narcissistic wounding. A "simple man" able to pass "for a boy again if he had been able to take his baldness off," Mr Darling does everything in excess, and we deduce from the opening chapters that he has a labile, infantile personality ungrounded in any secure sense of self. He takes to Nana's kennel when the children disappear, blaming himself for the disaster and assuming a disproportionate sense of guilt, which may be understood as his falling into a negative inflation and becoming fixated with the notion that no one is at fault, or suffers, as much as he. His mood fluctuates uncontrollably from joy to rage to petulance to arrogance to tears; he refers to his wife as "mother," and to the nursery as "my nursery." In his puerility, Mr Darling seems to identify most closely with his youngest son but in the histrionic charade he plays with Michael about taking medicine it is the child who proves to be father to the man.

Mr Darling's infantile behavior indicates that he has little or no mature connection either to feeling or instinct (for which psychic situation, again, the tie around the neck is an appropriate image marking, as it does, the separation of head from body). Accordingly, he acts now as the petulant child, now as the cynical, severe paternal figure serving a rigid ideal of the father as lawgiver. What he is *not* is a figure for mature masculinity. He denies creative masculine spirit, in the figure of Peter Pan, which is rendered inaccessible and unconscious as a result (i.e., relegated to Neverland and attributed to Wendy's childish fantasy). Laughing even at the idea of Peter Pan and seeing himself as strong (a claim he makes when sitting half in and half out of the kennel), Mr Darling shows himself to be, as we earlier saw in Pentheus, the unconscious victim of the same impulses he denies. In this way he serves as an embodiment of the Victorian shadow, as is evident in his temper tantrums, his spontaneous tears, his effeminacy, his alternating rigidity and emotionality.

The vehemence of Mr Darling's denial of Peter Pan suggests that Peter represents a part of the personality that has been split off from consciousness. Such a split-off part, though inactivated, is only apparently so. As Jung writes:

---

[144] *The Abandoned Child Within*, pp. 162ff.

In actual fact it brings about a possession of the personality, with the result that the individual's aims are falsified in the interests of the split-off part. If, then, the childhood state of the collective psyche is repressed to the point of total exclusion [as in Mr Darling's denial of Peter Pan], the unconscious content overwhelms the conscious aim and inhibits, falsifies, even destroys its realization. Viable progress only comes from the co-operation of both.[145]

The way in which we have so far described Mr Darling points to his manifesting a number of the negative qualities attributed to puer psychology (or pathology), but Mr Darling also shares several characteristics with the "old king" of alchemy. This old king is the "chief-dictator-father spirit" or senex into which extreme position the puer may swing unwittingly in his refusal to become grounded in time and adulthood, but in distinct opposition to which he must define himself if puer and senex values are not to remain unconsciously contaminated, the one by the other. Von Franz writes:

> The figure of the old king is usually portrayed . . . as defective, unredeemed, rigidified, sick, or even evil. The defective quality corresponds to an intensified egotism and hardening of the heart that must be broken down in the alchemical bath. Power hunger and concupiscence often also ingloriously characterize the old king . . . [who may] . . . embody a pure attitude of power and [be] characterized by a total lack of eros. The spirit, which in itself is no "adversary of the soul," degenerates in such personifications to the level of intellect, and in this contracted and rigidified form stands in the way of all the psyche's fertile and creative impulses. It is an enemy of emotionality and instinct, but precisely for this reason it secretly lets itself be negatively influenced by primitive impulses.[146]

To attribute to Mr Darling characteristics of the old king, or the wounded Fisher-King of Grail mythology, might seem harsh. However, there is much in his behavior to indicate a contamination, or lack of differentiation, of puer and senex qualities: his weak, labile ego causes him to act out traits of both puer and senex in an unconscious, irrational manner, and so we see in him similarities to Captain Hook as well as to Peter Pan. Although Mr Darling is described as "grander" than his wife, we are led to believe that this is solely by virtue of his being a male. (We are told, when the children are playing at mothers and fathers, of "the extra pomp . . . [occasioned by] . . . the birth of a male"). The psycho-

---

[145] The Psychology of the Child Archetype," *The Archetypes and the Collective Unconscious,* CW 9i, par. 277.
[146] "The Religious Background of the Puer Aeternus Problem," in von Franz, *Psychotherapy,* p. 312.

logical portrait Barrie gives us, then, is of a man who is not in the least bit grand but who remains unconsciously trapped in the realm of the Mother because he is caught at an instinctual level of identification in the role of son. So we see him behaving like his children, with Mrs Darling treating him accordingly.

Although there are in Mr Darling several positive qualities of the puer—like Peter Pan he is playful, spontaneous and loves to dance—the "fun" he has with his family may equally be understood as part of a protective shield which masks the viciousness we see him act out with Michael and with Nana. Mr Darling's victimization by the primitive impulses he either energetically denies or believes he controls is further captured in the image of him being brushed like a dog by his wife, in his having taken "a dog for a nurse" in the first place, in his banishment of Nana to the yard, and finally in his self-imposed punishment of going "down on all fours and . . . [crawling] into the kennel" until the children return.

Barrie dubs Mr Darling "quixotic," which brings to mind the delusional quality of Don Quixote's quest to right the wrongs of his world. Not unlike Cervantes' Knight of the Mournful Countenance—and arguably also to the point of delusion—Mr Darling is unconsciously impelled by forces which his fragile ego identifies as his own conscious choices and desires, as, for example, the determination to live in Nana's kennel. He does not appear to enjoy the stable sense of identity which Jeffrey Satinover associates with the development of a "proper narcissism" in early development. We know nothing of Mr Darling's childhood, but see that he exhibits many of the characteristics we later find in Peter Pan and the narcissistic personality: extreme highs followed by extreme lows; rapid shifts from positive to negative inflation, pointing to a damaged ego-Self axis or, in other words, to a basic mistrust of the world and an inability to embrace the ineluctable quality of life and of one's own destiny.

We see grandiosity and "lion courage," succeeded by feelings of failure and remorse; a stubborn need for control in an attempt to suppress a rising fear of the unknown and chaotic. ("Mr Darling was frightfully ashamed of himself, but he would not give in.") We see an egocentric need for attention and admiration; an inflexibility which results in black and white and often mistaken or paranoid thinking; a lack of either eros or insight, and so a tendency to act out emotions and impulses in an unrelated and often destructive manner; and, finally, a tendency to depression which often serves to mask the pain of the emotionally wounded. ("When he tied [Nana] up in the backyard, the wretched father went and sat in the passage, with his knuckles to his eyes.")

Overall, Mr Darling's quixotic, unstable and essentially narcissistic personality points to his alleged success in the social and business world being the result of a rigid persona supported by a somewhat paranoid system of defenses. In this regard, Erich Neumann writes of the juxtaposition of rigidity and chaos as a protection against what Kohut later calls "disintegration anxiety," the threat of falling apart or being flooded by the unconscious;[147] and James Hillman observes that "the dissolution of any paranoid system will release panic."[148]

We witness this process activated in Mr Darling: when his carefully constructed safeguards against all eventualities are rendered ineffectual by the arrival of Peter Pan in the nursery, he behaves in an erratic, irrational manner. Just as Pentheus's refusal of Dionysus spells his own destruction by the very Bacchanalian forces he despises, the more vehemently Mr Darling denies the reality of Peter Pan, or an incursion from the unconscious, the greater his panic and the less effective his precautions to protect his children.

Hillman points out that "where panic is, there too is Pan,"[149] and whether we understand in Peter Pan a dim vestige of the instinctual goat-god, a figment of the childish imagination, a figure for the unconscious, a symbol of autonomous creativity or spirit of renewal, the effect of his intrusion into the rational order of life at No. 14 returns Mr Darling to the level of instinct. So what Barrie gives us in the character of Mr Darling is, perhaps, under the softening guise of fantasy, an otherwise quite brutal portrayal of what may happen when puer and senex qualities of psychic energy have remained unconscious, and consequently undifferentiated, unrealized and unintegrated: they manifest autonomously in their negative aspects as puerility and irrational rigidity, with little evidence of creative reciprocity between the two.

In many ways Mr Darling's neurotic behavior provides a picture of how a distortion of the archetypal configuration of *puer-et-senex* often appears in conscious life: in extreme narcissism, and in the effeminacy and decadence associated with Victorian life at the turn of the century. Missing is a realization of the chthonic masculine as well as a differentiated relationship to the mature feminine which would enable Mr Darling to acknowledge both his personal shadow and that of the collective.

Barrie gives several indications in his opening paragraph that in visiting No. 14 we are entering a world dominated by feminine, specifically maternal, values: there is an implicit resistance to growth, differentiation and conflict—so

---

[147] Cited in Kathrin Asper, *The Abandoned Child Within,* p. 157.
[148] *Pan and the Nightmare,* p. xxxi.
[149] Ibid.

long considered aspects of masculine energy—in statements such as, "All children, except one, grow up," and "Two is the beginning of the end." More importantly, the first image we have of Mrs Darling is of her delight at the gift of a flower from the two-year-old Wendy who is "playing in a garden." Barrie's image is of Paradise, and of Demeter and Persephone—mother and daughter—before Persephone's abduction by Pluto/Hades to the Underworld. Mrs Darling's cry, "Oh, why can't you remain like this for ever!" expresses a lament for the passing of springtime and for the inevitability of process and change, and at the same time nostalgia for a world that is static, perfect and devoid of conflict. Her cry marks her resistance to an intrusion of chthonic masculine energy into the gentle refinement of her female domain. It is the cry of Demeter who refuses to allow the masculine, in the form of Hades, to objectify the mother-daughter dyad and who begs Zeus to permit Persephone to return to her for six months of the year.

In an ironic reversal at the end of the novel, when she again assumes the role of Demeter, Mrs Darling makes Peter Pan a "handsome offer: to let Wendy go to him for a week every year to do his spring cleaning." We understand the strength of the mother-daughter bond in Barrie's novel when we realize the extent of Wendy's identification with and idealization of her mother and when, in the final chapter, we learn how the powerfully introverted maternal instinct embodied in Mrs Darling is passed unchanged and unchallenged from mother to daughter for successive generations:

> As you look at Wendy you may see her hair becoming white, and her figure little again, for all this happened long ago. Jane is now a common grown-up, with a daughter called Margaret; and every spring-cleaning time, except when he forgets, Peter comes for Margaret and takes her to Neverland, where she tells him stories about himself, to which he listens eagerly. When Margaret grows up she will have a daughter, who is to be Peter's mother in turn; and thus it will go on . . .[150]

As much as Mr Darling has a passion for exactitude, Mrs Darling also loves "to have everything just so," and she conforms in many ways to a collective idea of woman- and mother-hood that is narrowly traditional and suggestive of her own unconscious tendency to be murderously exacting. Husband and wife are presented as nothing-but-father and nothing-but-mother, respectively, their individual personalities subsumed by their collective parental personae. Mrs Darling fulfills the role of the conventional wife, supporting her husband, taking care of

---

[150] *Peter Pan*, p. 225.

the household, the children, and all personal and social matters; she can keep the books perfectly, remain placid when her husband is irrational, and dances "gayest of all" as occasion demands. Jung suggests that such an exaggeration of the maternal element results in the type of mother who comes to regard her husband

> as an object to be looked after, along with children, poor relations, cats, dogs, and household furniture. Even her own personality is of secondary importance; she often remains entirely unconscious of it, for her life is lived in and through others, in more or less complete identification with all the objects of her care. First she gives birth to the children, and from then on she clings to them, for without them she has no existence whatsoever.[151]

Although this description may seem overly condemning when applied to Mrs Darling, it does bring the singular quality of her maternal instinct into relief: she keeps her husband's books perfectly, it is true, but "as if it were a game," and quickly substitutes "pictures of babies without faces" for the figures "she should have been totting up"; she treats her husband like a child, as mentioned above, on a mythological level playing Cybele to his Attis by "coddling" him and so figuratively rendering him impotent, his masculine spirit reduced to nothing more than a laughable childish charade as he hides in Nana's kennel; and she spends a great deal of time "tidying up her children's minds"—an activity, or attitude to life, that indicates a need for power, control and absolute right of possession that traditionally belongs to the father.

This type of fanatical insistence on "maternal rights" may arise when the instinct to bear children dominates the personality to the point of becoming an impersonal drive. (Mrs Darling draws "babies without faces" in her husband's books.) Jung writes: "Eros [then] develops exclusively as a maternal relationship while remaining unconscious as a personal one . . . . [and such] an unconscious Eros always expresses itself as will to power"[152]—which manifests as the devouring aspect of the archetypal Mother, a quality we see on the personal level in Mrs Darling's self-effacing but suffocating love for her children, and in her psychological emasculation of her husband.

We may speculate that as a nothing-but-mother, Mrs Darling grew up as the nothing-but-daughter of a woman much like herself, identifying with her mother's maternal values to the detriment of her own feminine initiative. A

---

[151] "Psychological Aspects of the Mother Complex," *The Archetypes of the Collective Unconscious,* CW 9i, par. 167.
[152] Ibid.

strong overidentification with the mother in this way may result in the type of woman whom Jung describes, with little apparent sympathy, as a "pallid maiden . . . often visibly sucked dry by the mother." This "empty vessel" attracts all of a man's unconscious projections and she readily forms herself according to his image of the feminine:

> Such women may become devoted and self-sacrificing wives of husbands whose whole existence turns on their identification with a profession or a great talent, but who, for the rest, are unconscious and remain so. Since they are nothing but masks themselves, the wife, too, must be able to play the accompanying part with a semblance of naturalness.[153]

Mrs Darling seems to have been just such a type of woman, whose feminine indeterminateness "sucks up all masculine projections and this pleases men enormously."[154] Barrie describes Mr Darling's courtship of her in the following way: "The many gentlemen who had been boys when she was a girl discovered simultaneously that they loved her, and they all ran to her house to propose to her except Mr Darling, who took a cab and nipped in first."[155]

Mrs Darling accepts the first suitor to arrive on her doorstep and Mr Darling, it would seem, marries his wife more because he is impelled by unconscious impulse (projection) and accident than by conscious relatedness and love, because Mrs Darling appears to embody something of the mystery and fascination of the archetypal feminine. She is, after all, "the chief one" at No. 14 until the birth of Wendy, and she has an elusive, enigmatic quality which is that of the woman whose innocence (or emptiness) suggests the "great feminine secret . . . . absolutely alien to man":[156]

> Her romantic mind was like the tiny boxes, one within the other, that come from the puzzling East, however many you discover there is always one more; and her sweet mocking mouth had one kiss on it that Wendy could never get, though there it was, perfectly conspicuous in the righthand corner.[157]

Barrie's depiction, however sentimental, is also subtly ambivalent. On the one hand, in the kiss that may never be taken and the "tiny box" about which Mr

---

[153] Ibid., par. 182.
[154] Ibid., par. 169.
[155] *Peter Pan*, p. 28.
[156] "Psychological Aspects of the Mother Complex," *The Archetypes of the Collective Unconscious,* CW 9i, par. 183.
[157] *Peter Pan*, pp. 27f.

Darling never even knew, it affords Mrs Darling a certain sense of selfhood and inner integrity. It paints the feminine as essentially *other*, mysterious and exotic ("from the puzzling East"). The "tiny box," however, also serves as a negative image of control; it is equally the locked inner chamber of Mrs Darling's affections (and, we may surmise, of the affections of Barrie's own mother), as inaccessible and taboo as the elusive kiss.

Throughout the novel, there is a marked ambivalence in Barrie's picture of Mrs Darling in particular and of mothers in general, an ambivalence echoed by Peter Pan who takes Wendy to Neverland because the lost boys need a mother, yet remembers little or nothing of his own mother, and considers he and Tinker Bell "don't want any silly mothers" anyway. When the children are on their way home from Neverland, Barrie's authorial voice intrudes to denounce Mrs Darling as a woman who has "no proper spirit." By this Barrie means the type of mother who declares "What do I matter?" and sacrifices everything—including her own personality—for her children and her role. (Recall the selfless devotion of Sylvia Llewelyn Davies to her five boys.) "So long as mothers are like this their children will take advantage of them," Barrie tells us, yet this self-sacrificing love may mask the seductive quality of the negative mother—the witch in the gingerbread house—promising her children ease and security in a potentially devouring embrace which nevertheless shields them from consciousness of moral conflict and so from life.

However, as soon as he has conjured again a sentimental image of her as "a very sad-eyed woman . . . because she has lost her babes," Barrie decides he does indeed like Mrs Darling best. Barrie's ambivalence is more clearly embodied in Peter Pan who projects onto Mrs Darling what must be an inner archetypal image of the mother as he has no experience of a personal mother himself; at the same time he energetically rejects her outstretched arms. On the one hand Peter whispers to Tinker Bell, "She is a pretty lady, but not so pretty as my mother"; on the other he warns Mrs Darling, "Keep back, lady, no one is going to catch me and make me a man."

Peter Pan is convinced that if he does not repulse Mrs Darling's offer of mothering he will become a solemn man with a beard—that is, only-senex. In the context of Barrie's tale he is right. We see what happens to John, Michael and the lost boys who come under Mrs Darling's care: the ambivalence they once felt about "grown-ups," and the "No!" with which they resisted growing up themselves, is forgotten (or becomes unconscious). Whereas Peter Pan defines himself, and so creates and recreates himself continually, by saying "No!" to the

he gnashed the little pearls at her — "I don't want ever to be a man"

adult world, the Darling children and the lost boys are soon adult and "done for":

> So it is scarcely worth while saying anything more about them. You may see the Twins and Nibs and Curly any day going to an office, each carrying a little bag and an umbrella. Michael is an engine-driver. Slightly married a lady of title, and so he became a lord. You see that judge in a wig coming out at the iron door? That used to be Tootles. The bearded man who doesn't know any story to tell his children was once John.[158]

In John's inability to remember any stories we see Barrie's association of the only-senex quality of the adult world with the death of imagination. We recall how Mr Darling either denies the reality of Peter Pan or denounces him as a "fiend," and we wonder if Barrie ever felt himself a fiend in Arthur Llewelyn Davies' eyes for stealing away the affection of his children. Although it would seem that storytelling is kept alive and passes from generation to generation through the mother-line (as was true of Barrie's own experience), stories—and the indulgence of fancy—are clearly confined to the nursery and to childhood: Mrs Darling is confident that Wendy will outgrow her fascination for Peter Pan, and to Wendy, who from the beginning emulates the quality of mothering she experiences in her own mother and who consequently "grew up of her own free will a day quicker than other girls," Peter Pan is soon "no more to her than a little dust in the box in which she had kept her toys."

Nothing changes at No. 14 because of the rigidity and fixity of the conscious structures. Wendy is little different from her mother, despite her experience of Neverland. Although initially she resists the tyranny of Mrs Darling by following Peter Pan, she is so identified with her nothing-but mother that even in Neverland—that is, unconsciously—she both acts out the "mother" and initiates the return to her real mother on the mainland, all earlier ambivalence overcome.

Jung writes that when there is a disturbance of instincts in the relation of parent to child (particularly in the relation of mother to child), archetypal fantasies are produced which "come between the child and its mother as an alien and often frightening element."[159] There is sufficient evidence in Barrie's tale to pin the origin of any disturbance of instinct in the Darling family on the conscious attitudes of the parents, especially those of the mother. Figures that might stand for

---

[158] Ibid., p. 219.
[159] "Psychological Aspects of the Mother Complex," *The Archetypes of the Collective Unconscious,* CW 9i, par. 161.

natural wisdom (Liza the maid) and instinct (the dog) are either immature and consequently ignored (Liza is little more than ten years old) or banished (Nana, who provides an image of distorted, over-domesticated instinct at best, is chained in her kennel).

We may argue that Peter Pan and the lure of Neverland appear as intervening fantasies arising out of the children's need to resist and separate from their parents, a need symbolized in their flight. In the experience of ambivalence which the children naturally and necessarily feel toward the parents (are mothers good or bad? are parents necessary?), Peter Pan represents one compelling alternative or pole while the other is kept alive by Wendy's stories of Mr and Mrs Darling. Eventually fear of separation and abandonment wins out and the children return to No. 14. Negative emotions toward mother, father and adulthood are again repressed. A final image is of the closed family circle from which "ecstasy" Peter Pan is barred, as Barrie, that entertaining but idiosyncratic genius from Scotland, was himself relegated to the position of outsider, always "listening in" on the Llewelyn Davies, unable to identify with many of the values embodied in the decidedly English parents of "his boys."

However, we know that Peter Pan is not entirely forgotten. He survives in the imaginations of generations of daughters, although Mrs Darling's dim sense of foreboding on the night he abducts Wendy and her brothers from the nursery is insufficiently strong to keep her from leaving her children alone. Barrie also tells us that there was a commotion in the firmament that night. There is much to suggest, then, that the perpetuation of Peter Pan and the inevitability (if unreliability) of his springtime return are symbolic of orchestrations of the archetypal psyche against which imperative the conscious ego has little recourse.

Such a reading would make Pan a figure for a quality of the Self, which appears now and again as fate to shape destiny and further the process of individuation; such a figure manifests a potentiality for positive, creative development, unless thwarted and perverted by an inflexible ego's will to power or unconscious enthrallment to a petrifying complex.

Neverland: Where We Beach Our Coracles on Magic Shores

In Neverland we discover the fantasy realm of the puer and all the vitality lacking in the world of collective values represented by Mr and Mrs Darling and life at No. 14. Spirit, spontaneity, creativity, the aggressive masculine and the courageous feminine, are all relegated to the unconscious, where we meet them in Peter Pan and Captain Hook, and the pirates and fairies, mermaids and redskins of Neverland.

At the conscious level, as represented by the Darling parents, aggression manifests in unfairness, spirit in childish tantrum; creativity and spontaneity are channeled appropriately and "tidied up" like so many clothes in a drawer, and feeling is replaced by sentimentality. Hence the novel's ambivalence toward the lost spirit of childhood: Barrie is at once nostalgic for Neverland, yet he does not hesitate to expose Neverland's darker side and he cautions his reader about the disruptive and chaotic result of Peter Pan's incursions into the adult world.

Barrie intimates that to sketch Neverland is "to draw a map of a child's mind." There are a number of layers to any map of Neverland, as if another is always showing through; so Neverland serves much like a palimpsest. The result is "all rather confusing, especially as nothing will stand still," and Barrie's description of the "magic shores" of Peter Pan's island invites us to think in terms of the different levels, or qualities, of psychic experience. Following Jung's model of the psyche, we would think of ego consciousness, the personal unconscious and the collective unconscious. That Neverlands "vary a good deal" and are therefore idiosyncratic indicates their relation to the contents of the personal unconscious: John's Neverland contains a lagoon with flamingoes, Wendy's has a "pet wolf forsaken by its parents," and in them all are innumerable versions of shared conscious experience such as "first day at school, religion, fathers, the round pond, needlework, chocolate pudding day, three-pence for pulling out your tooth yourself . . ." and so on and on. The collective unconscious, on the other hand, is suggested in the

> astonishing splashes of colour here and there, and coral reefs and rakish-looking craft in the offing, and savages and lonely lairs, and gnomes who are mostly tailors, and caves through which a river runs, and princes with six elder brothers, and a hut fast going to decay, and one very small old lady with a hooked nose.[160]

Barrie's many allusions place Neverland in a long line of imaginative countries which have served for centuries as literary metaphors for the "other world" of the unconscious and archetypal psyche. These countries belong to folklore and fairy story (tailors, gnomes, princes and witches), legend and adventure tale (coral reefs, savages and lonely lairs), epic and poem (the "caves through which a river runs" bringing to mind Coleridge's sacred river which descends "through caverns measureless to man down to a sunless sea" in "Kubla Khan").[161]

One of Neverland's precursors is clearly Tir Nan' Og, the Otherworld or Un-

---

[160] *Peter Pan*, p. 32.
[161] *Poetical Works*, p. 297.

derworld of Celtic mythology, variously named The Isles of the Blest, The Land of the (Happy) Dead, The Land of the Living, The Fortunate Isles, The Isle of Content, The Land of Youth or the Forever Young. The location of the Otherworld is uncertain; what is certain, though, is that it was thought to lie far away beneath or beyond the known seas, and to be accessible through the great pre-Celtic burial mounds guarded by the Sidhe (faery folk).

T.W. Rolleston, in his extensive study of Celtic myth and legend, retells the myth of the Otherworld's inhabitants, the Sidhe. After their defeat by the Milesians, held by legend to be the first wholly human invaders of the land, the Tuatha De Danann (Peoples of the Goddess Danann), a mythical race with sovereignty of Ireland,

> do not withdraw. By their magic art they cast over themselves a veil of invisibility, which they can put on or off as they choose. There are two Irelands henceforward, the spiritual and the earthly. The Dananns dwell in the spiritual Ireland. . . . Where the human eye can see but green mounds and ramparts, the relics of ruined fortresses or sepulchres, there rise the fairy palaces of the defeated divinities; there they hold their revels in eternal sunshine, nourished by the magic meat and ale that give them undying youth and beauty; and thence they come forth at times to mingle with mortal men in love or in war. The ancient mythical literature conceives them as heroic and splendid in strength and beauty. In later times, and as Christian influences grew stronger, they dwindle into fairies, the People of the Sidhe; but they have never wholly perished; to this day the Land of Youth and its inhabitants live in the imagination.[162]

Barrie alludes to the Celtic world of Faery with the title of his second chapter, "Come Away, Come Away." These are words central to the refrain of an early (1889) poem by W.B. Yeats, "The Stolen Child," which tells of the enchantments and lure of this Land of Youth, the Otherworld of Faery:

> Come away, O human child!
> To the waters and the wild
> With a faery, hand in hand,
> For the world's more full of weeping than you can understand.

In the final stanza, a warning: What to the human child will be forever lost if he follows the faery band are the simple, immediate joys of life in *this* world:

> He'll hear no more the lowing
> Of the calves on the warm hillside

---

[162] *Celtic Myths and Legends,* pp. 136ff.

The entrance to a sidh, or burial mound
(New Grange, County Lough, Ireland; built about 2500 B.C.)

> Or the kettle on the hob
> Sing peace into his breast,
> Or see the brown mice bob
> Round and round the oatmeal-chest.[163]

In this and others of Yeats's poems about the Otherworld of the Sidhe, the demarcation between the two realms appears to be unclear and dangerously permeable. While passage to the Land of Faery may not be difficult, its ease is deceptive, for return is seldom possible and never without the Sidhe's exacting a high price. This we learn from the legend of Oisin who, to his peril, "saw the wonders of the Land of Youth with mortal eyes and lived to tell them with mortal lips."[164] In Yeats's "The Hosting of the Sidhe," the price of knowledge of the Land of Youth is no more nor less than the "mortal dream" that constitutes our humanity:

> . . . . Away, come away:
> Empty your heart of its mortal dream.

---

[163] *Collected Poems*, pp. 20f.

[164] Rolleston, *Celtic Myths*, p. 272. The story tells how Oisin is enchanted by Niam, daughter of the King of the Land of Youth. She takes him to the Otherworld of Faery on a white steed and he sees many marvels and meets with countless adventures. When, after what seems to him like a sojourn of three weeks, he longs to return home, satiated as he is with the delights of Niam's realm, he is given the white fairy steed but told that he must never "touch the soil of the earthly world with his foot, or the way of return to the Land of Youth would be barred to him for ever."

After several adventures, Oisin turns to help some men who are struggling with a huge boulder. As soon as Oisin touches the stone, the enchantment is broken. He transforms into "a man stricken with extreme old age, white-bearded and withered, who stretched out groping hands and moaned with feeble and bitter cries. And his crimson cloak and yellow silken tunic were now but coarse homespun stuff tied with the hempen girdle, and the gold-hilted sword was a rough oaken staff such as a beggar carries who wanders the roads from farmer's house to house." It seems that Oisin becomes a figure analogous to that of the Wandering Jew. Having seen what no mortal eye should see, he is cursed and his curse is to belong neither to this nor to the Other world: his sojourn in the Land of Youth having been over three hundred years long, he has missed the coming to Ireland of Patrick with his teaching of the Christian message. In Yeats's "The Wanderings of Oisin," Oisin tells of his time in the Land of Youth to Saint Patrick for whom the Faery World is Hell and the fairy princess a devil. St. Patrick replies to Oisin:

> You who are bent, and bald, and blind,
> With a heavy heart and a wandering mind,
> Have known three centuries, poets sing,
> Of dalliance with a demon thing.

The winds awaken, the leaves whirl round,
Our cheeks are pale, our hair is unbound,
Our breasts are heaving, our eyes are agleam,
Our arms are waving, our lips are apart;
And if any gaze on our rushing band,
We come between him and the deed of his hand,
We come between him and the hope of his heart. [165]

In his introduction to *Peter Pan*, Michael Hearn speculates that in placing his hero and the lost boys in an underground home on a magical isle, Barrie "was playing with the fact that, except for George and Jack, the Llewelyn Davies boys had not been baptized when infants; in a sense, the Neverland is a child's Purgatory."[166] Peter Pan, like Adam in the Garden of Eden, has clearly been charged with naming the beasts and birds of Neverland, for when alone and in search of the kidnapped children he regrets "he had given the birds of the island such strange names that they were very wild and difficult of approach."[167] This may lead us to understand the island as a childhood paradise, or purgatory, but Neverland as a Land of the Dead and Peter Pan as guide of souls to that Land ("when children died he went part of the way with them, so that they should not be frightened")[168] seem to link Neverland more closely to Celtic lore about the afterlife than to Christian belief.

The Celtic Otherworld holds many of the blessings of a prelapsarian Eden: "everyone is beautiful, and there is an abundance of beautiful things, and the joys of life are endless."[169] This is not unlike Neverland, which promises an idealized version of the real world of childhood where dreams come true and almost everything and anything is possible. However, while early testimony, literature and archaeological findings indicate that the Celts believed in a life after death, the Otherworld was not simply a joyful paradise:

It was also—even primarily—an alternative to reality, a world that the hero might enter upon the invitation of a king or a beautiful woman. Inasmuch as this world, no matter how beautiful, is not quite human (there is, for example, no winter), the hero never stays; but the alternative—and thus the tension—is always present.[170]

---

[165] *Collected Poems*, p. 61.
[166] *Peter Pan*, p. 20.
[167] Ibid., p. 174.
[168] Ibid., p. 34.
[169] J. Gantz, *Early Irish Myths and Sagas*, p. 15.
[170] Ibid., p. 17.

Gantz's commentary is useful to bear in mind in our consideration of the darker aspects of Barrie's alternative fantasy world, as is Rolleston's reminder that the Celtic conception of the realm of the dead resembled that of Egyptian religion rather than the underworlds of Greek and Roman belief (Hades and Dis, respectively):

> The Other-world was not a place of gloom and suffering, but of light and libera-
> tion. The Sun was as much the god of that world as he was of this. Evil, pain, and
> gloom there were, no doubt, . . . but that they were particularly associated with the
> idea of death is . . . a false supposition founded on misleading analogies drawn
> from the ideas of the classical nations.[171]

At first glance, Neverland presents an endless round of adventure and freedom, yet while in many ways a land of "light and liberation," it is not without an admixture of evil, violence and cruelty. However, on Peter Pan's island, evil actions that an ethical ego must surely abhor, such as Hook's massacre of the Indians, the deaths of the pirate crew, and the attempted death-by-drowning of Tiger Lily, rarely evoke sorrow, remorse or suffering. Neverland, like the world of the fairy tale, is amoral, a timeless realm of unending cyclical process in which there appears to be little consciousness of pain or progress.

Although Peter Pan "hates lethargy," and everything on the island gets "under way again" when he returns from one of his frequent excursions, existence in Neverland is caught in a continual round, an "eternal return"[172] of make-believe. Barrie describes what is happening in Neverland on the evening Pan arrives with Wendy, John and Michael:

> On this evening the chief forces of the island were disposed as follows. The lost
> boys were out looking for Peter, the pirates were out looking for the lost boys, the
> redskins were out looking for the pirates, and the beasts were out looking for the
> redskins. They were going round and round the island, but they did not meet be-
> cause all were going at the same rate.[173]

The action is ritualized. The picture that comes immediately to mind is of a mandala, which traditionally symbolizes wholeness and balance but perhaps, in this instance, a quality of rigidity and stuckness. In Neverland, it is "good form," or fair play, that keeps the odds even and everything in balance, yet the only emphasis we might term *moral* is the conformity of Pan and Hook to this code.

---

[171] *Celtic Myths and Legends*, p. 89.
[172] See Mircea Eliade, *The Myth of the Eternal Return, or Cosmos and History*.
[173] *Peter Pan*, p. 79.

So Peter rescues Tiger Lily from drowning not because he is compassionate, like Wendy, but because he cannot tolerate the pirates' transgression of good form: "It was two against one that angered him, and he meant to save her."

There is, however, a paradoxical quality to good form: to embody and enact it one must be unaware one has it. It is unconscious and natural: "[Hook] remembered that you have to prove you don't know you have it before you are eligible for Pop."[174] Consequently, Captain Hook is "arrested" and rendered impotent when he is about to "claw" his bo'sun, the lovable Smee, because Smee has just proven he has "good form without knowing it, which is the best form of all":

> "To claw a man because he is good form, what would that be?"
>
> "Bad form!"
>
> The unhappy Hook was as impotent as he was damp, and he fell forward like a cut flower.[175]

We may speculate that the origin of "good form" is the inherent ordering potential of the psyche, in other words the archetype of the Self. However, Hook's reaction to Smee would suggest that a lack of self-consciousness, and an unconscious identification with autonomous psychic process, is the ideal condition of being in Neverland. We are reminded of Barrie's statement that "Two is the beginning of the end," and that an absence of self-consciousness persists only in early infancy.

As long as life adheres to an unconscious pattern of behavior there can be

---

[174] Ibid., p. 180. As Andrew Birkin explains in *J.M. Barrie and the Lost Boys,* "Pop" links Hook to Eton as surely as does Barrie's 1920 notebook entry at the time of the sixteenth consecutive annual revival of the play *Peter Pan:* "Hook. Eton & Magdalen. . . . Studied for Mods. Took to drink in 1881, elected M.P. following year, etc." Pop was a debating society at Eton started in 1816 by Charles Fox Townshend. It began in a house belonging to a Mrs Hatton who had originally kept a sock or tuck shop, the Latin name for which is Popina. Cyril Connolly, who believed his only hope to be elected to Pop was "as a wit," writes in *Enemies of Promise:* "The whole school ruled in theory by sixth form and the captain of school, was governed by Pop or the Eton Society, an oligarchy of two dozen boys who . . . were self-elected. . . . Pop were the rulers of Eton, fawned on by masters and the helpless sixth form. Such was their prestige that some boys who failed to get in never recovered; one was rumoured to have procured his sister for the influential members. Besides privileges—for they could beat anyone, fag any lower boy, walk arm-in-arm, wear pretty clothes, sit in their own club and get away with minor breaches of discipline, they also possessed executive power which their members tasted, often for the only time in their lives."

[175] *Peter Pan,* p. 180.

only repetition—no change or development, so no memory and therefore no story. From the standpoint of consciousness this represents paralysis, impotence; no creative impulse asserts itself to break free of the perpetual and self-perpetuating cycle of unreflected existence. Life is petrified when held in such rigid balance, fixated at a particular stage of development. It persists in an unconscious round of autonomous activity, a state of endless being, forever outside of time and so excluded from a history that would confer meaning.[176]

Again we meet with paradox: redemption from life as meaningless "eternal return," as represented by Neverland, would necessitate an incarnation, that is, a movement into time and so into tragedy. Such a radical transformation from a condition of virtual non-being to a state of becoming, with its attendant pain, sacrifice and commitment, meets fierce resistance both from Peter Pan (who refuses to grow up) and from Hook (who flees in terror from the tick-tock of the crocodile that symbolizes the passage of time, process and the inevitability of an end in death). Their refusal constitutes a refusal of consciousness.

There are numerous images of the timeless quality of Neverland and the refusal of the island's inhabitants to enter time. Every morning the lost boys cut the trunk of the Never tree that grows in the center of their underground home:

---

[176] In *Memories, Dreams, Reflections,* Jung describes his experience in Kenya when, alone on the broad savanna, he watched the herds of animals grazing as if in "the stillness of the eternal beginning, the world as it had always been, in the state of non-being; for until then no one had been present to know that it was this world." (p. 255)

Objective existence—and the possibility of meaning—is conferred on the instinctual, natural world by consciousness. Humankind, then,

> is indispensable for the completion of creation; in fact, [man] himself
> is the second creator of the world, who alone has given to the world
> its objective existence—without which, unheard, unseen, silently
> eating, giving birth, dying, heads nodding through hundreds of mil-
> lions of years, it would have gone on in the profoundest night of non-
> being down to its unknown end. Human consciousness created ob-
> jective existence and meaning, and man found his indispensable place
> in the great process of being. (Ibid., p. 256)

Later Jung adds that modern man, "robbed of transcendence by the shortsightedness of the super-intellectuals . . . . has fallen a victim to unconsciousness. But man's task is the exact opposite: to become conscious of the contents that press upward from the unconscious. Neither should he persist in his unconsciousness, nor remain identical with the unconscious elements of his being, thus evading his destiny, which is to create more and more consciousness. As far as we can discern, the sole purpose of human existence is to kindle a light in the darkness of mere being." (Ibid., p. 326)

By tea-time it was always about two feet high, and then they put a door on top of it, the whole thus becoming a table; as soon as they cleared away, they sawed off the trunk again, and thus there was more room to play.[177]

The boys' resistance to growth and development is also symbolized in the hollow trees which serve as each boy's personal entrance to their home. The boy is fitted to the tree rather than the other way around, and "if you are bumpy in awkward places or the only available tree is an odd shape, Peter does some things to you, and after that you fit." Taking care that, once fitted to your tree, you "go on fitting . . . keeps a whole family in perfect condition" (that is, static, childlike, innocent, prepubescent). Peter has difficulty fitting John, the eldest of the Darling children, to his tree, which suggests that mature sexuality has no place in Neverland. This is supported by Peter's insistence that "it is only make-believe, isn't it," when he acts as the boys' father, and by his puzzlement concerning Tiger Lily: "There is something she wants to be to me, and she says it is not my mother," to which Wendy responds vehemently "No, indeed, it is not." Peter Pan is essentially asexual; he is forever the son, although he persistently denies his need of a mother.

Despite the fact that Peter Pan consciously resists mothering on the personal level (by, for example, refusing to become a member of the Darling family), he presents many symptoms of remaining entrapped in an archetypal Mother-son entanglement. He clings to make-believe rather than enter fully into life and he unconsciously seeks a mother in every female child, fairy and Indian princess. Wendy's forthright response to Peter's concern about Tiger Lily's romantic designs on him is both instructive and amusing, as is the passionate addition to their conversation by that "abandoned little creature" Tinker Bell, who "squeaked out something impudent" from her boudoir, ending her protest with a resounding, "You silly ass!" Sexual awareness belongs to the female rather than the male in Barrie's fictional world.

The symbolic value of the tree has been extensively amplified by Jung, von Franz and others. As far as *Peter Pan* is concerned, it is useful to recall the relation of the tree to the Great Mother or the Great Goddess,[178] and note the symbolism of the boys' entering their underground home through the trunk of hollow trees. This suggests at least three symbolic possibilities: a return to the archetypal Mother through death (the lost boys are supposedly those babies who

---

[177] *Peter Pan*, p. 106.
[178] See, for example, above, p. 61.

fall from their prams and die because of their nurses' neglect); an incapacity to leave the embrace of the mother emotionally in order to enter fully and passionately into life as an independent adult; and a failure to develop sufficient masculine impulsion to realize one's individuality and creative potential. However, all true symbols are irreducibly complex and their many possible meanings are often contradictory. Jung tells us that by the image of the philosophical tree the alchemists depicted the individuation process, in which case the tree also symbolizes an "encounter with life and the world . . . [and so with] experiences that are capable of moving us to long and thorough reflection, from which, in time, insights and convictions grow up."[179] We may play with the idea that it is this tree, the Tree of Life, whose growth the children retard every day.

Jewish legend tells us that there were two trees in the Garden of Eden:

> In paradise stands the tree of life and the tree of knowledge, the latter forming a hedge about the former. Only he who has cleared a path for himself through the tree of knowledge can come close to the tree of life which is so huge that it would take a man five hundred years to traverse a distance equal to the diameter of the trunk, and no less vast is the space shaded by its crown of branches.[180]

While the fruit of the Tree of Knowledge confers consciousness (knowledge of the opposites, good and evil, and so of the essential structure of consciousness), the Tree of Life promises immortality. The legend encourages us to eat repeatedly the fruit of the Tree of Knowledge in order to forge a way through its dense foliage to the Tree of Life, for "the recovery of our lost wholeness can only be achieved by tasting and assimilating the fruits of consciousness to the full."[181] Essential to this redemptive process is the individual's continual awareness of and connection to both trees. We conceptualize this experience of connectedness as the ego-Self axis in psychological terms: that is, ego-consciousness's acknowledgment of its own relativity in face of a greater power, on the one hand, and ego's realization of a transpersonal, or archetypal, reality as the ground and support of its being, on the other.

Again, the tree serves as a symbol for such a vital axis both in the individual and in the world, as mythology's *omphalos,* world navel or *axis mundi.* In Norse mythology Yggdrasil is the World Tree from which all of life proceeds, and the

---

[179] *Mysterium Coniunctionis,* CW 14, par. 313.
[180] Edward F. Edinger, *Ego and Archetype: Individuation and the Religious Function of the Psyche,* p. 20 (quoting Louis Ginzberg, *Legends of the Bible).*
[181] Ibid., p. 21.

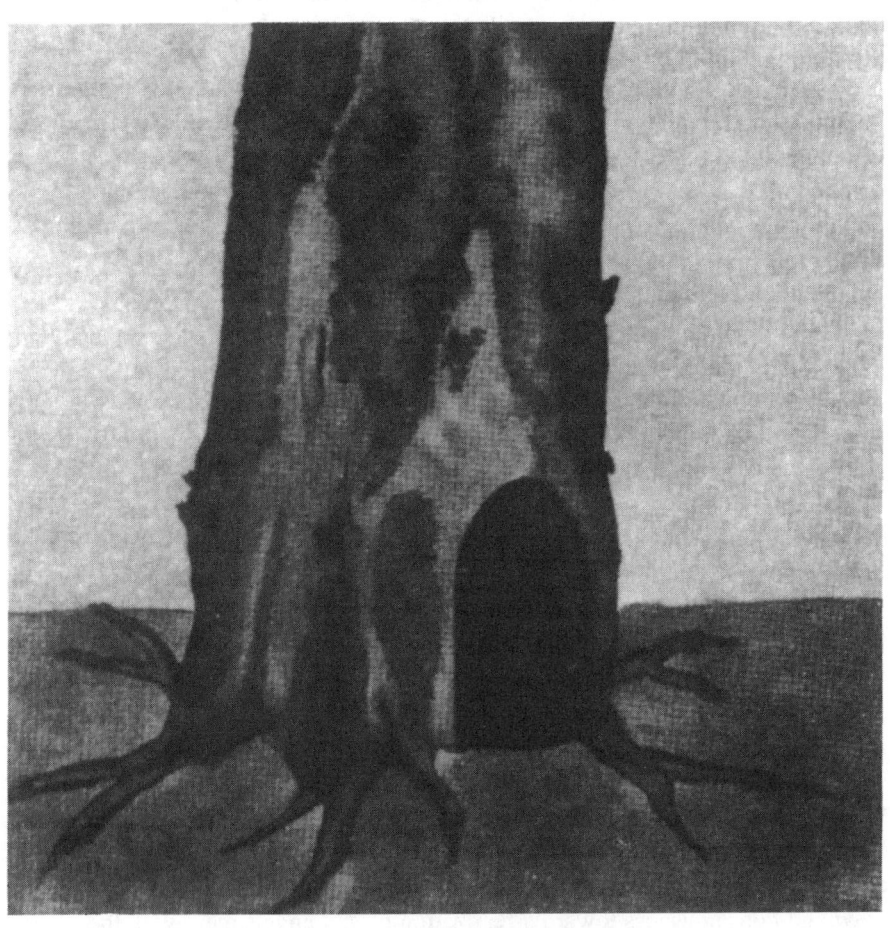

The tree as a symbol of renewal
("The Dark Door," dream image painted by the dreamer)

oak was sacred to the Celts because its roots were said to reach to the Underworld. In the Christian mythological universe, the tree is associated with eternal life, with death, with sacrifice and redemption: the branches reach to heaven, the roots to hell, and these two nonhuman realms are linked by the trunk, the middle, earthly, human world.

In many ways, *Peter Pan* addresses the problem of our imaginatively bridging the gap and realizing the tension between two disparate realms, between this twentieth-century world and an Otherworld or alternative reality. Barrie suggests that one may reach the Otherworld through dream, imagination and play ("in the two minutes before you go to sleep [Neverland] becomes very nearly real"), but only if one is a child and a little girl in particular. Thus, evidence of Peter Pan's having visited the nursery "seemed so natural to Wendy that you could not dismiss it by saying she had been dreaming." So, it is to the successive infant daughters of the Darling lineage, or to a young feminine aspect of consciousness, that passage to Neverland is open and Peter Pan a reality, an inner quality of the child-soul: " 'Oh no, he isn't grown up,' Wendy assured her [mother] confidently, 'and he is just my size.' "

We may argue that in Barrie's tale Wendy serves as a carrier of anima attributes; she represents a quality of conscious femininity that supports (in male, female or collective attitudes) a capacity for openness to the unknown Otherworld of imaginative fantasy and the unconscious. In classical Jungian terms, the anima is the contrasexual feminine element in the male psyche which, in its positive aspect, enables the man to develop a relationship both to the outer world and to the unknown inner realm whose reality is intimated in dreams, fantasies and moods.

If we follow this line of reasoning we must ask of *whose* male psyche is Wendy, as anima, a part. The obvious answer leads us to Barrie and an impossible labyrinth of enquiry we have no intention of entering. However, as much as an intrusion of unconscious material (in this case embodied in Peter Pan) may draw ego-consciousness toward a realization of and engagement with the objective psyche, a quality of consciousness (in this case a quality of conscious femininity embodied in Wendy) may also unwittingly initiate the process. So Jung writes that many "unconscious processes may be indirectly occasioned by consciousness, but never by conscious choice."[182] A positive engagement between ego-consciousness and unconscious fantasy is inevitably enhanced when anima

---

[182] "The Psychology of the Child Archetype," *The Archetypes and the Collective Unconscious,* CW 9i, par. 261.

qualities of relatedness and receptivity are to some degree already a part of one's conscious orientation. In terms of Barrie's novel, Peter Pan's arrival in the nursery is "indirectly occasioned" by Wendy's interest in story; both Peter Pan and Wendy are essential to the development of the action.

If we read the tale on the symbolic level as a story of psychic dynamics, then Wendy clearly represents a function "which filter[s] the contents of the collective unconscious through to the conscious mind."[183] Without Wendy, a bridge to the archetypal world would not be possible. Without the stories of her adventures in Neverland which she passes on to the next generation, the opportunity to link the two worlds, symbolized in the daughters' innate knowledge of Peter Pan, would never be realized.

Yet Wendy is still a child, albeit a curious one. She is also something of a paradox, being at once immature and yet already molded by the maternal instinct that shapes her experience of family and the adult world. Even the wolf of her imagination, often a symbol of the instinctual wildness and fierce individuality of the soul, is "a pet wolf forsaken by its parents." Wendy is, after all, fashioned after her mother. She emulates Mrs Darling and is chosen by Peter as a mother to the lost boys, providing a powerful illustration of how, even in the young, "the quiet voice of nature" is drowned by "opinions, beliefs, theories, and collective tendencies . . . [that] back up all the aberrations of the conscious mind."[184] In terms of Edwardian mores, however, Wendy would qualify as a "good" girl, affirming the cultural assumption that woman's natural ambition was to be absorbed into motherhood. In the novel, Wendy is the only one of the children connected with maturity and sexuality. She makes the others leave Neverland and supports Barrie's perspective that women are more strongly inclined to grow up than boys, if merely by virtue of their biology.

Mrs Darling, the only figure of adult human femininity in the tale, hardly remembers Peter, and Wendy, Margaret, Jane . . . are too young and not sufficiently individual (that is, not sufficiently differentiated from collective values and their own mothers) to serve as effective intermediaries between the two worlds. They fail to bring about either a transformation of the prevailing conscious attitude at No. 14 or a lasting reconciliation between consciousness and forgotten (or unconscious) contents of the psyche as represented by Peter Pan, Captain Hook, the crocodile, Tinker Bell, *et al.* John, we learn, does not even recall one story to tell his own children. Although Wendy's insistence on their

---

[183] "The Syzygy: Anima and Animus," *Aion,* CW 9ii, par. 40.
[184] Ibid.

return to the mainland alters the pattern of behavior and so breaks the recurring round of adventure on the island, with the result that the children are kidnapped by the pirates and Hook is eventually killed by Pan, this is done in service of a cultural ideal of motherhood.

Wendy's impulse is ambiguous. In one way it constitutes a refusal to remain a child, an asexual being, for she decides to leave Neverland after Peter Pan confesses that his feelings for her are those of a devoted son. In another way, her wish to return to London is conservative. Although outwardly adaptive and supportive of approved collective values, it is inwardly repressive: Wendy quickly forgets Neverland and so no appreciable change in conscious attitude takes place through her realization in conscious life of something of the qualities of the archetypal world she encountered in the form of Peter Pan, Hook and other denizens of Peter Pan's island. The rigid distinction between female and male roles in the external world prevails, and feminine and masculine qualities of psyche remain untransformed. As we have already noted, the family circle closes at the end of the novel to exclude Peter Pan but to include all the children (as well as Mr Darling) in the stultifying embrace of an unconsciously negative mother. Nothing changes, except for the fact that we are made aware that nothing changes through the medium of Barrie's tale.

The "tragedy" Wendy recognizes when she first sets eyes on Peter Pan may, then, be as much her own as Peter's. It is reflected in part in Barrie's intimation that Neverland and the adult world are mutually exclusive and unable to affect each other for better or for worse. Access to the magic shores of Neverland seems to be barred to grown-ups:

> On these magic shores children at play are for ever beaching their coracles. We too have been there; we can still hear the sound of the surf, though we shall land no more.[185]

Barrie's words evoke the Romantic idyll of childhood as a separate country, and bring to mind Wordsworth's notion that "Heaven lies about us in our infancy" when we play on the shores of the world, our child-souls still close to "that immortal sea / Which brought us hither."[186] In Wordsworth's imagination, life in the "prison-house" of the world leads us "inland," far from those magical shores, and we forget our soul's beginnings in "God, who is our home." However, the poet, and the poet-soul in each of us, retains the capacity, "though in-

---

[185] *Peter Pan,* p. 33.
[186] Above, p. 80.

land far we be," to sight the shores of childhood and "travel thither" through the power of poetic intuition.

We saw earlier that in classical mythology Hermes/Mercurius, as mediating psychopomp and guide of souls to the Otherworld, is also a figure for the movement of poetic inspiration and imagination which bridges the gap between this world and the shores of another. In psychological terms, Hermes/Mercurius signifies the bridge between ego-consciousness and the objective psyche. This essentially religious function of the psyche, which classical mythology recognizes in the figure of Hermes, is variously represented in mythology worldwide. For our purposes, it is sufficient to note the concern with poetic intuition that lies at the heart of the prophetic tradition of the Old Testament. Celtic mythology brings us Manannan *(mac Lir,* son of the sea), a trickster with magical powers and possessions who ferries souls to the Land of the Happy Dead (which, as we have seen, is paradoxically also the Land of the Living and of Youth).

Peter Pan, while he too serves as a guide and bridge between two worlds, cannot enter the conscious world of the Darlings without the cooperation of Wendy as the receptive feminine aspect of consciousness, and he cannot commit to life without sacrificing his sovereignty in Neverland. Caught between two worlds, he is lonely, an isolate, no matter how fascinating and desirable to earth-bound children his fairy dust and powers of flight. In this way he may represent the type of the poet who, by virtue of having been sprinkled with the fairy dust of poetic intuition, is forever set just a little apart. We think of Coleridge's warning at the end of "Kubla Khan" to beware the poet inspired to the point of madness because he has "drunk the milk of Paradise."[187] Access to the Otherworld is both a blessing and a curse. This is the subject of numerous tales from the Celtic and Northern traditions which tell of the isolation and fears, as well as the magical gifts, of one who has been touched by something or someone from the Otherworld, the man or woman, for example, who has enjoyed the love of a faery or water creature. The one so blessed knows something of both worlds but belongs fully to neither, existing on the margin of the seashore, as it were, in the liminal twilight region of the imaginal.

This essentially intermediate region is also known to the teller of tales as the place from which story arises. It is both without and within: at once a physical geography whose landmarks tell countless histories of soul, and an imaginal inscape that speaks of our experience of the world once it is given voice through

---

[187] *Poetical Works,* p. 298.

story. So Peter Pan, if understood as a quality of psyche or soul, lives by virtue of Barrie's story, but equally there can be no story without Peter Pan. Again, the supposed boundaries between the real and the unreal, tangible and imaginal, material and spiritual, are questioned. What remains an irrefutable inner prerogative or psychic fact to Wendy ("[Peter Pan] is just my size") appears to her father as the insubstantial phantasm of a childish imagination; and Barrie, as storyteller and fashioning ego, has the power to shape his tale as he wishes "in the way authors have." The story, then, is at once arbitrary, as conscious constructs and fictions can only ever be, and an embodiment of Peter Pan as a far from arbitrary psychic imperative.

If we extend Calvino's theory of narrative, which holds that meaning or "mythic significance is something one comes across only if one insists on playing around with narrative functions . . . inventing new developments in composition,"[188] we may argue that in good (that is, meaningful) storytelling, rational consciousness and archetypal immediacy, intellect and nature, meet in our experience of the tale. A story is meaningful because it presents us with something startling and provocative. Again we return to the idea introduced in our earlier discussion of literary fantasy, namely that story ideally concerns an encounter between two worlds.

I suggest that meaning resides in the *relation* we imagine to obtain between these two worlds: between such perceived disparities as Edwardian London and Neverland, fact and fiction, linear and holistic consciousness, intellect and intuition. In this way, all meaningful or soulful storytelling may be described as a *literature of encounter,* for it forces us to reflect on the meeting of our intellect with our nature, and so on our identity. How we understand the order of existence and how we relate to nonexistence—the eternal, the archetypal, the Other —depend upon our sense of place, purpose and relation to the world, in other words upon our sense of identity. The converse is of course also true. Fantasy literature, by its very structure, concerns the question of identity: it addresses the imaginative process of coming to grips with the inherent strangeness of the world in which we live, represented in the impossible strangeness of the secondary world of the fiction.

Earlier we noted that for Blake imaginative process is primary ("What is now proved was once only imagin'd"),[189] and Jung writes the following about the psychic, imaginal basis of reality:

---

[188] Above, p. 69.
[189] Above, p. 31.

It is my mind, with its store of images, that gives the world colour and sound; and that supremely real and rational certainty which I call "experience" is, in its most simple form, an exceedingly complicated structure of mental images. Thus there is, in a certain sense, nothing that is directly experienced except the mind itself. Everything is mediated through the mind, translated, filtered, allegorized, twisted, even falsified by it. We are . . . enveloped in a cloud of changing and endlessly shifting images.[190]

To this Hillman adds the importance of narration and narrative structure:

The fantasy [narrative] in which a problem is set tells more about the way the problem is constructed and how it can be transformed (reconstructed) than does any attempt at analyzing the problem in its own terms.[191]

If we concur with Blake, Jung and Hillman that our experience of ourselves and of the world is essentially psychic and comes to us in images, then we may look to imaginative phenomena—in this case Barrie's narrative—to tell us something of both the phenomenology of imagination as a function of psyche and the way in which we form our imaginative constructs of human identity. We may turn to art to learn better how to create and continually recreate ourselves, and to remember that the fully and consciously lived life is a life of deeply committed symbolic action. Story, then, confronts us with soul, and storytelling engages us in an activity of soul-making.

Peter Pan and Captain Hook: "Hook or Me This Time"

We suggested earlier that Peter Pan represents something of the nonrational, a previously unconscious content that has broken through the veil of conscious, rational experience. If Peter Pan is indeed the result of Barrie's attempt to create a figure for such an experience of the archetypal psyche, this would explain his equivocal, ambiguous, elusive character and our struggle to understand him. Jung's warning is therefore reassuring—namely, that when we undertake a psychological commentary of an archetypal image,

clear-cut distinctions and strict formulations are quite impossible . . . seeing that a kind of fluid interpenetration belongs to the very nature of all archetypes. They can only be roughly circumscribed at best. Their living meaning comes out more from their presentation as a whole than from a single formulation. . . . It is a well-nigh hopeless undertaking to tear a single archetype out of the living tissue of the psy-

---

[190] "Spirit and Life," *The Structure and Dynamics of the Psyche,* CW 8, par. 623.
[191] *Archetypal Psychology: A Brief Account,* p. 45.

che; but despite their interwovenness they do form units of meaning that can be apprehended intuitively.[192]

The difficulty in attaching a "unit of meaning" to Peter Pan supports the argument that he is not only an image of a potentially pathological personal complex (puer, negative mother, etc.) but also a significant mythologem: he personifies a quality of the archetypal core of the complex that determines its shape and dynamism but remains beyond the reach and understanding of the ego. If story ideally presents an encounter between nature (archetype) and intellect (ego-consciousness), then Peter Pan (as nature) and his magical island of Neverland both challenge and compensate the conscious attitude of Mr and Mrs Darling. Their attitude, as we have seen, is extremely one-sided, overly concerned with the opinion of neighbors and with "stowing out of sight" all but the "prettier thoughts" of the children. Despite the puerility and sentimentality of the Darling parents and their somewhat mawkish affection for Wendy, John and Michael, what appears to be missing from their conscious orientation are those positive qualities of consciousness symbolized in the archetypal image of the child, particularly the child-god or divine child, for which Peter Pan is in many ways an appropriate figure.

As an embodiment of "the treasure hard to attain" or the essential but lost value, the archetypal image of the divine child has a numinous quality often indicated by the way in which the child appears: as a pearl or golden ball, for example, in a flower or on a star. That Peter carries something of the numinosity of the divine or transpersonal psyche is intimated in Barrie's description of his relation to the stars:

> [The stars] are not really friendly to Peter, who has a mischievous way of stealing up behind them and trying to blow them out; but they are so fond of fun that they were on his side tonight. . . . So as soon as the door . . . closed on Mr and Mrs Darling there was a commotion in the firmament, and the smallest of all the stars in the Milky Way screamed out: "Now, Peter!"[193]

Peter Pan appears from an elsewhere that is at once the mysterious unknown of nature, clad as he is in leaves from an unfamiliar tree, and the past: Mrs Darling dimly remembers him from her own childhood. The qualities for which Peter stands, however, are of no great import in the conscious life of the Darlings.

---

[192] "The Psychology of the Child Archetype," *The Archetypes and the Collective Unconscious,* CW 9i, pars. 301f.
[193] *Peter Pan,* p. 49.

The window is closed against him and, if not flatly denied, he is certainly devalued by the adult world.

In "The Psychology of the Child Archetype," Jung suggests that what has been lost or devalued often turns up in an unexpected form and place—for example, in the shape of a dwarf, elf, child or animal, or in anything from stone to furrow. When we are confronted with such an image, we are also confronted,

> at every new stage in the differentiation of consciousness to which civilization attains, with the task of finding a new *interpretation* appropriate to this stage, in order to connect the life of the past that still exists in us with the life of the present, which threatens to slip away from it.[194]

Although Jung is here talking in terms of collective culture, the same applies at the level of personal psychological growth: dwarf, elf, child or animal may appear in cultural tales and myths in connection with a lost collective value or in the dreams of individuals whose childlike qualities of psyche have been forgotten. What is either lacking or too dominant in consciousness may be found, or will constellate its opposite, in the unconscious, for all things bring their opposites into being: one cannot know up without down, rich without poor.[195] In *Peter Pan* there is evidence in the impoverished conscious attitude of the Darlings of a *need* for Peter to appear at the nursery window and a *need* that he be recognized. The energy he embodies promises to redeem all that the Darlings have lost, forgotten and repressed: relatedness to imagination, to the past and to natural, instinctual wisdom, the poverty of which is seen in Mr Darling's mistreatment of Nana and Mrs Darling's daily effort to tidy the children's minds.

If, however, we fail to recognize the child-god, in whatever form he or she may appear, we fail to recognize our own inner potential for renewal. In many ways this constitutes a failure in our encounter with the numinosity of the child-god; it is therefore a failure of connection and a failure of interpretation. We remain cut off from, and uncomprehending of, the childhood aspect of the collective psyche that the child-image personifies, and so run the risk of finding ourselves rootless, lacking in orientation and consequently highly suggestible. This development we have already seen in Mr Darling, who becomes increas-

---

[194] *The Archetypes and the Collective Unconscious,* CW 9i, par. 267.
[195] What is often forgotten in such easy and satisfying oppositions is the space betwixt and between! A wealth of psychological and symbolic meaning surely lies in a subtle and painstaking discrimination of the myriad shades of grey that stretch between the black and white of any given situation.

ingly disoriented and puerile the more vociferously he denies any such tendency in himself. A lack of connection to the past is also evident in Mr Darling's having no memory of Peter Pan. It is, then, not surprising that Jung's description of the person who has suffered a dissociation between past and present provides an apt psychological sketch of Barrie's Edwardian father figure. Jung writes:

> Certain phases in an individual's life can become autonomous, can personify themselves to the extent that they result in a *vision of oneself*—for instance, one sees oneself as a child. . . . Such dissociations come about because of various incompatibilities; for instance, a man's present state may have come into conflict with his childhood state, or he may have violently sundered himself from his original character in the interests of some arbitrary persona more in keeping with his ambitions. He has thus become unchildlike and artificial, and has lost his roots. All this presents a favourable opportunity for an equally vehement confrontation with the primary truth.[196]

The "primary truth" may not, of course, be acknowledged as such, as is the case with Mr Darling.

In Peter Pan's own lack of memory, and in his being forgotten by generations of adults, Barrie provides another powerful image of the failure to establish a creative link with the past and, more precisely, with the mythological "idea of the child." This brings to mind Barrie's comment, quoted earlier, that his chief horror of adulthood was that the games of childhood would be forbidden and would have to be given up. Such a taboo generates the conscious need for secrecy and activates the psyche's autonomous mechanism of repression. Alternatively, writes Jung, an unbroken link with the childhood aspect of the psyche allows us a connection with "the original condition."[197] This in turn affirms a

---

[196] Ibid., par. 274.

[197] Ibid., par. 275. By "original condition" Jung refers to the state of undifferentiated *participation mystique* which the baby is assumed to enjoy with the mother in the prenatal and early postnatal stages of development. It is also suggested that for peoples living in a state of unconscious *participation mystique* with the world, a predominance of psychic content appears "out there" in the form of nature gods and spirits rather than "in here" as qualities of subjective experience and personality. These distinctions, however, tend to equate consciousness with solar, ego-consciousness. Recent infant studies and archaeological investigations of Neolithic goddess images point to the existence of a formerly unsuspected degree of discriminating consciousness in their subjects, newborn infants and Neolithic peoples respectively. The highly discriminating consciousness now attributed to Neolithic peoples may have been qualitatively *different from,* but not necessarily qualitatively or quantitatively *inferior to,* the type of differentiated ego-consciousness

profound realization of well-being and wholeness, a sense of trust in the world and the order of things, which we ascribe to the structuring principle of the Self, the psyche's apparently inherent tendency toward equilibrium and balance. A vital connection to this aspect of the Self affords us the capacity to maintain an openness and flexibility, and so a conscious humility, in the face of life.

However, everything has its shadow side, which may dominate the personality if one remains stuck at a stage of development or unconsciously identified with a quality or aspect of psyche that is taken for the whole. The shadow side of the child archetype shows itself in an undifferentiated, primitive morality which adheres slavishly and uncritically to the past, to natural laws and tradition. The result is an intransigent championing of uncompromising ideals which tends to retard rather than renew growth. We see this tendency in Mr Darling's adherence to the "right" way to do things, and in the importance of "good form" to both Pan and Hook, even at the risk of death.

Jung discusses a number of other qualities and attributes of the figure of the divine child in addition to its function as a link with the past. It signifies futurity and renewal and, as an image of possibility, it is symbolic of the transcendent function of the psyche. The god-child often enjoys unusual strength and gifts, yet suffers extreme vulnerability. He or she usually experiences a miraculous birth but endures life-threatening adversity in early childhood, similar to the child-hero. Let us begin with the last: the motifs of the miraculous birth, adversity in early childhood, gifts, strengths and vulnerability.

Peter Pan tells Wendy: "I ran away the day I was born" because "I heard father and mother . . . talking about what I was to be when I became a man," and

---

Western culture has valued above all others, particularly since the beginning of the Renaissance. The complex symbolic language which appears on figurines and at sites where goddess images have been found is a language we may no longer be able to "read," yet in all probability it constitutes a symbol system that not only informed religious rite but also supported a symbolic way of life and being in the world.

There would seem to be two types of consciousness: one belonging to the earth with its chthonic deities, the other to the mountain tops and sky with its more Olympian gods. It is primarily to the latter, the mythologies of Classical antiquity, that modern psychology has turned for its symbolic reading of the human psyche while comparatively little Celtic myth, for example, has been treated to such an analysis. Human beings, however, live neither in the earth nor in the sky but somewhere between the two. In many ways it would seem that Barrie struggles to bridge the gap between these two ways of being in the world or qualities of consciousness, for he overlays Celtic, Biblical and Classical mythologies throughout *Peter Pan*.

he boasts to Hook: "I'm youth, I'm joy . . . . I'm a little bird that has broken out of the egg."[198] So we are led to compare Peter Pan's story with tales of the miraculous births and extraordinary feats of infant child-gods discussed earlier (Dionysus, Hermes, Pan, Jesus). The image of Peter Pan as little bird links him to the motif of the winged messenger, angel or helpful bird of myth and fairy tale. It suggests both his autonomy (the shadow of which is, of course, his isolation as an orphan), and his being a part of nature and consequently a figure for an aspect of the objective, instinctual psyche.[199]

All this tells us that Peter Pan is not like other boys: not quite human, not fully divine; vulnerable yet immortal. Like many heroes of antiquity, he is vulnerable because of his special gifts and strengths. We think of Achilles, whose heel, the only vulnerable portion of his otherwise immortal body, caused his downfall. Likewise, Phaeton's and Icarus's youthful ambition and powers of flight led to their respective deaths. Peter Pan's capacity to fly and his many magical gifts, which he uses for good and ill, only serve to antagonize his archenemy, Hook, and despite his singular attributes the orphaned Pan is desperately lonely and "does so need a mother."

---

[198] *Peter Pan,* p. 196. In *Symbols of Transformation,* CW 5, pars. 388f., Jung writes that "man derives his human personality only secondarily from what the myths call his descent from the gods and heroes." Which is to say, archetypal figures, "endowed with personality at the outset," shape the personality. Mythological motifs support this view:

> In the first place [it is] the god [quasi-personal archetype] who transforms himself, and only through him does man take part in the transformation. Thus Khnum, "the maker, the potter, the builder," shapes his egg on the potter's wheel, for he is "immortal growth, his own generation and his own self-birth, the creator of the egg that came out of the primeval waters." The Egyptian Book of the Dead says: "I have risen like the mighty hawk that comes forth from his egg," and: "I am the creator of Nun, who has taken up his abode in the underworld. My nest is not seen and my egg is not broken." Yet another passage speaks of "that great and glorious god in his egg, who created himself for that which came forth from him." Therefore the god is also called Nagaga-uer, the "Great Cackler." (Book of the Dead 98:2: "I cackle like the goose, and whistle like the hawk.")

Peter Pan, we recall, is known for his crowing and cackling, especially when he feels triumphant and all-powerful, in other words, like a god.

[199] In *The Little White Bird,* a tale which had "no moral application" according to the Llewelyn Davies boys' nurse, Mary Hodgson, Barrie wrote of an island in the Serpentine, Kensington Gardens, where all the birds are born that later become babies. According to Barrie, all children were once birds and he insisted that "Children in the bird stage are difficult to catch." (Birkin, *J.M. Barrie and the Lost Boys,* p. 62)

Another characteristic of the divine- or hero-child is that he suffers adversity as an infant, often in the form of abandonment and exposure to the elements and wild beasts. We learn something of his divinity from his miraculous survival, the symbolic significance of which, in the psychology of the individual, is highly valued by Jung:

> The "child" is all that is abandoned and exposed and at the same time divinely powerful; the insignificant, dubious beginning, and the triumphal end. The "eternal child" in man is an indescribable experience, an incongruity, a handicap, and a divine prerogative; an imponderable that determines the ultimate worth or worthlessness of a personality.[200]

The greatest adversity suffered by Peter Pan, the lost boys, the pirates and Hook is also abandonment. While the lost boys fell from their prams when their nurses were looking the other way, Peter found the window closed and entry into his nursery barred when he decided to return to his parents. Smee asks "What's a mother?" and when, by way of example, Hook points to the Neverbird on her nest of eggs, "there was a break in his voice, as if for a moment he recalled innocent days when——."[201]

Our discussion of abandonment, nostalgia for mothers and the "innocent days" of an idyllic childhood in *Peter Pan* will initially take us away from the image of the "eternal child" as symbolic of a "divine prerogative." We will return to the divine, mythological dimensions of the image after considering its implications for personal psychology. In the individual, early experience of abandonment often manifests in those traits, many of which are characteristic of the narcissistic personality and the puer shaped by a negative mother complex, that are important to our understanding of Barrie's hero. These are traits that seem to have become synonymous with Peter Pan to the regrettable occlusion of his numinosity.

We have already noted a negative effect of abandonment in Peter's incapacity to trust. Never having experienced a "good-enough mother," in Winnicott's sense, Peter Pan has little trust for anyone but he is especially mistrustful of mothers and mothering in general, and of Mrs Darling in particular. Peter is even mistrustful of Wendy in her role of "mother" to the lost boys. Peter Pan's

---

[200] "The Psychology of the Child Archetype," *The Archetypes and the Collective Unconscious,* CW 9i, par. 300.
[201] *Peter Pan,* p. 121. It is interesting to note that the novel's sole image of a positive mother, the only mother figure with which Peter Pan relates, is that of the Never bird whose eggs are not yet hatched.

defensive mistrust and declarations of fierce independence ("we don't want any silly mothers") are complicated by his tragic neediness, which stems from the deeply ingrained fear that to admit need and vulnerability is to open himself again to the risk of abandonment. Peter's neediness and mistrust feed his consequent acts of denial and displays of ambivalence. He dare not admit his hunger for a mother and for the stories mothers tell their children, so his need becomes projected onto the lost boys: Wendy and her stories are for them. He idealizes the absent mother and is then tormented by his endless search for the perfect parent he has never known and who, if she were to appear, he would always repudiate as inadequate. Peter's ambivalence is most extreme in his simultaneous idealization and destruction (rejection) of Mrs Darling: "She is a pretty lady, but not so pretty as my mother. Her mouth is full of thimbles [kisses], but not so full as my mother's was."[202]

In the two-year old, demonstrations of ambivalence may indicate the beginning of a healthy independence. However, we must remember that Barrie says in his opening chapter, "Two is the beginning of the end"! If this stage of development is not successfully negotiated, a debilitating ambivalence may grow to characterize the core of a neurotic structure typical of the narcissistic personality and of the puer as eternal adolescent. When faced with choice, the narcissist and the puer alike tend to be unable to sacrifice one alternative in order to commit fully to the other: they each want both—everything—for fear of ending up, once again, with nothing. An often uncompromising, unrelated black-and-white thinking results from such a crux: unable to suffer sustained conflict or withstand denial, and faced by an unacceptable choice, the overwhelmed ego snatches at straws.

One avenue of escape from the inevitable conflict occasioned by choice is by way of a preposterous and highly undesirable third alternative. The typically extreme character of this "answer" demonstrates the lack of sufficient ground on which the ego rests, and so its failure to connect to feeling or to a reality structure other than its own. An example of such a rash decision impelled by fear is found in the pirates' rapid change of attitude toward Wendy when they are faced with the mysterious and deadly "ghost" which terrorizes their ship. Quickly named as the Jonah bedeviling the pirate craft, Wendy is instantly transformed in the pirates' eyes from desired object/mother to scapegoat and jinx. At one moment Wendy is prized and protected; at the next, she finds herself the first

---

[202] Ibid., p. 207.

candidate for the plank and a watery grave.

In marked contrast to his spontaneity and love of adventure, Peter Pan demonstrates an exacting rigidity in his ideas about childhood, manhood and motherhood. Although perhaps to a lesser degree than the lost boys, Hook and members of the Darling family, he is nevertheless a prisoner of matter—of Mother—and being stuck in matter he remains matter's victim. In psychological terms, this tendency to fixity results from a failure to distinguish the personal from the archetypal Mother, and manifests in a negative mother complex. Never having known his own mother, Peter's idea of mothers suggests a product of almost pure projection, a complex imago which has little or no basis in actual experience and in which both archetypal and conscious fantasy vie for the leading role. Jung writes on projection and imago as follows:

> Just as we tend to assume the world is as we see it, we naively suppose that people are as we imagine them to be. In this latter case, unfortunately, there is no scientific test that would prove the discrepancy between perception and reality. Although the possibility of gross deception is infinitely greater here than in our perception of the physical world, we still go on naively projecting our own psychology into our fellow human beings. In this way everyone creates for himself a series of more or less imaginary relationships based essentially on projection. . . . A person whom I perceive mainly through my projections is an *imago* or, alternatively, a *carrier* of imagos or symbols. All the contents of our unconscious are constantly being projected into our surroundings, and it is only by recognizing certain properties of the objects as projections or imagos that we are able to distinguish them from the real properties of the objects. But if we are not aware that a property of the object is a projection, we cannot do anything else but be naively convinced that it really does belong to the object.[203]

Although, as Jung suggests, "It is the natural and given thing for unconscious contents to be projected,"[204] the growth of the conscious personality depends on projections being recognized and eventually, if painfully, withdrawn. We become engaged in this natural rhythm of unconscious projection/conscious recognition mainly through relationship to others: love opens the way to what was once unconscious, for we are first drawn to others because we see in them, and are attracted by, something in ourselves of which we are as yet not aware. We initially encounter such new and different material as belonging to another (that

---

[203] "General Aspects of Dream Psychology," *The Structure and Dynamics of the Psyche,* CW 8, par. 507.
[204] Ibid.

is, in projection). Only if and when projections are withdrawn do we realize that the quality, vice or virtue which first commanded our attention is in fact not just "out there" in another, but also "in here" in ourselves.

As with all psychic processes, projection may present a positive or negative face. It seems that when the projection is seen as negative, the ego becomes intransigent, resisting any disturbance of the status quo or a change in attitude which recognition and withdrawal of the projection would demand. The psyche's conservative tendency takes over to defend a beleaguered ego against disruption and change, and rigidity sets in. To acknowledge a trait one abhors in another as a quality of one's own initiates a demanding process of self-knowledge and acceptance in the healthy personality. In one with a minimal sense of self, it assaults the fragile ego with the threat of disintegration.

Jung's comments on projection as a bridging function, linking us emotionally to others and to unknown parts of ourselves, are helpful in our understanding of how the psychic situation of "stuckness" (evident in Peter Pan, Mr Darling, and Hook in particular) may initially be constellated in the personality:

> So long as the libido can use . . . projections as agreeable and convenient bridges to the world, they will alleviate life in a positive way. But as soon as the libido wants to strike out on another path, and for this purpose begins running back along the previous bridges of projection, they will work as the greatest hindrances it is possible to imagine, for they effectively prevent any real detachment from the former object. We then witness the characteristic phenomenon of a person trying to devalue the former object as much as possible in order to detach his libido from it. But as the previous identity is due to the projection of subjective contents, complete and final detachment can only take place when the imago that mirrored itself in the object is restored, together with its meaning, to the subject. This restoration is achieved through conscious recognition of the projected content, that is, by acknowledging the "symbolic value" of the object.[205]

If we consider *Peter Pan* as a whole, we may argue that in its symbolic entirety the tale presents a narrative image of a psychodynamic field. Life, in both Edwardian London and Neverland, proceeds with predictable regularity until the action begins because of a surprise, eccentric event: Peter Pan's appearance at the nursery window sets our field in motion. Action is no more nor less than an opening to new possibilities, an indication that, on the level of the individual personality, one's desire or libido "wants to strike out on another path." Ac-

---

[205] Ibid.

cording to Jung, however, no change can take place unless former unconscious attachments (previous investments of libido) are recognized and withdrawn.

As readers, we have license to propose a number of possible developments for Barrie's characters. Depending on one's perspective, the lost boys may be found and Peter Pan may become a man, no longer doomed to suffer for all eternity as an isolate; the Darlings—parents and children alike—may experience an enhancement of consciousness and so of life; the pirates may be redeemed from a daily round dominated by fear and violence, which would in turn free the Indians from the need to be constantly on the warpath, etcetera, etcetera. However, as with Wendy, who overidentifies with her mother whether she is in Neverland or London, so with Mr Darling, the Darling children, the lost boys, Hook and his pirates alike: it proves impossible for them to effect and suffer the necessary sea-change required to detach libido from the Mother in order to channel it elsewhere. Mr Darling's enthrallment by the negative pole of the archetypal feminine is evident in his childish behavior and his dependence on his wife; the strength of both Peter Pan's and Hook's possession by an unconscious Mother imago is seen in the extreme vehemence of their resistance to mothers and to sentiment. In short, they are all stuck.[206]

Peter Pan's search for a mother is eternal. His need determines his return every springtime to the nursery window and, like the youthful sons of mythology such as Attis and Adonis who cannot escape the mother's embrace even in death, he never knows what it is to be free of her image. His annual appearance as a boy-child clad in leaves aligns him with the dying and resurgent gods of antiquity, and so, once again, with the Mother, for the young gods return by way of death to the archetypal Mother in order to be reborn. Jung tells us that this motif finds a parallel in the theme of being lost and found again,[207] a theme central to Barrie's novel. It concerns the lost boys and the Darling children in particular and links them to the same paradoxical mythologem of the young Near

---

[206] "Stuckness" results from our experience of opposites and the fear of loss which must accompany any movement or choice. Being stuck between opposites, unable to go backward or forward, is also a classical view of neurosis. When not mediated or bridged, the opposites appear as chaotic and unacceptable options (a situation in which we discover several of Barrie's characters). Another example of psychological stuckness is when one remains fixated at a certain stage in life: the life that is not lived falls into the unconscious and, if unrealized, tends to disturb the direction of consciousness. (Peter Pan is an excellent figure for the unconscious content that disrupts the conscious life of the Darling family.)

[207] "The Dual Mother," *Symbols of Transformation,* CW 5, par. 531.

Eastern sun-gods: the need to die in order to live, embodied in the heroic impulse to return to the Great Mother, as matrix and source of life, to be renewed.

This impulse is presented mythologically in numerous images, some of the most obvious being the hero's fight with the dragon, encounter with the witch, night-sea journey and quest to the underworld. The hero's task is always attended by the risk of failure, the possibility of his being "devoured" by dragon/underworld/Great Mother should he fail to slay the metaphorical beast of the unconscious and commit the symbolic matricide necessary to ensure a safe return home and a renewal or expansion of consciousness. Consequently, when thinking of Peter Pan's often vicious attack on "mothers," it is important to understand his resistance symbolically and to remember Jung's cautionary words about the way in which we may most usefully treat symbolic material:

> It is not the real mother who is symbolized, but the libido of the son, whose object was once the mother. We take mythological symbols much too concretely and are puzzled at every turn by the endless contradictions of myths [and literary works with archetypal content]. But we always forget that it is the unconscious creative force which wraps itself in images. When, therefore, we read: "His mother was a wicked witch," we must translate it as: the son is unable to detach his libido from the mother-imago, he suffers from resistances because he is tied to the mother.[208]

The psychological picture in *Peter Pan* is complicated still further when we remember that in the male psyche the archetypal image of the anima (the man's inner image of a sexual counterpart and feminine Other) first appears mingled with the image of the mother. "The mother is the first feminine being with whom the man-to-be comes in contact, and she cannot help playing, overtly or covertly, consciously or unconsciously, upon the son's masculinity."[209]

We see this contamination, or confounding, of mother and contrasexual imagos in Mr Darling. His relationship to Mrs Darling is as much that of son as husband, which suggests that his wife is the object or carrier of his unconscious projections of both mother and lover: he expects her to be both and acts accordingly. In Neverland this contamination is compounded by Wendy's lack of differentiation from her mother. Wendy slips as easily into the role of mother as that of daughter, just as her father metamorphoses from husband to son to patriarch. Even Peter Pan, for whom "make-believe and true were exactly the same

---

[208] "Symbols of the Mother and of Rebirth," ibid., par. 329.
[209] "Psychological Aspects of the Mother Archetype," *The Archetypes and the Collective Unconscious,* CW 9i. par. 162.

thing," finds it necessary to confirm that Wendy's game of playing mother to his father is indeed make-believe.

Sexual differentiation and gender roles are unclear, and the absence of clear boundaries at the conscious level, as represented in the Darling family, is reflected in the confusion that reigns in the unconscious, in Neverland, as seen in Pan, Hook and the pirates. As noted earlier, Peter Pan's innocence is evident when he cannot understand what Tiger Lily wants to be to him if it is not a mother, and when he "does something to" the boys' growing bodies so that they continue to fit their hollow trees! However, neither Tiger Lily nor Tinker Bell is as innocent, or ignorant, as any of the male inhabitants of Neverland, and certainly the mermaids do not hesitate to try to drown Wendy in order to keep Peter Pan to themselves.

Symbolically, the mermaids' attempt to drown Wendy suggests Wendy's vulnerability: as a newly acquired or burgeoning attribute of consciousness, more strongly aligned with adulthood than eternal childhood, she is in danger of being swallowed by the instinctive psyche. The mermaids embody a negatively conservative and regressive pull of the unconscious which opposes the ego's push toward sexual maturity and collective adaptation, evident in Wendy's insistence that the children return to the mainland. They attempt to pull back into the unconscious the young feminine impulse that promises to draw Peter Pan into the arena of conscious life. The mermaids may consequently be understood as primitive and essentially negative anima figures. K.M. Briggs writes that the mermaid is a

> sinister character . . . though harmless mermaids have been known. . . . It was considered a certain omen of shipwreck for a ship to sight a mermaid. . . . Like many other fairies the mermaids have a great desire for human children. In the folk-lore of a good many countries the mermaids and other water fairies are supposed to be very anxious to gain a human soul. Their lives are long, but when they die they perish utterly."[210]

A key characteristic of the mermaid is that she, like the siren, fascinates men to their death. In this way, we can see how Tinker Bell and the mermaids point to that otherworldly aspect of the anima which captivates and lures victims away from the "real" world, whereas the feminine as embodied in Wendy attempts to

---

[210] *The Anatomy of Puck: An Examination of Fairy Beliefs Among Shakespeare's Contemporaries and Successors,* p. 191. (Think of Peter Pan's desperation when it appears that Tinker Bell is about to die.)

turn Peter Pan and the lost boys back from a regressive and infantile attachment to childhood toward conscious, adult, worldly commitment.

In fact, Wendy's life is often in danger. Apart from the mermaids' attempt to drown her, Tinker Bell tries to kill Wendy more than once; she is shot by mistake by Tootles, and her life is threatened by the pirates. This indicates the strength of the negative anima as "nature being," as mermaid or fairy who, like the seal- or swan-woman of folklore, "indicates psychologically the original closeness of the anima with water, the unconscious, into which she is always ready to disappear and into which, in some stories, she does indeed disappear."[211] What is indicated by this symbolism is the difficulty to grasp and hold the positive anima-quality of psyche, that bridging function which enables the dialogue of conscious ego and unconscious, and that facilitates the ego's differentiation of imaginal, archetypal being (Tinker Bell, mermaids) from human being (Wendy). The imaginal being lures one into the phantasmagoric realm of unconscious fantasy, while the human being invites an engagement with real life.

In *Peter Pan,* the possibility of a mature sexuality seems to lie far from consciousness, with the "savages" (Tiger Lily) and perhaps with the mermaids and the fairies, although there is some confusion of sexual identity even with them. As Wendy explains to her mother, "[Fairies] live in nests on the tops of trees; and the mauve ones are boys and the white ones are girls, and the blue ones are just little sillies who are not sure what they are." Yet it is with the fairies that the Bacchanalian shadow of a supposed sexual innocence lies. When Peter sleeps above-ground to keep watch over Wendy in her little house, "some unsteady fairies had to climb over him on their way home from an orgy. Any of the other boys obstructing the fairy path at night they would have mischiefed, but they just tweaked Peter's nose and passed on."[212]

As with Peter's technique of fitting the boys to their trees, Barrie once again spares the details and so leaves much to the conjecture and imagination of the adult reader! It is tempting, however, to think of Neverland as a metaphor for Celtic Ireland at this point. In Celtic lore, the mythological race of the Tuatha De Danann (Peoples of the Goddess Danann) suffered defeat at the hands of human invaders and they and their nature religion were forced underground, at which time they became the Little People or Faerie Folk of Irish legend. The Faerie Folk came to symbolize the Tuatha De Danann's earlier sensual and spiritual connection to life and nature that influenced the beliefs of the Druids but suf-

---

[211] Rivkah Scharf Kluger, *Psyche in Scripture,* p. 94.
[212] *Peter Pan,* p. 103.

fered further suppression with the coming of Christianity. It is also likely that Neverland's fairies symbolize that remnant of the instinctive Pan-like aspect of Peter's nature, which was represented in the first production of the play by a live goat on stage, and which survives in the novel in Peter's "playing gaily on his heartless pipes."

The subtle confounding of masculine and feminine attributes that describes many of Barrie's characters provides yet another example of the powerful but unconscious hold of the maternal feminine. While much of Peter's charm lies in his prepubescent asexuality, the symbolism of Hook's appearance and personality points to a complex, undifferentiated and dark interrelation of masculine and feminine qualities. Hook dresses, with his long black curls, in the style of Charles II (see next page), whose court was renowned for its permissive admixture of effeminacy, sexual license and perversity; he has the cadaverous features of the devil yet eyes "of the blue of the forget-me-not"; he is as elegant and polite as he is sinister and cruel; he denies sentiment yet swipes an errant tear from his eye with a flourish of his iron claw; he is forced to rely on the strength of his ego and the solidity of his persona, whispering to his ego, "Don't desert me, bully," when his men threaten mutiny, for "in his dark nature there was a touch of the feminine, as in all the great pirates, and it sometimes gave him intuitions."[213]

Hook's authority is eventually undermined and he himself is unmanned by his refusal to admit his innate femininity into his conscious life: his fear of being taken for "a codfish" by his men leads him to break, "with almost diabolical cunning," the rules of the game in Neverland. While this dubious heroism sets Hook apart from his followers "in spirit as in substance" and results in the massacre of the Indians, it leads finally to his defeat by Pan and the death, in the jaws of the crocodile, he dreaded most of all.

Hook's nemesis, the crocodile, is a type of dragon or Leviathan, a symbol of primal powers and the alchemical *prima materia,* and also a complex amalgam of masculine and feminine qualities. According to *The Herder Symbol Dictionary,* the crocodile

> enjoyed special veneration in Egypt, where it was thought to have been born out of the water like the sun; it was revered as a powerful deity (Sebek), simultaneously solar and chthonic [i.e., masculine and feminine].[214]

Like the Old Testament Leviathan, the crocodile

---

[213] Ibid., p. 123.
[214] P. 49.

embodies the continuing effects of the primal chaos which threatens creation and must be vanquished. [It] . . . thus personifies the difficulties that must be overcome before an important goal can be attained.[215]

A creature of both land and water, the crocodile signifies the dual nature of humankind. It evokes great age and a nearness to the origins and source of life, as it has existed since long before recorded history. Jung names the snake as the commonest symbol "for the dark, chthonic world of instinct,"[216] but other cold-blooded animals, such as the crocodile, may be substituted. It is precisely this chthonic world that Hook dreads: the crocodile as devourer, signifying, by its association in *Peter Pan* with time (it has swallowed a ticking clock), "the necessity of passing through death to life."[217] By refusing death Hook symbolically refuses life and consciousness.[218] For Hook, to be devoured by the crocodile represents an irreversible defeat by process (time) and a final descent into hell, into the maternal matrix; hence the mixture of fear and awe in which the creature is held, as embodiment of the numinous, the alpha and omega of existence.

We also meet an admixture of fear and awe in Hook when he faces the descent into Peter's underground home, which "seemed to be but one more empty tenement in the void," another powerful image of the negative aspect of the archetypal Mother. Hook's terror is extreme:

> [He] let his cloak slip softly to the ground, and then biting his lips till a lewd blood stood on them, he stepped into the tree. He was a brave man; but for a moment he had to stop there and wipe his brow, which was dripping like a candle. Then silently, he let himself go into the unknown.[219] *p. 110*

In psychological terms, we may describe Hook's horror of death, the unknown and the feminine as a resistance against regression, or fear of the dissolution and fragmentation of identity. In mythological terms, it represents the dread of symbolic incest with the Great Mother, a terror of possible engulfment and obliteration in the primal chaos. This fear is embodied in the figure of the crocodile and underlies Hook's tyrannical rigidity (as it underlies Mr Darling's

---

[215] Ibid.

[216] *Aion*, CW 9ii, par. 385.

[217] J.C. Cooper, *An Illustrated Encyclopaedia of Traditional Symbols*, p. 44.

[218] Jung: "Consciousness can only exist through continual recognition of the unconscious, just as everything that lives must pass through many deaths." ("Psychological Aspects of the Mother Archetype, *The Archetypes and the Collective Unconscious*, CW 9i, par. 178)

[219] *Peter Pan*, p. 168.

paranoia). The picture we have of Hook as he steals into Peter Pan's underground home intent on murder, and finds himself facing a sleeping boy, is one of tortuous conflict. Libido seems to fight against libido, instinct against instinct:

> Thus defenceless Hook found him [Peter Pan in a dreamless sleep]. He stood silent at the foot of the tree looking across the chamber at his enemy. Did no feeling of compassion disturb his sombre breast? The man was not wholly evil; he loved flowers (I have been told) and sweet music (he was himself no mean performer on the harpsichord); and, let it be frankly admitted, the idyllic nature of the scene stirred him profoundly. Mastered by his better self he would have returned reluctantly up the tree, but for one thing.
>
> What stayed him was Peter's impertinent appearance as he slept . . . . such a personification of cockiness . . . . steeled Hook's heart.[20] $p. \, |||$

If Hook, with Mr Darling, is a representative of the father as spirit, one of his functions, as spirit, is to oppose pure instinctuality (personified as much in Peter Pan as in the crocodile). Hook's lack of conscious integration of the feminine, however, pushes him into a defensive position that is colored by the negative poles of both the maternal and paternal archetypes. His tyrannical cruelty (negative father) thrives only when he murderously denies his feelings (positive mother). In repressing the positive feminine, he unwittingly constellates the negative mother in whose maw he already symbolically but unconsciously lives: we must not forget that Hook's iron claw was fashioned to replace the arm Peter Pan cut off in battle and threw to the crocodile. The crocodile long ago devoured a part of Hook and enjoyed that tasty tidbit so much that she pursues Hook relentlessly in the hope of feasting on more of the same.[21]

The style of Hook's death brings us finally to those other essential character-

---

[20] Ibid., p. 169.

[21] This invites a comparison between Barrie's Captain Hook and Herman Melville's Captain Ahab. Both Hook and Ahab have lost a limb to the unconscious or chthonic world, in the form of the crocodile and white whale (Moby Dick), respectively; each is devoured in the end by the creature he hates; Hook suffers a sense of dissolution, Ahab feels himself to be "all aleak"; each is maimed, a maiming that in many ways represents a perverse identification with the Father and a debilitating severance from the Mother. We may also compare Hook's treatment of his men with Ahab's brutality, and recall Hook's sentimental description of motherhood when we think of Ahab's words as toward the end of the hunt for Moby Dick he shakes his fist at his "fiery Father" in heaven and demands what has become of his mother: "I now know thee, thou clear spirit, ... my sweet mother, I know not. Oh, cruel! What hast thou done with her?" (Melville, *Moby Dick,* pp. 616f.) See also Edward F. Edinger, *Melville's Moby-Dick: An American Nekyia.*

istics of the divine-child: futurity, renewal and possibility. In many ways, the on-going conflict between Hook and Peter Pan is an enactment of the old king's resistance to renewal and to youth as symbol of futurity. The blackness of Hook, with his iron claw, is a symbolic description of the ruler who is impotent or deformed and no longer suitable to be king. This motif of the out-worn, infertile king (Hook laments that there are "no little children to love me") occurs in mythology and literature world-wide, but a particularly interesting analogue to Barrie's tale comes from Ireland.[222]

The story concerns Nuada, King of the Tuatha De Danann, who loses his hand in battle. A silver hand is crafted for him, but Nuada's mutilation renders him unacceptable as king and another succeeds him. The new King Bres, however, is only part Tuatha and proves niggardly and tyrannical, stripping the Tuatha De Danann of their wealth. Finally the Tuatha demand the restitution of their realm. Nuada is reinstated as king when it is discovered that his hand of silver has been magically restored to a hand of flesh. Until his death Nuada is effectively supported by Lug, "a young warrior, fair and shapely, with a king's trappings" who arrives at Nuada's court and proves himself "a sage in every art."[223] Lug, whose name means light, is associated with youth, prowess, sunconsciousness and the arts; he infuses the Tuatha De Danann with vitality and creative spirit until their final defeat and relegation to the "faery regions" by the conquering Milesians. However, Lug, who as the God of Light resembles "the rising of the sun," appears in Irish mythology also as a god of the Underworld, "belonging on the side of his mother . . . to the Powers of Darkness."[224]

In this tale of Lug and Nuada we find no easy polarization of good and evil, light and darkness, puer and senex. Lug does not overthrow Nuada but benefits him and his kingdom with the gift of *all* his crafts, from poetry to the warrior's art. This is the story of a realization of occult and psychic libido—the power of the god—in the realm of the manifest. The same cannot be said of *Peter Pan.* In Barrie's tale there is no notable change in the realm of the manifest as a result of Wendy's experience of Peter Pan: at the end, life continues both in the conscious world and in Neverland in much the same way as before. Although Peter Pan and Hook cannot simply be equated with good and bad respectively, and al-

---

[222] The myth of the Grail and the wounded old Fisher-King originates, as far as we know, in the Celtic tradition.

[223] Alwyn Rees and Brinley Rees, *Celtic Heritage: Ancient Tradition in Ireland and Wales,* pp. 33, 35.

[224] Rolleston, *Celtic Myths and Legends,* p. 88.

though each shares many qualities, dark and light, of the other, they fail to cooperate as Nuada and Lug do.

One explanation for this may be that, as puer and senex, boy and old man, Peter Pan and Hook have not attained a sufficient degree of differentiation to permit each to relate to the other as distinct but complementary aspects of a single archetypal configuration or as two faces of the same dominant (as king and king's son; as the young Dionysus with the aged Silenus). The opposite is true of Lug. When he arrives at Nuada's court, he has first to distinguish himself from others, prove his arts and meet a number of challenges to test his powers. Only after Lug is known in all his many parts does Nuada invite him, as the "man of each and every art," to take the king's seat.[225]

In our story, Hook asks Peter Pan to identify himself many times but Peter's replies, if lyrical, are hardly definitive: "I'm youth, I'm joy," "[I'm] wonderful boy." He has no solid sense of identity apart from that reflected back to him by others, hence his desperate neediness and his fear to change the status quo lest he and his world suffer irreparable fragmentation. Neither is Hook secure enough in his own identity to open himself to Peter Pan. The two persist in a round of undifferentiated enmity, a rigid bond essential to the stability of both players, until Peter, making a ticking sound like the crocodile, tricks Hook and brings about his defeat, only, symbolically, to take his place. While Lug, as harbinger of consciousness, brings renewal and possibility to Nuada's kingdom, Peter Pan assumes the darker aspects of the Old King to the extent of having Wendy make him a new suit out of "some of Hook's wickedest garments":

> It was afterwards whispered among them that on the first night he wore this suit he sat long in the cabin with Hook's cigar-holder in his mouth and one hand clenched, all but the forefinger, which he bent and held threateningly aloft like a hook.[226]

In his essay, "Symbols of the Mother and of Rebirth," Jung argues that mythology illustrates how the "paradoxical background of . . . consciousness"— that is, what appears to be an "unconscious in conflict with itself"—can be projected onto and reflected in the "adversities and contrarieties of external nature."[227] This is a useful metaphor if we think of the enmity between Hook and Peter Pan, senex and puer, as presenting an image of the "unconscious in conflict with itself." Hook's deformity, his arcane knowledge which leads him to

---

[225] Rees, *Celtic Heritage,* p. 35.

[226] *Peter Pan,* p. 202.

[227] *Symbols of Transformation,* CW 5, par. 395.

concoct a poison "quite unknown to science," and his "looking the very spirit of evil breaking from its hole" as he emerges from Peter Pan's underground home, link him to the dark, chthonic gods of antiquity as well as to the devil of Christianity.[228] A ruthless pirate persona belies Hook's constant struggle against potentially overwhelming sentiment and we cannot forget that he is blessed with "blue eyes . . . as soft as the periwinkle."

Peter Pan, on the other hand, knows magic and the mercurial power of flight, is associated with the light through Tinker Bell and has Adamic dominion over beast, fish, fowl and fairy alike. Yet he, too, is likened to the devil more than once and assumes a Luciferian stance of such unremitting opposition to the adult father world that one questions whether he represents the hope of redemption or a senseless, destructive disturbance.

Both Hook and Peter Pan enjoy extraordinary powers, yet each suffers a desperate and self-destructive loneliness: Hook would kill the youth and youthful creativity he envies; Peter Pan is as ruthless and cruel as the "old man" he hates. Inwardly, each falls victim to a tortuous syllogism of his own making. Hook is tormented by the paradox of "good form," a construct that, regardless of its origin, appears a tenet of only-senex rationalism. He is totally identified with "good form" and consequently experiences "a presentiment of his early dissolution" in his inability to resolve this conundrum, which we may phrase as follows:

> It is bad form to think about good form.
> The highest good is good form;
> Therefore he who knowingly attains to good form enacts bad form.[229]

Peter has constructed for himself a comparable prison-house of logic which traps him in an only-puer position and sentences him to eternal childhood, a fate which even in Wendy's young eyes appears a tragedy. The paradoxical equation that keeps Peter out of life might read:

> All men lead solemn lives and have no fun.
> All boys grow up to become men;
> Therefore to grow up is to lead a solemn life and have no fun.

---

[228] Jung notes: "Ugliness and deformity are especially characteristic of those mysterious chthonic gods, the sons of Hephaestus, the Cabiri, to whom mighty wonder-working powers were ascribed." (Ibid., par. 183)

[229] The way in which Hook experiences the presentiment of his early dissolution suggests the beginnings of a dissociation of personality. He refers to himself in the third person, something he does "in his darkest hours only."

Peter, of course, wants always to have fun, hence his resistance to Mrs Darling who says she "should love [him] in a beard."

Life in Neverland, then, is less idyllic than it might at first appear. As we look more closely at Barrie's other world it betrays itself increasingly as a place of fear. As such, it presents an image of the "psychic distress" that Jung associates with a prepsychological primitive unconsciousness, but that may be constellated in the modern psyche suffering a "conflict-situation that offers no way out."[230] Neverland, after all, comes close during the night: Hook attacks under cover of darkness, violating the unspoken rules that underpin the inhabitants' collective round of activity, and returning all to a state of chaos in which natural man (the Indian tribe) and his own pirates are decimated and he himself suffers dissolution in the belly of the crocodile; and Peter Pan, as he creeps up on Hook's ship in the dead of night, knows "well that sudden death might be at the next tree, or stalking him from behind."

Against such psychic distress, neurosis provides a defense. We see a number of Barrie's characters desperately (neurotically?) trying to maintain the status quo rather than risk a choice which might result in a breakdown of the known order of things. Peter Pan looks for a mother to keep the lost boys happy; Mr Darling clings to his position, Mrs Darling to her maternal role, and Wendy, in Neverland, to her memories of how mothers and fathers are; Hook adheres to good form and the Indians to the tradition of attacking their enemies at dawn, etcetera. Choice and change are, however, unavoidable components of life and individual psychological growth, and each necessitates sacrifice. Childhood attachments must be sacrificed before libido formerly invested in the Mother (both actually and symbolically) may be redirected into the world. This constitutes a creative act, a liberation of masculine spirit in order to create world in the first place and then fructify what has been created.

In *Peter Pan,* however, Barrie provides no model for the release of masculine spirit from matter, Mother and inertia. No positive father figure enables a break with the maternal matrix and promotes initiation into independent, mature action. Mr Darling is ineffectual as a father. Together, he and Hook embody a perverse and degenerate masculinity rather than a generative phallic libido that, despite its potency, remains related to the feminine (as mythologically Hermes both serves and is related to Aphrodite).

Consequently, Peter Pan's struggle to define himself as youth and joy, against

---

[230] "The Psychology of the Child Archetype," *The Archetypes and the Collective Unconscious,* CW 9i, par. 288.

Hook as senex, is essential. The son must separate from the mother but he must also differentiate himself from, or symbolically kill, the father, in order to define himself in terms of his own phallic energy. The puer, by definition, must resist the senex. Paradoxically, however, as much as puer and senex must define themselves in opposition to each other, they need to realize themselves *through* each other. Such a movement of libido requires a grounding in the positive feminine, enabling sufficient basic trust on the part of the ego to surrender its autonomy, momentarily, in the faith that it will survive.[231]

Integration of the quality of consciousness we call senex supports, in its positive aspect, an actualization of the creative passion and fantasy symbolized by the figure of the puer. As we suggested earlier, the puer who engages the senex pole of the *puer-et-senex* archetype in a solely negative way remains a mother's son identified with a negative femininity and unable fully to trust life. He will never become the hero who claims his phallic power and proves his valor and independence by symbolically breaking from unconscious inertia, represented mythologically by the Great Mother and psychologically by an out-worn ego stance or infantile adherence to an earlier stage of development. As creative impulse, he will suffer perpetual relegation to the Otherworld.

For the puer to realize heroic qualities of consciousness, "Hook *or* me" must alternate with "Hook *and* me." There is a need for creative tension within the *puer-et-senex* configuration rather than denial of each pole by the other. First, however, there is a need for differentiation in order that the puer may later aspire to what Hillman terms an Icarian (vertical) flight to make contact with senex/father/spirit. Such a psychic condition would entail, for Peter Pan, a painful recognition and integration of shadow qualities: his similarities to Hook, his needs and vulnerabilities, and the fact that, although he fancies himself free and powerful, his freedom and power remain isolating illusions.

Jung says of the shadow of the puer that it "becomes fatal when there is too little vitality or too little consciousness in the hero for him to complete his heroic task."[232] In Peter Pan there is plenty of vitality, but too little consciousness. This is symbolized in Peter Pan's reaction to the loss of his shadow which is snapped off when Nana closes the window in an attempt to catch him. Although we might argue that Peter Pan should be glad to be free of his shadow, this would presuppose his awareness of its content. However, in psychological terms, Peter's physical attachment to his shadow (his request that Wendy sew it back on)

---

[231] See Erik Erikson, *Identity: Youth and Crisis.*
[232] *Symbols of Transformation,* CW 5, par. 393.

describes an unconscious identification of ego and shadow. Such an identification explains his lack of self-reflective, objective distance, without which there may develop neither self-knowledge nor the desire to change:

> If he thought at all, but I don't believe he ever thought, it was that he and his shadow, when brought near each other, would join like drops of water; and when they did not he was appalled. He tried to stick it on with soap from the bathroom, but that also failed. A shudder passed through Peter, and he sat on the floor and cried.[23]

Nana (instinct) knows that Peter Pan will return for the missing shadow, that he and his shadow are totally undifferentiated and joined "like drops of water." His "shadow problem" underlies Peter Pan's lack of insight, substance and psychology: as long as his shadow is not "seen," as a fictional character he remains a delightful if elusive idea but hardly a complex personality. This is evident in his refusal to become entangled in relationships and in his inability to separate from the painful dreams ("more painful than the dreams of other boys") which have to do "with the riddle of his existence" but whose content remains a mystery.

The differentiation of shadow as an initial step in the development of personality is, however, a function of ego-consciousness and, as we have seen in our discussion of the Darling family, in *Peter Pan* there is no figure representative of ego-consciousness strong enough to engage in such a task. Consequently, the shadow side of life, represented by Hook, his pirates and the Indians, etcetera, has long since been relegated to the unconscious, as is clear from the fictional necessity of Neverland in the first place, and the fact that most of the action takes place there. Particularly regrettable is the contamination or confounding of spiritual potential (Peter Pan) and shadow, for which Peter Pan's identification with his own shadow serves as fitting metaphor.

The problem is that of sacrifice. Whoever would be heroic requires an ego of sufficient strength and flexibility to surrender its sovereignty in the shadowy face of the unconscious. Only then does the personality as a whole acquire the courage and humility that enables it to maintain a sacrificial stance in the face of life, without which there can be no hope of transformation and spiritual growth. Fear of the unknown, however, paralyzes. And, as Jung argues, fear of death ties the unheroic, the neurotic, to the "mother" (and so to the neurosis).[24] In contrast, the heroic ego remains neither stuck (as does Peter Pan), nor dies (like Hook),

---

[23] *Peter Pan,* p. 52.
[24] *Symbols of Transformation,* CW 5, par. 398.

but overcomes its fear of death in the form of the dragon of material and spiritual inertia. Such an heroic movement of libido represents a symbolic matricide, a resistance to infantile dependence, regression and the unconscious, with which Peter Pan flirts but which is not realized at the conscious level (in the Darling family) or the unconscious (in Neverland).

Identified with his shadow, and suffering a consequent inflation, Peter Pan cannot conceive of sacrificing his sovereign status, so he fails to defeat the crocodile/dragon of the unconscious. While Hook is swallowed by it, Peter identifies with it, assuming its tick, amongst other qualities, in the final stages of his battle with Hook:

> Peter reached the shore without mishap, and went straight on; his legs encountering the water as if quite unaware that they had entered a new element. Thus many animals pass from land to water, but no other human of whom I know.[235]

Identification with the crocodile, as much as being devoured by it, symbolizes the vulnerability of a fragile ego or embryonic consciousness to being overwhelmed by the instinctive psyche. To escape the impasse in which Peter Pan and Hook find themselves demands an act of conscious sacrifice. As Jung writes:

> Animals represent instinct, and also the prohibition of instinct, so that man becomes human through conquering his animal instinctuality. . . . [Sacrifice as an] act of supreme courage and supreme renunciation is a crushing defeat for man's animal nature . . . . The sacrifice is the very reverse of regression—it is a successful canalization of libido into the symbolic equivalent of the mother, and hence a spiritualization of it.[236]

Arguably, the only canalization of libido we discover in *Peter Pan* lies in story rather than action: in the storytelling of Mrs Darling, Wendy and her female descendants, and in Barrie's fiction itself.

Although Peter Pan fantasizes at different times what an adventure it would be both to live and to die, the only characters prepared to suffer conscious sacrifice, seen in their willingness to die, are Tiger Lily and Tinker Bell. Tinker Bell drinks the poison Hook intends for Peter Pan, and Tiger Lily faces death at Hook's hand for the sake of the collective, her tribe. In both cases, an aspect of the young feminine is prepared to sacrifice itself either to sustain the collective

---

[235] *Peter Pan,* p. 188.
[236] *Symbols of Transformation,* CW 5, par. 398.

values of the tribe (Tiger Lily) or to ensure the survival of the youthful mascu-line spirit (Tink would die in Peter's stead). Such sacrifices represent a conser-vative tendency to maintain the existing status quo, as Peter Pan's evasion of sacrifice and suffering lies in his refusal to grow up and enter life. The impov-erishment of consciousness which results is represented in the inhibited personal psychology of each of the Darlings as well as the static collective condition of the family unit. Liberation from repetitive unconscious psychodynamics and patterns of behavior fails to take place; renewal is not effected and no fresh life or vitality enlivens the daily round at No. 14. To quote Jung again, "Con-sciousness can only exist through continual recognition of [i.e., sacrifice to] the unconscious, just as everything that lives must pass through many deaths."[237]

Although its hero claims the attributes of youth, joy and spontaneity, *Peter Pan* is in many ways the story of the inhibition of such life-affirming qualities. When Peter comes back for Wendy the springtime following her return from Neverland, Wendy discovers that he does not remember Hook or their earlier adventures. Even Tinker Bell is forgotten. Understood symbolically, this sug-gests what may happen when dynamic potential at the archetypal level of the psyche, namely a fresh configuration of the Peter-Hook/puer-senex dominant, fails to attain sufficient intensity to impact consciousness. It sinks back deep into the unconscious whence it originated, to all intents and purposes forgotten, ex-cept for the creative impulse itself which, in the figure of Peter Pan, may return sporadically to embark on yet another skirmish with ego-consciousness.

Beyond Mother and Father: Peter Pan, Puer, Phenomenon of Spirit

A conclusion? Peter Pan has little to do with conclusions, although a great deal to do with returns, renewals, recurring disruptions, insights, flights both physical and fantastical, games and gamuts, propositions and passions. A conclusion suggests the final proving of something, while my concern has been the elucida-tion, to use Peter Tatham's expression, of the symbolic geography of the *field* that is Peter Pan. However, before a final chapter in which I will speculate on reasons for Peter Pan's strong and continuing impact on English and American popular culture, a summary of our metaphoric mapping of Neverland is in order.

If we choose to understand Peter Pan from the perspective of personal psy-chology, we will have no difficulty finding in him the traits and behavior identi-fied with puer as neurosis or pathology. Among the most evident of these are his

---

[237] "Psychological Aspects of the Mother Complex," *The Archetypes and the Collective Unconscious,* CW 9i, par. 178.

often insufferable cockiness, his refusal to leave the provisional fantasy-realm of childhood in order to assume an adult identity and social responsibility, the labile quality of his emotions and attachments, his callousness, cruelty, vulnerability and neediness, his flightiness and his charm, to name but a few. In Mr Darling we have noted how ludicrous such behavior appears when it is writ large in the adult. We have suggested that, at an unconscious level in such an adult, the dynamics for which Peter Pan and Hook, puer and senex, stand, are stuck in constant conflict. At the end of Barrie's novel, Peter Pan/puer reigns supreme. He assumes some of Hook's more obvious attributes in his clothing and the crooking of his hand in imitation of the old pirate's hook, but all other Hook/senex potential remains unredeemed and forgotten, reabsorbed into the maw of the maternal matrix of the unconscious (the crocodile): the cycle of the masculine begins again, untransformed.

We know nothing of Mr Darling's parents, but with Peter Pan having received no effective parenting whatsoever, we see in Peter the result of the failure of an early emotional environment to support the process of a proper narcissism, or healthy introspection, which Jeffrey Satinover claims is essential to the constellation of the Self in the infant. According to Satinover, the constellation of the Self is perhaps best understood as

> the introspective apprehension of a coherent relationship prevailing amongst the various structures of the psyche. When the psyche is functioning in a stable and harmonious fashion; when there *is* a relationship amongst its parts, a functional unity exists and is perceived by the ego as the sense of identity.[238]

Lack of a sense of constant identity leads the puer into relationships which are notoriously short-lived and intense because they have less to do with relationship than with the puer's need to be reflected and thereby affirmed "through the eyes of another."[239] Hence Mr Darling's dependence on wife, family and colleagues for verification of his persona as businessman and father, and Peter Pan's imperious need for Wendy and Hook to give substance to his actions through their reactions. Consequently Wendy often feels slighted by Peter, as though she were merely an extension or externalized psychic function of him, and Hook is soon forgotten, with Peter able carelessly to dismiss his forgetfulness of his old enemy with the callous remark, "I forget them after I kill them."

Barrie's continual reworking of *Peter Pan* and his repeated exploration of

---

[238] "Puer Aeternus: The Narcissistic Relation to the Self," p. 76.
[239] Ibid., p. 100.

It is only the gay and innocent and heartless who can fly.

what I now feel we may call "the Peter Pan enigma" in most of his numerous other works, speak to the centrality of the image both personally and collectively, as Barrie's dramas and novels were generally well-received by his public. We may fantasize that Barrie was, for whatever reasons of personal psychology, addicted to the image of a childhood self, with its power to evoke for him the child's seemingly limitless gift of imagination, unfettered by the strictures of the mundane adult world. We may also suppose that this addiction was so strong that Barrie sought every opportunity to experience vicariously the wholeness and sheer vitality of the childhood self through his association with the Llewelyn Davies boys.

Many of his detractors have consequently accused Barrie of harboring an unhealthy regard for "his boys," but Nico, the youngest, dispels any such misgivings in one of many interviews with Andrew Birkin, author of *J.M. Barrie and the Lost Boys,* before the book's publication in 1979:

> Of all the men I have ever known, Barrie was the wittiest, and the best company. He was also the least interested in sex. He was a darling man.[240]

—and later, more explicitly, in a letter to Birkin:

> I'm 200% certain there was never a desire to kiss (other than the cheek!), though things obviously went through his mind—often producing magic—which never go through the more ordinary minds of such as myself. . . . All I can say for certain is that I . . . never heard one word or saw one glimmer of anything approaching homosexuality or paedophilia: had he had either of these leanings in however slight a symptom I would have been aware. He was an innocent—which is why he could write *Peter Pan.*[241]

All indications from the boys' surviving letters to Barrie, and from Barrie's own notebooks, suggest that he was fated to suffer, in Hillman's sense, the full *infirmitas* of the archetype of eternal youth, both through his art and, we may assume, throughout his life. Undoubtedly the pathology looms large, in Barrie's tormented sense of inadequacy as a man and his failure as a husband, in his moodiness, wit, humor, grandiosity and disregard for limits, in his sentimentality, his cruelty and the vagaries of his genius. However, especially toward the end of his life, Barrie left sufficient evidence in his work, letters and notebooks for us to conclude that Peter Pan stood for the transcendent powers of imagina-

---

[240] *J.M. Barrie and the Lost Boys,* p. xii.
[241] Ibid., p. 130.

tion and opened for him a window to the soul, enabling at times that profound engagement in the fullness of life itself that we tend to associate with childhood play alone.

In his Dedication to *Peter Pan,* Barrie wrote of how on one summer fishing trip in 1912 with Michael, the boy who more and more came to embody the whole compelling enigma of Peter Pan, he managed to bring Michael "back to the faith [in fairies] for at least two minutes."[242] Michael was at that time twelve and had "ceased to believe," hovering, as it were, at the point of no return between childhood and adolescence:

> "Whom do you want to see most, Michael?" "Of course I would like most to see Johnny Mackay." "Well, then, wish for him." "Oh, rot." "It can't do any harm to wish." Contemptuously he wished, and as the ropes were thrown on the pier he saw Johnny waiting for him, loaded with angling paraphernalia. I know no one less like a fairy than Johnny Mackay, but for two minutes Michael was quivering in another world than ours. When he came to he gave me a smile which meant that we understood each other, and thereafter neglected me for a month, being always with Johnny. . . . this episode is not in the play; so though I dedicate *Peter Pan* to you I keep the smile, with the few other broken fragments of immortality that have come my way.[243]

Barrie wrote, "Nothing that happens after we are 12 matters very much," and treasured in particular memories of "his boys" in that "golden year" between childhood and adolescence. The "broken fragments of immortality" to which he refers in his Dedication must surely be memories of those moments when, in the depths of play with "his boys," he was transported from this world to find himself vitally present in the other world of the imagination; indeed, we may say of Barrie as E. V. Lucas said of Michael: "For all his vivid interest in the moment, [he was ever] more in the world than of it, an elvish spectator rather than a participant."[244]

It seems, however, that Barrie was as inimical and enigmatic as his creation. Lady Cynthia Asquith, who at one time worked as Barrie's secretary, described Barrie to her husband as:

> An extraordinary plural personality. . . . For all that apparent haphazardness there seems to be plenty of shrewdness, plenty of canniness. As for the legend of his

---

[242] *Peter Pan and Other Plays,* pp. 85f.
[243] Ibid., p. 86.
[244] *J.M. Barrie and the Lost Boys,* p. 279.

being himself the boy who wouldn't grow up, I see no evidence whatever of this. On the contrary he strikes me as more than old, in fact I doubt whether he ever was a boy. But then, for the matter of that, Peter Pan isn't a boy, is he? He is a wish-fulfilment in fable form of the kind of mother—Barrie's an expert at her—who doesn't want her son to grow up.[245]

Yet there was, for all his canniness, dour demeanor and moody withdrawal, a lightness of being about Barrie that seems to belong to the imaginal realm but which he endeavored to realize in this world.[246] Consequently the boys' nurse, Mary Hodgson, complained bitterly of Barrie's spoiling the boys, sheltering them to a debilitating degree. Even Peter, the third and perhaps most cynical of the five, writes in the *Morgue,* his compilation of family letters and papers,

> The lighter side of life was thoroughly catered for. . . . I think it was of far more interest to him [Barrie] that George and all of us should excel in games and fishing . . . than that we should acquire any real culture in Matthew Arnold's sense of the word.[247]

With his own ideal of childhood based on fantasy, the stories of his mother's girlhood, Barrie seemed condemned to construct and struggle to dwell imagina-tively in a fiction that alone could afford the sense of security and solace his own boyhood lacked. The Llewelyn Davies in every way filled Barrie's need for such a "storybook family." Peter Davies was later to write of his parents that they were perhaps too perfect to live long, referring to his mother Sylvia as "the widow, still so beautiful in her forty-fourth year, of the splendid Arthur."[248] Sylvia especially attempted to surround her boys with gaiety and light, insisting in a Will found several months after her death that "great care" must be taken of Michael in particular. The dying Sylvia tried to protect her boys from the fact of her death, forbidding them to see her toward the end, and as they grew older the boys seemed naturally to take it upon themselves to protect Barrie from the more brutal facts of their own lives: the twenty-one-year-old George, before his

---

[245] Dunbar, *J.M. Barrie: The Man Behind the Image,* p. 307.

[246] Birkin, *J.M. Barrie and the Lost Boys,* p. 201. Birkin quotes Nico, who wrote of Bar-rie, "He was the most wonderful of all companions, and the wittiest man I shall ever know, and all the usual talk about his being obsessed with thoughts of his mother and with general gloom is largely distortion (I cannot recall his once talking about his mother in all the years I knew him). . . . A creature of moods, yes indeed: maybe to be expected of a man of genius; hours of silence, but many, many more hours of humour."

[247] Ibid., p. 219.

[248] Ibid., p. 192.

death at the front in 1915, spared Barrie the horrors of trench warfare, insisting in his letters,

> Don't you get worried about me, I take every precaution I can, & shall do very well. It is an amazing show, & I am unable to look forward more than two or three hours. . . .
>
> The sing of a bullet passing near doesn't worry me very much now. It just warns me if it is possible to crouch as low as I can. . . .
>
> On the whole, then, my dear Uncle Jim, there's nothing for you to be anxious about. . . .
>
> I'm far too timorous a man (I am a man now, I think) to run any more risks than I must. . . .
>
> Would you send out some Cambridge sausages from Fortnum & Mason? . . .
>
> Meanwhile, dear Uncle Jim, you must carry on with your job of keeping up your courage. . . .[249]

The lightness of the Otherworld of play and imagination, a lightness on which Barrie thrived (when he was not morosely withdrawn in this world), is perhaps only partly a consequence of Barrie's innocence, of which Nico speaks. However, as we have seen in *Peter Pan,* as well as in the way in which Barrie chose to indulge "his boys," there appears a marked absence of the counter-quality to lightness, namely the weight and dark materiality of the chthonic side of life. What was by nature dark was rendered in the lightest possible hues, although in actuality both Barrie's life and the story of the Llewelyn Davies were characterized more by tragedy than comedy and good fortune. Possibly this attraction to the light speaks as much to the collective consciousness of the era in which Barrie lived as it does to his own psychology and creative genius, an idea to be explored in my final chapter.

Paradoxically, whereas lightness, freedom and space may be the necessary conditions for play, play itself is far from light, in that it has the capacity to ground one in the wholeness of one's being. In a discussion of the importance of play in childhood, Anthony Stevens cites Johan Huizinga's claim, in *Homo Ludens,* his work on the subject of play, that "in play there is something 'at play' which transcends the immediate needs of life." This is because the archetypal activities of human life are filled with possibilities for play. Notes Stevens:

> Hence Schiller's famous aphorism, "Man is only truly himself when he is at play."

---

[249] Dunbar, *J.M. Barrie: The Man Behind the Image,* pp. 226, 267, 268, 273, 275.

. . . Childhood is a period of immense vitality and inventiveness, when imagination is given free rein to complement the realities or compensate for the deficiencies of everyday existence. . . .

It is one of the misfortunes of growing up that we readily lose touch with this rich land of childhood . . . . Yet nothing is lost to the Self, and play, like the child who sponsors it, lives on as a propensity of the psyche to its dying day.[250]

What is of particular interest in our discussion of Barrie is Stevens's emphasis that fantasy, as *introverted* play,

is the product of play between the archetypes of the collective unconscious and the living circumstances of the individual. . . . Fantasy is not a regressive means of escape from reality . . . but the *modus operandi* of psychological growth: it is the stuff of life, leading us on into the future.[251]

Play and fantasy lead us into the future because they make us creators. They legitimize our re-formation and re-creation of the world, allowing us to remember and so re-deem the scattered fragments of ordinary life. They make us gods for an hour or a day, enabling an activity which affirms our sense of Self because it affords unlimited scope to our desire for realization, fulfillment and creative power in a world of our own making that is secret and therefore safe. The task of the artist is then to establish a vital connection between the hidden world of possibility and the world of actuality.

However, according to Winnicott, the "place" of play and fantasy is precarious, "because it belongs to the interplay in the . . . mind of that which is subjective (near-hallucination) and that which is objectively perceived (actual or shared reality)."[252]

This precarious place is the No-man's land, the betwixt and between, the intermediary realm of the imagination, that the artist must continually negotiate and re-negotiate or, to be more precise, interpret and re-interpret. This is where one may encounter the image of the god-child, that "divine prerogative" buried deep in the personality. The problem for the writer who, like Barrie, feels infinitely more at home and alive in the imaginal realm, is to interpret an experience or encounter in *that* world in the terms of *this* world. No such reassuring resolution occurs in *Peter Pan.* Barrie's two worlds are as opposed at the end as they are at the beginning, with nothing to suggest there is space in the Edwardian

---

[250] *On Jung,* pp. 87f.

[251] Ibid., pp. 88f.

[252] *Playing and Reality,* p. 61.

world of the Darlings for the intensity and richness of life discovered in Neverland. Barrie is unable, in the end, to show that reality does provide room for self-
fulfillment, a domesticating and comforting resolution we find, Elliott Gose argues, in other children's classics of the era, such as Kenneth Grahame's *Wind in
the Willows* and A. A. Milne's Winnie-the-Pooh stories.[253]

In Barrie we are faced with quite the contrary: an explicit devaluing and
questioning of cosy domesticity, and an iconoclastic strain that seems to run
throughout his work, although most evident in the figure of Peter Pan and other
Barrie heroes that serve as versions of Peter's enigmatic presence. As a result,
we discover in Peter Pan that quality of masculine energy described as the trickster, a familiar figure of myth and folklore who functions as "lawbreaker . . .
[and] . . . represents the expression of instinctual desires."[254]

The trickster element often represents an early stage in the development of
the heroic ego and expresses the transformative power of nature,[255] while itself
resisting transformation. Barrie's hero, likewise, resists transformation. In *Peter
Pan,* there is precious little evidence of the active sexuality of either a Don Juan
or the trickster. There is equally little promise of development, clear or otherwise, beyond infant-boy-trickster to mature hero, father and possibly Wise Old
Man. On the contrary, Peter Pan's iconoclasm threatens to solidify into an idol
to boyish (prepubescent) perversity and defiance for their own sakes.

This alone invites an understanding of Peter Pan as a very specific aspect of

---

[253] See *Mere Creatures: A Study of Modern Fantasy Tales for Children.*

[254] Barbara Greenfield, "The Archetypal Masculine," in Andrew Samuels, ed., *The Father,* p. 192.

[255] Ibid., p. 191. Greenfield argues that "The boy, Don Juan, and the trickster show us the
ego in its early stages of development, while the hero, the father and the wise old man
represent later stages of development. As a whole, the animus, or male archetype, unifies
these disparate figures because it exists as those principles which underlie them all." She
suggests that the most powerful mythological forms of the masculine archetype are those
of the father and the trickster, claiming the trickster as "an early incarnation of the father"
rather than an archetype separate from that of the father, as it is treated by Jung.
    Her view supports our earlier discussion of the inherent similarities of Peter Pan and
Hook and is useful when individual development and personal pathology are the issue.
However, what we may describe as the "creative iconoclasm" of the Self in its impulse to
further consciousness favors Jung's treatment of the trickster and his recognition of its
important and constant role in the archetypal drama of the psyche. Perhaps this presents a
case for "both/and" rather than "either/or" terminology; and for a concept of co-existing
levels of activity rather than a more linear development from one stage to the next, with
only faint traces of earlier characteristics evident in the later stages.

the archetypal psyche's character, seen in the psyche's unrelenting impulsion of ego- and collective consciousness toward some undefinable goal or condition. Peter Pan seems to me to be far more specifically *boy* than he is youth, Don Juan, trickster or potential senex: he is an embodiment of restless striving, of yearning or *Pothos,* which James Hillman translates from the Greek, and understands from the Greek god of that name, as "the longing towards the unattainable, the ungraspable, the incomprehensible, that idealization which is attendant upon all love and which is always beyond capture."[256]

Barrie very clearly establishes Peter Pan as the force, or archetypal image, of the eternal boy whose nature it is to oppose authority and old age, represented in Hook as Saturn/Chronos. This opposition Barrie considered essential, as is evident from his notebook entry of December 1920, when he was preparing an address to the graduating class of St. Andrews entitled "Courage":

> Great thing to form own opinion, don't accept hearsay. Try to get at what you really see in it all. Question authority. Question accepted views, values, reputations. Don't be afraid to be among the rebels. . . Speak scornfully of the Victorian age. Of Edwardian age. Of last year. Of old-fashioned writers like Barrie, who accept old-fangled ideas. Don't be greybeards before your time—too much advice is to make you so.[257]

Yet, as Barrie aged, and as the most precious of his boys were taken from him—by war, by drowning, by adulthood—the distance between this and his other world seems to have increased. Arguably, this is traceable in his changing perspective on Peter Pan: in early years Peter Pan is "the boy who *won't* grow up," later "the boy who *couldn't* grow up," and finally, after Michael drowned, "the lad that *will never* be old."[258] Peter Pan and his world remain constant: it is we and this world that change.

However, Peter Pan's constancy may also be an image of Barrie's intuitive knowledge that, as spiritual phenomenon and figure for "the awakened heart," Peter Pan *cannot* be forced to develop, grow old, transform. Puer, as image of the soul's yearning, cannot help but constellate its opposite or *otherness,* that undefinable goal for which it longs and toward which it drives. Whether that otherness manifests as senex, mother, homo- or heterosexual lover, "the presence of otherness feels like self-estrangement, self-alienation" and our experi-

---

[256] "Pothos," in *Loose Ends,* p. 53.
[257] Birkin, *J.M. Barrie and the Lost Boys,* p. 289.
[258] Ibid., p. 300, italics added.

ence of it initiates us into an awareness of our "essentially double nature."[29]

Once one becomes conscious of puer or twin consciousness, writes Hillman, one's "being is metaphorical, always on two levels at once," and there flits just beyond one's reach "always a reflection of an invisible other." One's desire is in danger of becoming "hooked" and pulled obsessively "towards the image that initiates the desire," that is, toward the image of the *puer aeternus.*[260] This idea, of the eternal boy as an "imaginal reflection of ourselves,"[261] Barrie captures nowhere more poignantly than in *Neil and Tintinnabulum,* in which he is really writing about Michael at the "golden" age of twelve:

> A rural cricket match in buttercup time with boys at play, seen and heard through the trees; it is surely the loveliest scene in England and the most disarming sound. From the ranks of the unseen dead, forever passing along our country lanes on their eternal journey, the Englishman falls out for a moment to look over the gate of the cricket field and smile. Let Neil's 26 against Juddy's . . . be our last sight of him as a child. He is walking back bat in hand to the pavilion. . . . An unearthly glory has swept over the cricket ground. He tries to look unaware of it; you know the expression and the bursting heart. . . . [He] gathers up the glory and tacks it over his bed. "The End," as he used to say in his letters. I never know him quite so well again. He seems henceforth to be running to me on a road that is moving still more rapidly in the opposite direction.[262]

Barrie kept his two worlds, and his sense of our essential doubleness, constantly before his public. Some of his late plays introduce the metaphor of the thin veil he imagined as separating this world from the other, and the difficulty some have of knowing on which side of the veil they stand.[263] Always there is a

---

[29] Hillman, "Pothos," in *Loose Ends,* p. 59.

[260] Ibid., pp. 59-60.

[261] Ibid.

[262] Birkin, *J.M. Barrie and the Lost Boys,* p. 203.

[263] *Mary Rose* is about a young mother who mysteriously disappears when visiting an island in the Outer Hebrides with her husband. She returns from the Land of the Dead twenty years later, unchanged in any way, to seek her child who is now a young soldier. After a strange, unconnected encounter with her adult son, the ghost of Mary Rose disappears, once again. *A Well-Remembered Voice* concerns a grieving mother who holds seances in an effort to contact her soldier son "on the other side." However, the young soldier appears to his father, whose grief is perhaps deeper yet less demonstrative than the mother's. Dick, the dead son, speaks to his father about a comrade who was killed: "You see he got into a hopeless muddle about which side of the veil he had come out on . . . and he got lost . . . I expect he has become a ghost!"

hero whose character is close to that of Peter Pan. In this way the figure of Peter Pan, the quintessential eternal boy, as image of our desire for the unattainable, remains alive, constantly on stage, refusing to allow us to forget, diminish or evade his mystery.

Finally, in creating Peter Pan, whose archetypal necessity it is to initiate transformation in others but refuse it for himself, Barrie succeeds in bringing us a hero who also stubbornly resists interpretation and continues to elude, or postpone, meaning. It is, quite simply, because he cannot change that the enigmatic Peter Pan never ceases to tease us, inviting us playfully into the future, provoking us to attempt interpretation and so to keep open the window to imagination and possibility. Herein lies his charm, his magic, his endless fascination and the force of his symbolic significance.

I'll borrow life and not grow old;
And nightingales and trees
Shall keep me, though the veins be cold,
As young as Sophocles.

And when I may no longer live,
They'll say, who know the truth,
He gave whate'er he had to give
To Freedom and to Youth.
—William Corey, Master at Eton c. 1850-1870.

Success achieved, he never stays
for only by never staying does he not depart.
—Dao Tzu, *Dao De Jing.*

5
Peter Pan
Past and Present, At Home and Abroad

Peter Pan's resounding, and sustained, success owes much to the possibility of Barrie's having touched an unacknowledged nerve in the collective British psyche of his time, and perhaps of our own. This is not to say there were no dissenters or adverse reviews when the play was first performed, but they were few and far between. Generally *Peter Pan* enjoyed an overwhelmingly positive reception by what was to become a devoted following.[264]

What was the cultural nerve that Barrie's hero touched? We must remember that Barrie introduced Peter Pan to Edwardian London in 1904. England had buried her queen only a few years earlier and just emerged from a matriarchal Victorian era, lasting over seventy years, which had sanctioned the Empire won by her "sons" for Queen and Country. There followed the comparatively short reign of Victoria's son, Edward VII, the dash and romantic drama of whose personal life challenged Victorian conservatism and sobriety.

Abroad, the power of the Empire was beginning to wane and the British had recently suffered humiliation in the Boer War (1899-1902). At home, common belief held that England, having reigned supreme since Waterloo, was the most powerful nation in the world and would continue to be so. The shadow side of nineteenth-century achievement had been well documented by such writers as Charles Dickens *(Oliver Twist, Hard Times),* George Gissing *(New Grub Street)* and others, with the horrors of the Industrial Revolution exposed in tales of the deplorable conditions of the working classes, but nothing stemmed the tide of progress. There was a complacency which pervaded the nation and effectively kept early twentieth-century British attitudes in the nineteenth century, oriented, as a whole, more to a glorious past than an uncertain future.

One of the main causes of the dramatic change in fortune that Britain experienced from the end of the Boer War to mid-century is discovered, according to historian Corelli Barnett,

---

[264] Perhaps the most vocal of the few dissenters was the writer Anthony Hope. The first performance of *Peter Pan* indulged in a scene in which the Beautiful Mothers adopted the Lost Boys, at which point Hope was reported to have groaned aloud, "Oh, for an hour of Herod!" (Birkin, *J.M. Barrie and the Lost Boys,* p. 117)

in the national character itself, as it had evolved by the early 20th century. For it is character which, at grips with circumstances, governs the destinies of nations as it does of individual men. It is the key to all policies, all decisions.[265]

The key to Britain's national character lay in the institution of her public school system. The public schools, many of which were explicitly High Church or Evangelical, "educated a segregated section of the community along lines designed to assure that those leaving them would be *gentlemen.* "[266] Picking up on Barnett's argument, above, Gathorne-Hardy comments somewhat harshly that

the public schools were above all engines to produce uniformity. They were designed to reward conformity, obedience to authority, and to crush originality and
rebellion. And they had succeeded. The saving graces of the upper classes had
once been their variety, individuality and spontaneity; now they were conventional, dull, self-satisfied and snobbish. And this whole slack, uncompetitive crowd
of "leaders" was brought up on a games ethic where the point was not to win but to
"play the game"; where team spirit was more important than victory, and anything
that was not cricket was not on. At a time of turbulent change, of an aggressive
Germany, of ferocious and unscrupulous competition, of—at the end of the 19th
century—intense scientific progress and speculation, the schools had become
static, they took for granted their position and their Empire, thinking that both
would last for ever, when the time had come to defend and change and fight.[267]

Gathorne-Hardy's uncompromising critique notwithstanding, the upper eche-
lon of late-nineteenth- and early-twentieth-century public schools served essentially as "social agencies," and "nurseries of the nobility and gentry, . . . deliber-
ately training their pupils as members of a ruling class."[268] The public school
provided a setting that was effectively a "total society" which, like all such so-
cieties (asylums, prisons, ships, monasteries, convents), functioned as a closed
world unto itself with its own common goals, institutional hierarchy, code of
conduct, system of rewards and punishments, shared loyalties, and the cohesive
public persona, "show" or "front" for which the legendary stiff upper lip was
indispensable. However, there also developed an exclusive language and an un-
der-life of secret loyalties and practices, forms of rebellion against the totalism
of the institution that, paradoxically, present "evidence of the most profound

---

[265] Quoted in Jonathan Gathorne-Hardy, *The Old School Tie,* p. 202.
[266] Asa Briggs, *A Social History of England,* p. 249.
[267] *The Old School Tie,* pp. 202f.
[268] E.J. Hobsbawm, *The Age of Empire, 1875-1914,* p. 178.

The Allahakbarries Cricket Team in 1905, with Michael Llewelyn Davies,
aged 5, as mascot. J.M. Barrie is in the back row, second from left.

involvement."[269] On the one hand, the public school supplied a vessel, a time and space, for the realization of adolescent tensions and passions, from the adolescent's need to conform and find an identity as part of the group, to the equally powerful need to rebel, to define himself against and through criticism of that same group. On the other hand, "intense passions and 'romantic friendships' consumed practically all public school boys,"[270] and the cloistered world of the community was so complete and compelling that many lost their individuality in a total identification that lasted a lifetime.

So Edgar Friedenberg writes:

> The British public school . . . made adolescence much more than an interregnum. It made it an epoch . . . its heroes became myths. . . . At best, [the schools] helped the adolescent make himself into a strongly characterised human being . . . at worst their impact made adolescence interminable and their victims permanently fixated Old Boys.[271]

The tendency of the public school experience to arrest its initiates in permanent adolescence is captured in Cyril Connolly's reminiscences, as is the archetypal tenor of the experience:

> For my own part I was long dominated by impressions of school. The plopping of gas mantles in the classroom, the refrain of psalm tunes, the smell of plaster on the stairs, the walk through the fields to the bathing places or to the chapel across the cobbles of School Yard, evoked a vanished Eden of grace and security.[272]

The institution of the Old Boy network provided a social cohesiveness to an otherwise "heterogeneous body of recruits," and its influence extended nationally, internationally and generationally.[273] However, Old Boy nostalgia for "pleasures lost forever," and public school ideals of good form, rightness, decency and honor between friend and foe alike, became overlaid and intensified, toward the end of the nineteenth century, by Victorian Romanticism and a revival of interest (often sentimental) in chivalry and the feudal Middle Ages (Sir Walter Scott, Alfred Lord Tennyson, the Pre-Raphaelites).

Despite the growing unease and sense of fragmentation recognized in the anti-Romanticism of the Modernists (Conrad, Joyce, Yeats, Eliot, etc.), this me-

---

[269] Gathorne-Hardy, *The Old School Tie,* p. 206.

[270] Ibid., p. 289.

[271] Ibid., pp. 209f.

[272] Ibid., p. 210.

[273] Hobsbawm, *The Age of Empire,* p 179.

dievalist emphasis extended into the twentieth century, influencing the pastoral nostalgia of the pre-First World War Georgian poets (Walter de la Mare, John Masefield, Rupert Brooke). Nostalgia for a lost rural idyll which evoked the essence of Englishness was not significantly challenged in the literature of the era until the war poets (such as Wilfred Owen, Stephen Spender, Louis Mac-Neice) revealed the brutal reality of trench warfare. Then, shortly after the war, T.S. Eliot gave us "The Waste Land" and James Joyce published *Ulysses*.

The gulf between the Edwardian pre-War romantic ideal and the harsh reality of fighting in the trenches is forcibly encapsulated if we compare the famous lines of Rupert Brooke, the "most beautiful man in England . . . and embodiment of patriotic, youthful sacrifice,"[274] with those of Wilfred Owen. Brooke writes, in his 1914 sonnet, "The Soldier":

> If I should die, think only this of me:
> That there's some corner of a foreign field
> That is forever England. There shall be
> In that rich earth a richer dust concealed:
> A dust whom England bore, shaped, made aware,
> Gave, once, her flowers to love, her ways to roam,
> A body of England's, breathing English air,
> Washed by the rivers, blest by suns of home.[275]

And Wilfred Owen, in "Anthem for Doomed Youth":

> What passing-bells for these who die as cattle?
> Only the monstrous anger of the guns.
> Only the stuttering rifles' rapid rattle
> Can patter out their hasty orisons.
> No mockeries now for them; no prayers nor bells,
> Nor any voice of mourning save the choirs,—
> The shrill, demented choirs of wailing shells;
> And bugles calling for them from sad shires.[276]

According to Gathorne-Hardy, the romantic, reified ethos inculcated by the public schools spread throughout the class system, from the 1870s to as late as the 1930s, with the proliferation and wide circulation of boys' weeklies and comics, read, it should be noted, as much by adults as by children and by people

---

[274] Jonathan Rutherford, *Forever England: Reflections on Masculinity and Empire*, p. 40.
[275] *The Norton Anthology of English Literature*, pp. 1918f.
[276] *The Norton Anthology of Modern Poetry*, p. 516.

"The Look into Eternity," 1903, by Ferdinand Hodler (1953-1918)

from all walks of life. Some of these publications (e.g., *The Boys' Own Paper, Rover*) enjoyed an extensive readership well beyond the end of the Second World War, as I recall from my own childhood experience of finding the boys' papers far more enthralling than those written for girls. They eulogized Britain's empire builders, featuring heroes with extraordinary prowess and a boundless optimism whose endeavors suggested "a compulsion to escape the idleness and comfort of domesticity."[277] The effect, by the 1900-1914 period, was that most English boys read little other than stories of dauntless imperial heroes, and school tales steeped in the fantasy and romantic idealism of the public school system and more often than not infused with a strain of *fin-de-siècle* decadence:

> It was a system where public schools, public school morality and way of life, the inevitable success and rightness of the success of the public school class were not only accepted axiomatically, unquestioned, but as it were deified. . . . the ideals, ideas, taboos and standards of the public schools—that thin wafer of privilege—had become national ones, . . . sunk deep into the unconscious of the nation.[278]

This penetration of the public school ethos to all levels of English culture from 1900-1914 goes a long way to explain, in Gathorne-Hardy's reading of social history, the character of England's engagement in the First World War—the horror and the glory—the heroism and the eccentricities:

> The penetration of the public school ethos . . . (its roots, however altered and buried, were feudal) . . . explains why England rose with such complete unity, not pacific at all but extremely belligerent. It explains why its soldiers were prepared to follow callow youths into battle. But it also explains why callow youths were able to take command. In some respects the public schools produced ideal officers for an army: a majority of conformist disciplined men who were yet absolutely confident they could lead; a good number of men capable of individual dash and resource but still within the system. . . . The First World War in particular was a public school war.[279]

There are a few more observations I feel to be useful before turning again to Barrie and Peter Pan. Social mores, and an all-male environment sequestered away from parental models and guidance, placed the public school adolescent in an often difficult situation regarding the healthy discovery and expression of his

---

[277] Rutherford, *Forever England,* p. 12.
[278] Gathorne-Hardy, *The Old School Tie,* p. 219.
[279] Ibid., p. 221.

sexuality. At best, during adolescence,

> the concrete possibility of a fulfilling love relationship is generally unrealistic, [and] teenagers turn to the imagination. They write diaries, make up stories, join theater groups, immerse themselves in romantic novels.[280]

The atmosphere of many public schools proved "romantic and sentimental to a degree," fertile soil for the cultivation of bizarre fantasies and passions and for what have long since become familiar stereotypes: the eccentric "who has many fringe non-conformities, often picturesque and amusing, adopted to express individuality, but who conforms to all the major social *mores,*" and the "bowler-hatted, stiff-collared, conventional Englishman, one whole drawer of whose office desk is stuffed with romantic poems."[281]

Also cultivated and silently condoned were the often passionate friendships between boy and boy, prefect and "fag," master and boy, teacher and protégé, a homoeroticism traceable in boys' school and adventure novels, and evident, to point to but a few examples, in the art and literature of the *fin-de-siècle* Art for Art's Sake Movement, the life and work of Lytton Strachey and the Bloomsbury Group, the later novels of Evelyn Waugh, P.J. Wodehouse and Anthony Powell, whose bowler-hatted hero puts on a dress to read the romantic verse secreted in his desk drawer.

The exclusivity and elitism of public school culture sanctified a degree of dandyism, dilettantism and decadence among upper-class youth, and created a rarified air that could not be brought intact into the real world. Eccentricity and whimsy were prized, as was the golden, slightly effeminate Apollonian beauty of a Rupert Brooke above a more chthonic masculinity. The "blythe spirits" of the era were seemingly intoxicated, if often bored, not from imbibing a true spirituality, but with a quality of life that was light, provisional and inherited from fathers who themselves had been shaped by an overarching idealism and self-confidence, the privileged attitudes of the elite. Perhaps only a culture thoroughly permeated by this ethos *could* tolerate the eccentricities and the type of youth or puer the public school system produced and, as a result, so fervently embrace Barrie's Peter Pan, who embodies the very qualities to which the nation was arguably already addicted. We may say, then, that Peter Pan is *essentially* English, a product and symptom of the cultural ethos described in the previous pages, and of a fascination for a certain type of indomitable heroism.

---

[280] Kaspar Kiepenheuer, *Crossing the Bridge: A Jungian Approach to Adolescence,* p. 6.
[281] Gathorne-Hardy, *The Old School Tie,* pp. 226ff.

Jonathan Rutherford writes that concepts of the Englishman, masculinity and the hero begin with the Victorian family:

> A central dynamic in the creation of . . . imperial manliness was men's childhood relationships with their mothers. Motherhood was the ideological centre of the Victorian . . . family. Mothers were endowed with a sacred mission to raise their children and provide a haven for their husbands. . . . In spite of this idealisation women commanded domestic power, and their control in the home was seen as a potential threat to male dominance. Motherhood came under intense scrutiny. Women were subjected to a variety of taboos and regulatory practices which sought to protect the conjugal rights of their husband and safeguard their sons from feminine influence. It was this patriarchal institution of motherhood and the fraught relationship of boys to it, which contributed to the making of a late Victorian masculinity characterised by narcissism, emotional immaturity and a preoccupation with self-sacrifice: qualities that found a popular expression . . . in the figure of Peter Pan — the Englishman as the eternal adolescent.[282]

We find a concrete example of this ideal of imperial heroism, characterized by "romanticism and a death wish," in Barrie's regarding his friend, Scott of the Antarctic, "as another variation on the Peter Pan theme."[283] We may also recall the earlier inclination of the English Romantic poets to be "half in love with easeful death,"[284] the fascination of the Pre-Raphaelites with death and decadence, as well as Peter Pan's extravagantly romantic, if innocent, declaration, "To die will be an awfully big adventure."

While in many ways an innocent, his overwhelming reception indicates that

---

[282] *Forever England*, p. 7.

[283] Dunbar, *J.M. Barrie: The Man Behind the Image,* pp. 253f. Scott wrote to Barrie just before his death, asking Barrie to help his widow and son, Peter, named after Peter Pan. Scott's words encapsulate the essential quality of heroism revered by Barrie and the nation as a whole:

> We are showing that Englishmen can still die with a bold spirit fighting it out to the end. It will be known that we have accomplished our object in reaching the Pole and that we have done everything possible even to sacrificing ourselves in order to save sick companions. I think this makes an example for Englishmen of the future. . . . Goodbye. I am not at all afraid of the end but sad to miss many a simple pleasure which I had planned for the future on our long marches—I may not have proved a great explorer, but we have done the greatest march ever made and come very near to great success. . . . We are very near the end but have not and will not lose our good cheer . . . it would do your heart good to be in our tent, to hear our songs and the cheery conversation as to what we will do when we get to Hut Point.

[284] John Keats, "Ode to a Nightingale," in *Poetical Works,* p. 207.

"TO DIE WILL BE AN AWFULLY BIG ADVENTURE."

Peter Pan was not, either in history or fiction, the isolate he believed himself to be. Peter Pan takes his place, and plays an important role, in a long and distinguished tradition in which feelings and concerns attributable to adult, adolescent and child alike, and generally held to be taboo or inappropriate, are explored under the softening, protective guise of fantasy and animal story: Kipling's *Just So Stories* and *Jungle Book*, Kenneth Grahame's *The Wind in the Willows*, A.A. Milne's Winnie-the-Pooh stories, J.R.R. Tolkein's Hobbits, the more recent animal worlds of Richard Adams's novels, Maurice Sendak's *Wild Things*. Thus Barrie's crocodile and Tinker Bell are part of an ancestral line of creature- and fairy-characters that stretches back through Puck, Caliban, Ariel, and Sir Gawain's Green Knight, to Grendel. And while Milne's Christopher Robin (linked to the imaginative realm of the Hundred Acre Wood) is perhaps more earthbound than Peter Pan, he is certainly of the same boyish persuasion, as is Sebastian, the sadly ineffectual hero of Evelyn Waugh's *Brideshead Revisited*, who is trapped in a permanent adolescence, unable to go anywhere without Aloysius, his teddy bear.

The list of permanent adolescents in English history and literature is extensive. Also of note is the fact that the public school ethos spawned not only memorable literary figures but other institutions that enshrined and inculcated in their members the same values and type of culture. In 1908, four years after the first performance of *Peter Pan*, Lord Baden-Powell, fresh from service in India with the British Army, founded the Boy Scouts Brigade as a form of "sexual purity crusade" for young boys:

> [Baden-Powell's] vision of the outdoor life was resolutely anti-urban, masculine, anti-sensual and censorious of all expressions of sexuality. It drew upon the myth of the regenerative powers of rural England, . . . the bulwark against emasculating decadence and the degenerative influences of civilisation.[285]

Numerous boys' clubs followed and were to gain momentum to the degree that boys' clubs and camps for public school boys later enjoyed royal patronage under George VI. The hierarchical structure of the Boy Scouts, however, best emulates the public school communities, with the Scouts' special inside language and system of badges and rewards, its essentially militaristic model, moral code and discipline, its common goals and proud adherence to traditional values. We may speculate that the early twentieth-century proliferation of creature- and fairy-fantasies provided a much-needed outlet for the exploration of

---

[285] Rutherford, *Forever England*, p. 56.

passions, feelings and relations, about which society, for the most part, still maintained a stubborn silence. The Scouts and other boys' clubs, on the other hand, served to perpetuate the values and control of the old order—as well as gratify Old Boy nostalgia for boyhood—in reaction to a world whose fragmentation was intuited if not yet fully acknowledged.

Both Andrew Birkin and Janet Dunbar confirm that Barrie's own educational experience at Dumfries Academy, which he attended during his adolescent years, was the happiest time of his life. This was because he met a like-minded school-mate on his first day "who shared his own appetite for high adventure," while another boy left a lasting impression as "a Presence—[with] something winged about him." Not surprising, then, is Barrie's strong fascination for the English public schools ("They draw from their sons a devotion that is deeper, more lasting than almost any other love") and his self-declared affection for at least one of them was great:

> Eton became a source of romance for him, like the aristocracy—an institution which he could tease and flirt with, but never fully embrace—and it was not long before the stage Captain Hook was proclaiming "Floreat Etona!" as he projected himself into the mouth of the crocodile.[286]

Certainly *Peter Pan,* both the play and the novel, is steeped in the ethos and mystique of the public school. The references to Eton's elite society, Pop, and to Hook's and Peter Pan's insistence on good form and playing the game are clear enough, but embedded in the structure of the tale itself lie the values and dynamics of the institution: Neverland suggests the exclusive boys' club, apart from parents, in a world of its own, with its singular population and hierarchy, moral code and set of values; Neverland, like Pop, is reserved for an elite set of, in this case, "lost" boys, and the enemy the boys all love to hate is Old Age, father, prefect and master, adult responsibility and sexuality, each represented to various degrees, or satirized, in the figures of Mr Darling and Captain Jas. Hook.

The intense conflict the adolescent suffers between the equally attractive poles of conformity and individuality finds an analogue in Peter Pan's fascination with, and rejection of, Mrs Darling in particular and the institution of motherhood in general. An addiction to adolescence is evident in Peter Pan's opting for a state of eternal boyhood and in his vehement objection to becoming a man, a fate synonymous with bowler-hatted, besuited misery, the end of fun and high adventure and, for Barrie, the death of imagination. In Neverland, power, death

---

[286] Birkin, *J.M. Barrie and the Lost Boys,* pp. 8, 10, 196.

and warfare are just part of the game. Homoeroticism is expressed in loyalty to the leader, and there is a blissful ignorance of sexuality, which belongs to the mysteries of adult womanhood and the secret lives of fairies and mermaids.

If we propose that Peter Pan was received in England by a nation collectively enthralled by boyhood, yet puzzled by an intuition that it was time to outgrow the same boyish spirit that had inspired glories and ignited heroes of the past, what of America's response to Barrie's eternal youth?

In 1896 Barrie and his wife visited America, where Barrie's wily theatrical agent, Addison Bright, arranged that his client should meet the legendary Broadway producer, Charles Frohman.

> The two men were exact contemporaries; both had sprung from humble origins and conquered their chosen professions; both men worshipped mothers and children, yet both were childless themselves. . . . Little wonder that, with so much in common, these two men joined forces and formed such a close, lasting and profitable friendship.[287]

Barrie himself described Frohman as having energy "like a force of nature," and as being passionate about his schemes: "They were a succession of many-coloured romances to him, and were issued to the world not without the accompaniment of the drum."[288] It was this energy and passion and romanticism that swept *Peter Pan* onto the New York stage on November 6th, 1905, less than a year after the play had been sprung on its London audience. America proved even less critical than England, embracing Barrie's sentimentality and treating the play "with a seriousness that mystified and amused its author—every aspect of it was lapped up and swallowed whole, except possibly its humour."[289] Peter Pan appealed to the American mythologies of individuality, freedom, opportunity and gigantism:

> The Never Land symbolized the New World, while Peter Pan—the Great White Father—was seen to represent the Spirit of Youth and Freedom, hailing the children of the Old World to leave their antiquated nurseries and fly away to the Never Land of Liberty.[290]

Frohman threw himself into the elaborate New York production. He later toured the play, which had become his mission, the full length and breadth of

---

[287] Ibid., pp. 38f.
[288] Ibid., p. 126.
[289] Ibid.
[290] Ibid.

North America, feeling it his duty to "bring Peter Pan into the life of every child in the country."[291] Peter Pan rapidly lost his fictive status and became the "best beloved of all American children."[292] It was as though he had quite literally walked off the stage to preside as god of innocence and eternal youth, those ideals that have dominated the American psyche since America's initial vision of herself as the New Jerusalem. These values have been imaged throughout her history in figures as various as Huck Finn, James Dean, Shirley Temple, Elvis Presley, the Camelot-court of the Kennedy presidency, and Bill Clinton, golden-boy president.

In the speculative spirit of this chapter, I suggest that a possible explanation for Peter Pan's continued power to fascinate, especially in England and America, as well as for Barrie's life-long struggle with that errant creation of his own imagination, lies in the fact that *Peter Pan* speaks to the psyche at both the conscious and unconscious levels. *Peter Pan* as symbolic field returns us to the complexity and ambiguity of Hillman's *puer-et-senex* configuration. Peter Pan alone, however, either divorced from the full context of his story and myth, or diminished to a simple embodiment of only-positive, only-puer qualities of freedom, spontaneity and youth, appeals to the child's need for high adventure and fantasy, the adolescent's romantic idealism and the adult's nostalgia for an imagined lost Eden of heroic potential.

Identification with only-Peter Pan allows us to escape reality by flying off to a Neverland of the imagination or to explain away Peter Pan's allure by criticizing him through the lens of pathology. Understood in the context of his myth, however, the enigmatic Peter Pan forces us to look again at the conflictual dynamics of adolescence, that turbulent period when one is caught between two worlds, and one's whole being seems to hang on the slender thread of the chance remark or decision of the moment, precisely because the dynamics of adolescence reflect those of all periods of transition. If, then, we agree that adolescence is not only a distinct time of life but representative of "an ever-present pattern of transformation,"[293] we may see the tensions and conflicts of our teenage years reactivated in any period of change and growth. By logical extension of our argument, we may imagine a similar dynamic to pertain both at the collective level of the individual psyche and in the cultural collective. While this pattern of transformation

---

[291] Ibid., p. 127.
[292] Ibid.
[293] Kiepenheuer, *Crossing the Bridge*, p. 14.

may have especially sweeping consequences during the period of physical and sexual maturation, it is in no way limited to that age. . . . In the course of a life, then, there are ever new "puberty-steps," beckoning particularly when we are stirred and weakened by a physical or emotional crisis, as we were by the radical changes in younger years.[294]

Read as imaginal field, for its mythic and archetypal context, Barrie's novel affords us a descriptive image of the dual dynamic at work in the psyche caught in adolescent or transitional space. Barrie's Peter Pan-field explores how that space operates, how it invites self-embodiment and self-realization through play, in Winnicott's sense of the term, and how equally it threatens dissolution and alienation. The way of transition is fraught with dangers while one is in No-man's land, betwixt and between the old and new orders, the previous and future sense of self. This is a liminal, border experience "in which powers liberated from among one's own resources can serve both to overcome the crisis and to pave the way for new growth"[295]—*or not*. Ego may fail to suffer and explore the conflict consciously enough to enable a new way forward to present itself through the natural, transcendent function of the psyche. In the context of Barrie's novel, we might say that new growth does not happen if the nursery window remains shut, with ego and conscious attitudes decisively closed against the disturbing impulse from the unconscious that is Peter Pan.

Given the radical uncertainty and real possibility of annihilation with which we live, and have lived, for over half a century, it is not surprising that collectively we tend to evade suffering and assuage our fears by splitting off and denying or projecting shadow and evil. The propensity to separate Peter Pan from his story, or from his symbolic and archetypal field, and to identify exclusively with his lightness of being, reflects this tendency of consciousness to split off and suppress traumatic and unacceptable content, especially during periods of radical uncertainty. In the past century, previously unimaginable frontiers of knowledge and understanding have been crossed in disciplines of discovery and expression from the pure, applied and social sciences to art, literature, industry and entertainment. The result has been a series of paradigm shifts that ask us, individually and collectively, to radically revise our world-view and therefore to relocate meaning and our sense of identity in an as yet indeterminate new order. This presents a potentially insupportable challenge to the already beleaguered

---

[294] Ibid., pp. 14f.
[295] Ibid., p. 4.

ego but one that must be engaged if we are to meet the new millennium crea-
tively and meaningfully, and thus as consciously as possible.

Popular readings of *Peter Pan* tend to divide and narrow Barrie's imaginal
field, inviting overidentification with a one-dimensional Peter Pan as only-puer.
Any potential for spiritual weight and profundity is lost with the denial of both
Peter Pan's shadow and his archetypal resonance. The problem seems to lie in
the impulse to escape rather than face reality, as if the only proper place for the
flight of the soul is somewhere else, apart from suffering in this world. The collective tendency to avoid the agony of conscious transformation in the here-and-
now results in an intensification of focus on the "light," because that way presents an easier path than the struggle toward an integration of the conflicted opposites. This is not surprising. The rapidity with which we have been hurtled
from a Modern to post-Modern condition and are now faced with finding our
way in the virtual realm of cyberspace, heightens the dichotomy between what is
held as conscious, manageable reality and what has been put on hold to be dealt
with later, or banished from consciousness altogether.

In the process of putting things on hold, however, consciousness suffers im-
poverishment, and the personal and collective shadow accrues more power and
potentially destructive energy. We see this in so many aspects of life: in the
projection of value and meaning onto material possessions; in the search for
Connolly's "vanished Eden of grace and security" in ideology, cult and work-
place; in the quest for spiritual peace and freedom from conflict in drugs, sex
and alcohol (paradoxically, in the very body and matter the addict seeks to tran-
scend); in the search for novelty and heightened sensation in order to feel alive,
present and vital in, again, sex, drugs and physical risk-taking from fast cars to
body piercing to bunjy-jumping; in flight from the untenable old order which
has deceived the new (the two World Wars, Korea, Vietnam) into a frenetic
idolization of youth; in the violence which erupts when chaos, rather than any
distinct sense of a new order, appears to be the only alternative. The list is long.

To return to *Peter Pan* in America, we find that Barrie's hero was quickly
commercialized (even in 1905 Peter Pan clothing was manufactured and sold
throughout North America). He is further sentimentalized by the Disney animated film, with his lightness, brightness and rightness clearly differentiated
from the evil and darkness of his arch-enemy and archetypal counterpart, Hook.
In a more recent film, Steven Spielberg's *Hook,* we move from the pure fantasy
of animation to an emphasis on slapstick fun and games. In the movie, Peter Pan
(Robin Williams) is an aggressive executive totally absorbed in his work. The

two children he has neglected are magically stolen away by Hook; the middle-aged Peter has to fly to Neverland to rescue, finally, his lost creativity and youth (the children) from the clutches of the negative senex he has become as a ruthless pirate, or Hook, of the business world. The lost boys teach the adult Peter Pan all that he has forgotten about fairies, flying, good form and make-believe since he joined the "real" world at age twelve.

While the trickster qualities of Peter Pan are emphasized in Robin Williams's portrayal, there persists in the film an uneasy relation between the trickster's potential for transformative (positive), white magic, and his profoundly disruptive and disturbing (negative) energy that we see debased and trivialized in the violence and amorality of popular cartoon tricksters, such as Roadrunner. The trickster, after all, can do all that is taboo in the adult world; "He acts out an impulse over which he has no control."[26] Certainly Peter Pan has a comparable vitality but, as in the example of Roadrunner, he is robbed of shadow and substance when the dark, chaotic quality of his energy is depotentiated by being presented in terms of slapstick. Hollywood nevertheless recognizes that the successful businessman, who has forgotten that he is also Peter Pan and has settled unconsciously into an only-senex way of being which threatens family life, must return to Neverland to engage, this time, in conscious conflict with Hook. This encounter is no longer another episode in an endless round of good fun and good form: the adult Peter fights Hook for his children's lives, and so, symbolically, for his own creative vitality.

In psychological terms, the unconscious identification of ego and negative senex must be broken: the hold that the negative senex (Hook) has on the conscious attitude (Peter as businessman and father) must be destroyed if a revitalization of life and spirit is to take place. Unfinished business has to be faced and made conscious. Such a confrontation returns us, at any age, to a No-man's land of psychic turmoil like that experienced in adolescence.

In Joel Schumacher's movie *The Lost Boys,* Peter Pan and his tribe of lost boys are vampires. Schumacher emphasizes the loneliness and marginality of adolescence. His lost boys move among the general populace during the daytime but enact extremist fantasies of life, death, cruelty and passion at night. Yet their world is not elsewhere in another place and time but present, though unrecognized, in the here-and-now. Schumacher presents the orders of darkness and light as parallel realities.

---

[26] Gose, *Mere Creatures,* p. 10.

When neither ordinary youths by day, nor active vampires by night, the boys hang in their underground cave, upside-down, as bats—a fitting image of the adolescent's sense of hovering in suspension between two worlds. Scenes of the daytime world focus on the candy-floss and merry-go-rounds of an amusement park. The nighttime world of the vampiric youths is filled with violence, blood, and a desperate savagery, like that of a trapped animal. The darkness of Schumacher's vision suggests the psychopathic violence that may accrue as the shadow-side of a candy floss conscious attitude, so distorted by sentiment that it inures one from real feeling, transformative suffering, and so from the fullness of life. We participate vicariously in such examples of pathological extremes in the movie theater and in front of the television, at a safe distance both from the screen and from the horror to which we have become numbed. As movie and television viewers, we are the passive recipients of a fully developed program of images. While as viewers we may interpret what we see, when presented with images of violence and cruelty, we nevertheless remain absolved of responsibility for our personal potential for evil which is, quite literally, projected, and rendered harmless in a fictive, flickering illusion.

Schumacher's representation of two worlds, to all intents and purposes in mutual opposition and denial, yet interdependent, returns us to the problem of the imaginal field that has, perhaps, been ignored in Barrie's work: the necessarily antithetical relation of Peter Pan to Hook, of Edwardian England to Neverland; the ambiguities of the narrative and ambivalence of Barrie's narrative voice; the sinister undertone, so easily dismissed in the context of a children's fantasy, of Peter Pan's careless remark to Wendy ("I forget them after I kill them") when she upbraids him for having forgotten Hook.

In his book on the myth of Daedalus, Peter Tatham argues that Daedalus and Icarus belong together, forming what Hillman talks of as "syzygy consciousness," a juxtaposition where, in Jung's words, "the One is never separated from the Other, its antithesis."[27] In such a relation, "together, they perturb and further the process: separate, they make things in their own likeness, keeping to order."[28] So, too, do Peter Pan and Captain Hook form a syzygy consciousness. Together they, with the other syzygies or antithetical pairs in the novel, present an image of the process and experience of individuation.

Certainly, in the context of Barrie's tale, Peter Pan is not only the puer as golden youth. In his relation to Mr and Mrs Darling and Capt. Hook he most

---

[27] Tatham, *The Makings of Maleness*, p. 252.
[28] Ibid., pp. 251f.

definitely perturbs, but he is also potentially Hermes, that generative, transformative impulse of the life force and winged messenger, bringing soul messages from the depths of the psyche. The problem becomes, or remains, one of encounter and interpretation. How to listen? How best to meet and realize the Hermetic gift? How to bring an immature phallic energy, as represented generally in the male characters and narrative action of *Peter Pan,* to creative maturation? How to negotiate our present, and any future period of transition whose dynamics we have described as adolescent? How to activate *phallos* in order to transform the provisional life and ground the unfulfilled potential of an ego (or era) caught in the chaos and turbulence of an unresolved adolescent sea-change? How to enhance consciousness by successfully negotiating transitional periods, addressing conflict and encountering the unknown, to attain a renewed sense of self and world?

Jung reminds us that "an archetypal content [i.e., that which is undifferentiated, disturbing, unconscious] expresses itself, first and foremost, in metaphors."[29] The difficult role of the ego is one of interpretation:

> We are confronted, at every new stage in the differentiation of consciousness to which civilization attains, with the task of finding a new *interpretation* appropriate to this stage, in order to connect the life of the past that still exists in us with the life of the present, which threatens to slip away from it. If this link-up does not take place, a kind of rootless consciousness comes into being no longer oriented to the past, a consciousness which succumbs helplessly to all manner of suggestions and, in practice, is susceptible to psychic epidemics.[30]

Peter Pan provides a metaphor for the unknown new: rootless consciousness is the *dis*ease of contemporary society as it faces an uncertain future.

The radical uncertainty of our future finds its own metaphor in our rapidly evolving electronic technology. In many ways, the elusive promise embodied in Peter Pan is the promise also of cyberspace. The new electronic era invites us to enter an indeterminate virtual realm where, it seems, everything and anything is possible, where we may create ourselves as we desire, where freedom and creativity know no bounds. Yet the very metaphors we use to describe this virtual zone are ambiguous: Netscape, Web, Internet, Windows, Paths—images of boundless potential, but also metaphors for entrapment and delusion.

---

[29] "The Psychology of the Child Archetype," *The Archetypes and the Collective Unconscious,* CW 9i, par. 267.
[30] Ibid.

On the one hand, Internet users access a seemingly unlimited network of information; on the other, the value and structure of that same information must be questioned, if one is not to run the risk of having one's mind made up for one, as an unwitting adherent of, to quote Derrick de Kerckhove, a "collective, techno-cultural morality" which generates an "average and averaging psychology."[301] Who are we when flying in the Neverland of cyberspace? How does the individual relate when caught in the electronic flow of "psychotechnologies" which

> erode the walls of our private identity . . .[and] create the condition of an expanded self, springing from the personal self to the farthest reaches of all that we can survey with our ever-expanding, all-probing perceptual and motor extensions.[302]

De Kerckhove argues that our protection against psychotechnologies that threaten to make us extensions of themselves is to include them within our personal psychology. To do as he suggests requires considerable consciousness, and the courage to confront the shadow-side of the new technoculture and our connection to it. Confronted with the seductive pull of cyberspace in which boundaries are dissolved and identity becomes virtual, we must concern ourselves ever more vigilantly with consciousness, with the interface between self and world, lest we disappear into the twilight consciousness of a global media network.

Jung reminds us that "without a reflecting psyche the world might as well not exist," and Erich Neumann argues for a "new form of humanism . . . in which man will learn to make friends with himself and to experience his own shadow side as an essential component of his creative vitality."[303] Syzygy consciousness is essential to our evolution as conscious beings. Boundaries must be set if we are to define the problems that beset us, and create a secure setting, or vessel, for their solution.[304] Possibility and meaning are born of conscious connections, for which one needs ground, value, a place to stand. In psychological terms, ego's realization of possibility succeeds in proportion to its capacity for groundedness: puer as psychic potential is realized only through historicity (positive senex) and materiality (positive feminine).

We may argue that Barrie's relation to Peter Pan as spiritual phenomenon

---

[301] *The Skin of Culture: Investigating the New Electronic Reality,* p. 210.
[302] Ibid., p. 216.
[303] Quoted in Edward F. Edinger, *The New God-Image: A Study of Jung's Key Letters Concerning the Evolution of the Western God-Image,* p. 145. (See *C.G. Jung Letters,* vol. 2, pp. 482ff, and Neumann, *Depth Psychology and a New Ethic,* p. 146)
[304] Tatham, *The Makings of Maleness,* p. 145.

presents us with a failure of interpretation. Barrie seemed in love with the only-puer in Peter Pan, or identified with the archetype of eternal boyhood in its light aspect only. It was perhaps for this reason that he could not write the proposed play "The Old Age of Peter Pan," while his last work, "The Boy David," ostensibly about the Biblical David, also honors the memory of his own lost brother. Alternatively, we may claim that genius lies in the capacity to live, more surely than others, from an intermediate, imaginal place between two worlds. If this is so, the genius of Barrie was, throughout his career, to work from the imaginal zone in order to keep the enigma of Peter Pan before our eyes and at the forefront of his public's consciousness. Such is Barrie's task and prerogative as an artist; it is ours to attempt an interpretation. And while Barrie does not supply the answer, he seems to point the way when he writes, in "A Well-Remembered Voice," of the veil that conceals, as it reveals, that Other realm. In the play, Dick, a youth killed in the trenches of the First World War, appears to his father, Mr Don:

DICK. . . . . I wish you people would understand what a little thing [death] is. . . .

MR DON. Tell me, Dick, about the—the veil. . . . I suppose the veil is like a mist?

DICK. The veil's a rummy thing, father. Yes, like a mist. But when one has been at the Front for a bit, you can't think how thin the veil seems to get; just one layer of it. . . . We sometimes mix up those who have gone through with those who have not. . . .

Mr Don does not want to let his son go. His suffering reflects a confusion of archetypal and personal reality, and may serve us as a metaphor for our difficulty with, and the enigma of, Peter Pan. When we overly personalize, pathologize and diagnose Peter Pan, we diminish him. As a figure for a divine prerogative that we describe as "eternal child," he belongs finally on the other side of Barrie's veil. His gifts become ours, *if* they become ours, through grace followed by the hard work of conscious integration, not through arbitrary appropriation. So, as Barrie insists, Peter Pan cannot get past a certain age, and that is as it must be, whilst we, as carriers of consciousness, cannot afford to remain stuck in a condition of permanent adolescence.

Jung intuited a *telos*, or purposiveness, to the individuation process which supports the task of ego to suffer, repeatedly, transition to new levels of consciousness. From the fresh vantage point of each new level of awareness, ego will re-meet and re-interpret soul messages from the unconscious psyche, again and again, each time challenged to integrate a startlingly different aspect of the

Self into consciousness. In the context of Barrie's novel, Peter Pan, as soul message, will disrupt ego's equilibrium again and again. The question of how to embody transformative spirit and meet the creative autonomy of the psyche, as represented in Peter Pan, is the age-old question of all artists and all those who live their lives fully because symbolically.

How to realize spirit in and through matter remains the task of consciousness at each step in the on-going process of psychic evolution, both in the individual and the collective. Projections that lead us to identify with, and unconsciously appropriate, archetypal energy by attempting, as it were, to lift Peter Pan off the page into life, may be dissolved and withdrawn only through the creative act of conscious interpretation. Our gods must be recognized as gods and allowed, as gods, to die repeatedly that they may be reborn and return to us anew to disrupt, disturb and initiate yet another stage of development. Peter Pan belongs to the archetypal realm of possibility and his is the tale of our continual struggle to realize and so incarnate something of our experience of the transcendent psyche and so of the world. Taken in its entirety, Barrie's novel affords a narrative image of the difficulty of such a struggle, as it describes the dynamics of the imaginal place, or cyberspace, of transition.

It is not an easy place to stand, betwixt and between. It asks us to find our orientation and meaning in terms of our proximity and relation to the Other, whether that be another person, place, work, idea, ideology, object or image, conscious or unconscious. This is to discover meaning, not through appropriation, identification or control, through violence or submission, but in constantly evolving relation to psyche and world, both within and without. It requires us to see the transparency of things, to look beyond and through image, story, behavior and pathology to the archetypal reality, in all its paradox, its admixture of light and darkness, on the far side of the veil.

So we attend and listen, actively awaiting the emergence of a fresh image and narrative, another "flash of enlightenment from the unconscious and the forbidden" (to quote Calvino again),[305] another encounter to move us forward in a new consciousness of self, soul and world.

---

[305] See above, p. 69.

Bibliography

Adler, Gerhard, *Studies in Analytical Psychology.* New York: W.W. Norton, 1948.

Armitt, Lucie. *Theorizing the Fantastic.* London: Arnold, 1996.

Asper, Kathrin. *The Abandoned Child Within: On Losing and Regaining Self-Worth.* Trans. Sharon E. Rooks. New York: Fromm International, 1993.

Auden, W.H. *Collected Shorter Poems 1927-1957.* London: Faber and Faber, 1977.

Bachelard, Gaston. *On Poetic Imagination and Reverie: Selections from the Works of Gaston Bachelard.* Ed., trans. and intro. Colette Gaudin. Indianapolis: The Bobbs-Merrill Co., 1971.

Barrie, J.M. *Peter Pan.* Intro. Michael P. Hearn. Illus. Susan Hudson. Montreal: Tundra Books, 1988. (Originally *Peter and Wendy.* London: Hodder and Stoughton, 1911.)

_____. *Peter Pan and Other Plays.* New York: Oxford University Press, 1995.

_____. *Peter Pan and Wendy.* Adapted for children by Jane Carruth. Illus. Anne Grahame Johnstone. London: Award Publications Limited, 1988.

Berry, Patricia, ed. *Fathers and Mothers.* Dallas, TX.: Spring Publications, 1990.

King James Bible. London: Oxford University Press, n.d.

The New English Bible. London: Penguin, 1974.

Birkin, Andrew. *J.M. Barrie & the Lost Boys.* London: Constable, 1979.

Blake, William. *Complete Writings.* Ed. Geoffrey Keynes. London: Oxford University Press, 1971.

Briggs, Asa. *A Social History of England.* New York: Viking, 1984.

Briggs, K.M. *The Anatomy of Puck: An Examination of Fairy Beliefs Among Shakespeare's Contemporaries and Successors.* London: Routledge and Kegan Paul, 1959.

Byron, Lord. *Poetical Works.* Ed. F. Page. London: Oxford University Press, 1970.

Calvino, Italo. *Invisible Cities.* Trans. William Weaver. London: Picador (Pan), 1979.

_____. *The Uses of Literature.* Trans. Patrick Creagh. San Diego: Harcourt Brace Jovanovich, 1986.

Campbell, Joseph. *The Hero with a Thousand Faces* (Bollingen Series XVII). Princeton: Princton University Press, 1949.

_____. *The Mythic Image* (Bollingen Series C). Princeton: Princeton University Press, 1974.

Clark, Giles. "The Transformation of 'Spiritual Image' and 'Instinctual Shadow' into 'Instinctual Spirit.' " Diploma Thesis, C.G. Jung Institute, Zurich, 1977. Unpublished.

Coleridge, Samuel Taylor. *Poetical Works.* Ed. Ernest Hartley Coleridge. London: Oxford University Press, 1969.

Connolly, Cyril. *Enemies of Promise*. Harmondsworth, UK: Penguin, 1961.

Cooper, J.C. *An Illustrated Encyclopaedia of Traditional Symbols*. London: Thames and Hudson, 1978.

de Kerckhove, Derrick. *The Skin of Culture: Investigating the New Electronic Reality*. Toronto: Somerville House, 1995.

Dijkstra, Bram. *Idols of Perversity: Fantasies of Feminine Evil in Fin-de-Siècle Culture*. New York: Oxford University Press, 1986.

Doty, William G. *Myths of Masculinity*. New York: Crossroad Publishing Co., 1993.

Dunbar, Janet. *J.M. Barrie: The Man Behind the Image*. Boston: Houghton Mifflin Co., 1970.

Edinger, Edward F. *Ego and Archetype: Individuation and the Religious Function of the Psyche*. New York: Putnam's Sons, 1972.

_____. *The Eternal Drama: The Inner Meaning of Greek Mythology*. Boston: Shambhala Publications, 1994.

_____. *Melville's Moby-Dick: An American Nekyia*. Toronto: Inner City Books, 1995.

_____. *The New God-Image: A Study of Jung's Key Letters Concerning the Evolution of the Western God-Image*. Wilmette, IL.: Chiron Publications, 1996.

Eliade, Mircea. *The Myth of the Eternal Return or Cosmos and History* (Bollingen Series XLVI). Trans. Willard R. Trask. Princeton: Princeton University Press, 1974.

Eliot, T.S. *Collected Poems 1909-1962*. New York: Harcourt, Brace and World, 1963.

_____. *Selected Essays*. London: Faber and Faber, 1976.

_____. *Selected Prose of T.S. Eliot*. Ed. Frank Kermode. London: Faber and Faber, 1975.

Erikson, Erik H. *Identity: Youth and Crisis*. New York: W.W. Norton and Co., 1968.

Euripides. *The Bacchae*. Trans. William Arrowsmith. Chicago: Chicago University Press, 1968.

Frye, Northrop. *Anatomy of Criticism: Four Essays*. Princeton: Princeton University Press, 1973.

_____. *Fables of Identity: Studies in Poetic Mythology*. New York: Harcourt, Brace and World, 1963.

_____. *The Secular Scripture: A Study of the Structure of Romance*. Cambridge, MA.: Harvard University Press, 1976.

Gantz, J., trans. *Early Irish Myths and Sagas*. London: Penguin Books, 1983.

Gathorne-Hardy, Jonathan. *The Old School Tie: The Phenomenon of the English Public School*. London: Viking, 1971.

Gittings, Robert, ed. *Letters of John Keats*. London: Oxford University Press, 1970.

Goethe, Johann Wolfgang. *Faust*. Trans. Barker Fairley. Toronto: University of Toronto Press, 1985.

Gose, Elliott. *Mere Creatures: A Study of Modern Fantasy Tales for Children.* Toronto: University of Toronto Press, 1988.

Grimm Brothers. *The Complete Grimm's Fairy Tales.* New York: Pantheon Books, 1944.

Hanson, Bruce K. *The Peter Pan Chronicles.* New York: Carol Publishing Co., 1993.

The Herder Symbol Dictionary. Trans. Boris Matthews. Wilmette, IL.: Chiron Publications, 1978.

Hillman, James. *Archetypal Psychology.* Dallas: Spring Publications, 1983.

_____. *Loose Ends.* Dallas: Spring Publications, 1978.

_____. *Pan and the Nightmare.* Zurich: Spring Publications, 1972.

_____. *Revisioning Psychology.* New York: Harper and Row, 1977.

_____, ed. *Facing the Gods.* Dallas: Spring Publications, 1980.

_____, ed. *Puer Papers.* Dallas: Spring Publications, 1979.

Hobsbawm, E.J. *The Age of Empire, 1875-1914.* London: Little, Brown and Co., 1988.

Homer. *The Odyssey.* Trans. Robert Fitzgerald. New York: Random (Vintage), 1990.

Hudson, Susan. *The Eternal Peter Pan: The Wisdom of J.M. Barrie.* Illus. Susan Hudson. Montreal: Tundra, 1987.

Jacoby, Mario. *Individuation and Narcissism: the Psychology of Self in Jung and Kohut.* Trans. Myron Gubitz and Francoise O'Kane. New York: Routledge, 1991.

_____. *Longing for Paradise: Psychological Perspectives on an Archetype.* Trans. Myron Gubitz. Boston: Sigo Press, 1985.

Joyce, James. *A Portrait of the Artist as a Young Man.* London: Penguin, 1976.

Jung, C.G. *C.G. Jung Letters* (Bollingen Series XCV). 2 vols. Ed. Gerhard Adler and Aniela Jaffé. Princeton: Princeton University Press, 1973.

_____. *The Collected Works of C. G. Jung* (Bollingen Series XX). 20 vols. Trans. R.F.C. Hull. Ed. Herbert Read, Michael Fordham, Gerhard Adler, William McGuire. Princeton: Princeton University Press, 1953-1979.

_____. *Memories, Dreams, Reflections.* Trans. Richard and Clara Winston. Ed. Aniela Jaffé. New York: Vintage Books, 1965.

Keats, John. *Poetical Works.* Ed. H.W. Garrod. London: Oxford University Press, 1970.

Kelley-Laine, Kathleen. *Peter Pan: The Story of Lost Childhood.* Dorset: Element Books Ltd., 1997.

Kerényi, Karl. *The Gods of the Greeks.* London: Thames and Hudson, 1951.

_____. *Hermes: Guide of Souls.* Zurich: Spring Publications, 1976.

Kiepenheuer, Kaspar. *Crossing the Bridge: A Jungian Approach to Adolescence.* Trans. Karen R. Schneider. La Salle, IL.: Open Court Press, 1990.

Kiley, D. *The Peter Pan Syndrome.* New York: Avon, 1984.

Kluger, Rivkah Scharf. *Psyche in Scripture: The Idea of the Chosen People and Other*

Essays. Toronto: Inner City Books, 1995.

Kohut, Heinz. *The Restoration of the Self.* New York: International Universities Press, 1977.

Lee, John. *The Flying Boy: Healing the Wounded Man.* (Austin Men's Center, Texas.) Deerfield Beach, Fla.: Public Health Communications Inc., 1998.

McGuire, William, ed. *The Freud/Jung Letters* (Bollingen Series XCIV). Trans. Ralph Manheim, R.F.C. Hull. Princeton: Princeton University Press, 1974.

Melville, Herman. *Moby Dick, or The Whale.* Ed. and intro. Harold Beaver. London: Penguin, 1986.

Merivale, Patricia. *Pan the Goat-God: His Myth in Modern Times.* Cambridge, MA.: Harvard University Press, 1969.

Monick, Eugene. *Phallos: Sacred Image of the Masculine.* Toronto: Inner City Books, 1987.

Murray, H.A., ed. *Myth and Mythmaking.* New York: George Braziller, 1960.

Neumann, Erich. *The Child: Structure and Dynamics of the Nascent Personality.* Trans. Ralph Manheim. London: Maresfield Library, 1973.

_____. *Depth Psychology and a New Ethic.* Foreword by C.G. Jung. Boston: Shambhala Publications, 1990.

The New Larousse Encyclopedia of Mythology. New York: Prometheus Press, 1973.

The Norton Anthology of English Literature. 4th ed. Ed. M.H. Abrams. New York: W.W. Norton and Co., 1979.

The Norton Anthology of Modern Poetry. Ed. Richard Ellman, Robert O'Clair. New York: W.W. Norton and Co., 1973.

Ovid. *Metamorphoses.* Trans. Rolfe Humphries. Bloomington, IN: Indiana University Press, 1955.

Peake, Mervyn. *Peake's Progress: Selected Writings and Drawings of Mervyn Peake.* Ed. Maeve Gilmore. London: Penguin, 1981.

Rees, Alwyn and Rees, Brinley. *Celtic Heritage: Ancient Tradition in Ireland and Wales.* London: Thames and Hudson, 1961.

Roberts, Timothy R. *Myths of the World: The Celts in Myth and Legend.* New York: Metro Books (Friedman/Fairfax Publishers), 1995.

Rolleston, T. W. *Celtic Myths and Legends.* London: Senate/Studio Editions, 1994. (First published by The Gresham Pub. Co., n.d.)

Rose, Jacqueline. *The Case of Peter Pan or The Impossibility of Children's Fiction.* Philadelphia: University of Pennsylvania Press, 1992.

Rutherford, Jonathan. *Forever England: Reflections on Masculinity and Empire.* London: Lawrence and Wishart, 1997.

Samuels, Andrew, ed. *The Father.* London: Free Assoc. Press, 1985.

Satinover, Jeffrey. "Puer Aeternus: The Narcissistic Relation to the Self." In *Quadrant,* vol. 13, no. 2 (1980).

Schwartz-Salant, Nathan. *Narcissism and Character Transformation: The Psychology of Narcissistic Character Disorders.* Toronto: Inner City Books, 1982.

Shelley, Mary. *Frankenstein.* London: Oxford Classics, 1986.

Shelley, Percy Bysshe. *Poetical Works.* Ed. Thomas Hutchinson. London: Oxford University Press, 1970.

Stevens, Anthony. *On Jung.* New York: Routledge, 1990.

Stevenson, Robert Louis. *Dr. Jekyll and Mr. Hyde.* London: Penguin (Puffin), 1985.

Tatham, Peter. *The Makings of Maleness: Men, Women, and the Flight of Daedalus.* London: Karnac Books Ltd., 1992.

Tolkien, J.R.R. *Tree and Leaf.* London: Allen and Unwin, 1975.

Townsend, John Rowe. *Written For Children: An Outline of English-Language Children's Literature.* Middlesex, England: Pelican Books, 1980.

von Franz, Marie-Louise. *The Feminine in Fairy Tales.* 2nd ed. Boston: Shambhala Publications, 1993.

_____. *An Introduction to the Psychology of Fairy Tales.* Zurich: Spring Publications, 1970.

_____. *Psychotherapy.* Boston: Shambhala Publications, 1993.

_____. *Puer Aeternus: A Psychological Study of the Adult Struggle with the Paradise of Childhood.* 2nd ed. Boston: Sigo Press, 1981.

Wind, Edgar. *Pagan Mysteries in the Renaissance.* London: Faber and Faber, 1960.

Winnicott, D.W. *Playing and Reality.* New York: Routledge, 1991.

Woodman, Marion. *The Pregnant Virgin: A Process of Psychological Transformation.* Toronto: Inner City Books, 1985.

_____. *The Ravaged Bridegroom: Masculinity in Women.* Toronto: Inner City Books, 1990.

Wordsworth, William. *Poetical Works.* Ed. Thomas Hutchinson. London: Oxford University Press, 1969.

Yeats, W. B. *Collected Poems.* New York: Macmillan Publishing Co., 1956.

Index

abandonment, 92, 102, 125-126
Actaeon, 60
adolescence/adolescent, 17, 24, 26, 159-160, 163, 167-168, 170, 173-175, 177
Adonis, 15, 58, 60-61, 129
alchemical/alchemy, 39, 133
Alighieri, Dante Gabriel, 57, 76
ambivalence, 22, 63, 77, 79, 82, 89, 98-99, 102-103, 125-126, 174
anima, 114, 130-132
animus, 152n
Ansell, Mary (wife of J.M. Barrie), 79
Aphrodite, 39-40, 58, 60, 140
Apuleius: "Amor and Psyche," 44
archetype(s)/archetypal, 17, 19, 23, 32, 36, 50, 54-56, 74-75, 77, 115-120, 124, 129-130, 132, 136, 138, 141, 144, 147, 150-154, 160, 171-172, 175-178
  archetypal field, 75, 171
  child, 120, 123
Artemis, 58
art/artist(s), 31-32, 54-55, 58, 65-67, 69-70, 72, 75-77, 78, 119, 151, 178. *See also* creative/creativity
Asper, Kathrin: *The Abandoned Child Within,* 92
Athena, 38, 62, 64
Attis, 45n, 58, 61, 129
Auden, W.H.: "La Musée des Beaux Arts"

Bacchus, 15, 20, 46. *See also* Dionysus
Barrie, J.M., *21,* 23, 28, 29, 34, 62-68, 153,*159,* 167-169, 172, 174, 176-177
  ambivalence of, 63, 77, 79, 82, 89, 98-99, 102, 174
  authorial voice of, 77, 79, 81
  early life, 71-73, 79, 168, 177
  influences acknowledged by, 85n
  and mythmaking, 69-79
  mother of (Marg. Ogilvy), 72-73, 79, 149
  personality of, 79, 147-149
  wife of (Mary Ansell), 79
  "The Boy David," 177
  The Little White Bird, 70, 73n, 124n
  Mary Rose, 154n
  Neil and Tintinnabulum, 154
  "The Old Age of Peter Pan," 177
  Peter Pan (Peter and Wendy, novel), 66-67, 81-156, 170-172, 175, 178
    American reaction to, 169-173
    British reaction to, 157-169
    as fairy tale, 83
    film versions, 16, 35, 172-173
    synopsis, 12-13
  Peter Pan (play), 15, 34, 67, 73n, 82, 133, 157, 167-169
  Peter Pan in Kensington Gardens, 73n
  A Well-Remembered Voice, 154n, 177
Birkin, Andrew: *J.M. Barrie and the Lost Boys,* 24, 109n, 147, 149, 168
Blake, William: "The Marriage of Heaven and Hell," 31, 57, 65, 118-119
Boy Scouts, 167-168
Breughel, Pieter: *Landscape With the Fall of Icarus,* 54
Brooke, Rupert, 161, 164
  "The Soldier," 161
burial mounds, 104, *105. See also* Celtic mythology; sidh/Sidhe

Cabir(i), 48, 139n
Cain, 54, 57
Calvino, Italo: "Cybernetics and Ghosts," 69-71, 77, 118, 178
  Invisible Cities, 35
Campbell, Joseph: *The Hero with a Thousand Faces,* 69
Carroll, Lewis, 34
Celtic mythology, 84, 104, 106-108, 114, 117, 123n
  burial mounds, 104, *105*
  Oisin, 106, *106*
  sidh/Sidhe, 104, *106*
  Tir Nan' Og, 103-104
  Tuatha De Danann, 104, 132, 137
chaos, 135, 140, 172
child, childhood, 11-17, 24, 28, 38, 63-64, 71-75, 80, 82-89, 100-104, 107, 112, 114-118, 121-122, 125, 131, 140, 144, 147-151, 169. *See also* eternal boy
  archetype, 120, 123
  divine, 20, 120, 123-125, 137
  -god(s),120-121, 124-125, 128
  as symbol, 50, 125
  of the tree, 61
  two year old, 126

Christ/Christian/Christianity, 50-51, 61, 64, 67-68, 133, 139
chthonic, 15, 36, 39, 95-96, 133, 135, 136n, 139, 150, 164. *See also* instinct
collective, 16, 19-20, 28, 32, 35, 50-51, 62, 73, 75, 85, 88-89, 92, 96, 102, 115-116, 120-121, 143-144, 153, 157-158, 164, 167-171, 178
collective unconscious, 75, 78, 103, 115, 151
complex(es), 19-20, 25-26, 28, 52, 60, 62, 74, 76-77, 87, 102, 116, 120, 125, 127, 135-136. *See also* mother(s)/motherhood, complex; father(s) complex
Connolly, Cyril, 160, 172
Enemies of Promise, 109n
conscious/consciously/consciousness, 22-23, 28-29, 32-36, 39, 44, 48, 56-58, 61-62, 64-65, 68-70, 74-78, 83, 94, 101-102, 110, 112, 114-123, 127, 129-132, 135-138, 141, 143-144, 150, 152n, 153, 171-178
coracle(s), 116, *155*
courage, Barrie on, 153
creative/creativity, 57, 72, 76, 78, 103, 140, 144, 151, 175-176. *See also* art/artist(s)
crocodile, 110, 115, 133, 135-136, 138, 140, 143, 145, 167-168, *179*

Daedalus, 53-54, 174
Dante. *See* Alighieri, Dante Gabriel.
Darling family, 12-13, 82, 86, 88-89, *90,* 91-102, 111, 116-117, 120-121, 126-128, 129n, 131, 142-144, 151. *See also below,* by name
children, 12-13, 101, 111, 116, 129
John, 12-13, 99-101, 103, 108, 111, 115, 120
Liza (the maid), 12, 101-102
Michael, 12-13, 92, 94, 99-102, 108, 120
Mr, 12-13, 63, 89, 91-96, 101-103, 116, 118, 120-123, 128-130, 135-136, 139-140, 144-145, 168, 174
Mrs, 12-13, 26, 63, 67, 77, 81, 86, 89, 91, 94, 95-99, 101-103, 115, 120-121, 125-126, 130, 139-140, 143, 168, 174
Nana (the dog/nanny), 12-13, 91-92, 94, 102, 121, 141-142
Wendy, 12-13, 15, 63, 67, 81-83, 85-86, 88, 91, 96, 98, 101-103, 108, 111, 114-

118, 120, 125-126, 129-132, 138-141, 143-145, 174
daughter(s), 114
death, 17, 19, 44, 52-53, 58-59, 61, 64, 66, 85, 108, 110-111, 114, 123, 135-136, 142-144, 165, 168, 177. *See also* dying and resurgent gods
Demeter, 96
devil, 139
Diana, 60. *See also* Artemis
Dickens, Charles, 157
Dionysus, 15, 40, 42, *47,* 48, 46-52, 57, 62, 64, 95, 124, 138
as anticipation of Christ, 49
with beard, 20, 48
birth of, 46
characteristics, 46
connection with the father, 48
Disney, 16, 35, 172
dissociation(s), 122, 139n
divine child, 20, 120, 122-125, 127. *See also* god-child
Don Juan, 152, 152n, 153
Dostoyevsky, Feodor: *The Double,* 84
Doty, W.G.: "Hermes," 36
dragon, 133, 143
dream(s), 114, 121
Dunbar, Janet: *J.M. Barrie,* 168
dying and resurgent god(s), 15, 19, 46, 49-50, 59-64, 129-130, 133

Edinger, Edward: *The Eternal Drama,* 56
Melville's Moby-Dick, 136n
Edwardian, 62, 83, 85, 87-88, 115, 118, 122, 128, 151, 153, 157, 161
egg 124n, 125
ego, 25-26, 31, 50, 56, 60, 62, 65, 67-68, 78, 83-84, 91, 94, 102, 112, 118, 120, 126, 128, 131-133, 141-143, 145, 152n, 171, 173, 175-178
-consciousness, 22, 57, 65, 75, 84, 103, 112, 114, 117, 120, 122n, 142, 144, 153. *See also* conscious
development, 62
heroic, 152
-Self axis, 112
Eliot, T.S., 160
on James Joyce's *Ulysses,* 34
"The Waste Land," 34, 73n, 161
Erikson, E.: *Identity: Youth and Crisis,* 24

Eros (god), 38-39
eros, 94, 97
eternal boy/child/youth, 11, 16, 20, 23-24, 26, 28-29, 34, 74, 88, 125-126, 131, 139, 147, 153, 155, 165, 168-170. *See also puer aeternus*
  archetype of, 17, 147, 153, 176-177
  Barrie, J.M., as, 79, 147
  collective manifestations of, 16-17
  Jung on, 20, 125
  Peter Pan as, 15, 82, 88, 153-154, 168, 170
Eton, 109n, 168
Euripides: *The Bacchae,* 48-49

Faery/faery, 104, 106, 117, 132, 137. *See also* Celtic mythology; sidh/Sidhe
fairy(ies), 102-103, 131-133, 148, 169
fairy tale(s), 83, 88, 103, 108. *See also* fantasy; story(ies)
  "Beauty and the Beast," 83-84
  "Cinderella," 84
  "Girl Without Hands, The," 62
  the Gospels as, 84
  "Hansel and Gretel," 83-84
  link with modern fantasy, 84-85
  Peter Pan as, 83
  pschological understanding of, 83, 87
faith, 65-67
fantasy, 32, 34-35, 64, 73-74, 78, 84, 86-88, 102, 114, 118-119, 132, 151, 167
  Christian, 85
  vs. fairy tale, 84-86
  opposition of two worlds in, 85-86
  psychological vs. visionary, 86
  vs. directed thinking, 74-75
father(s), 19-20, 22, 27, 39-40, 42, 48-51, 57-60, 92, 102, 118, 122-123, 136, 140-141, 152, 152n, 164, 168. *See also* Darling, Mr; masculine
  archetype, 19-20, 50, 136
  complex, 25, 28
  Peter Pan as, 111, 131
  -puer connection 19, 49, 51-52, 58, 164
  and son, 50, 53-54, 56-57, 63
  rebellion against, 54-56, 139
feeling(s), 91, 103, 126, 136
feminine/femininity, 19, 29, 38-39, 48, 50, 52-57, 62, 95-99, 115-116, 131, 133, 135-136, 140-141, 143, 176

consciousness, 56, 114, 117
  qualities of Christ and Dionysus, 50
Frampton, Sir George, 63
Frohman, Charles, 169-170
Frye, Northrop, 69

Gantz, J.: *Early Irish Myths and Sagas,* 107-108
Gathorne-Hardy, Jonathan, 161, 163
  The Old School Tie, 158
God/Godhead, 19, 50, 56-57, 62, 116
god(s), goddess(es), 15, 17, 20, 23, 29, 32-33, 35, 38-40, 42, 45-50, 52-53, 56-58, 60-62, 75, 104, 108, 122n, 124n, 129, 132, 137-138, 151-152, 170, 178. *See also* Great Goddess; *and by name*
  -child, 123-4, 127, 151
  dying and resurgent, 15, 19, 46, 49-50, 59-64, 129-130, 133
Goethe, Johann Wolfgang, 38, 77n
  Faust II, 31, 39, 76
good form, 63, 85, 108-109, 123, 139-140, 160, 168, 173
Gospel(s), 66-67, 84
Gose, Elliott: *Mere Creatures,* 152
Great Goddess, 18, 39-40, 48, 50, 61, 111
Great Mother, 51, 111, 129, 135, 141. *See also* mother, archetype
Greenfield, Barbara: *The Father,* 152n

Hades/Pluto, 96
Haggard, Rider: *She,* 77n
Hearn, Michael: *Peter Pan,* 70, 77, 85n, 107
heaven, 114, 116
Helios, 52-53
hell, 114, 135
Hephaestus, 139n
Hermes, 15, 36, *37,* 38-40, 42-43, 46, 48, 50, 57, 59, 62, 117, 123, 140, 174
hero(s)/heroine(s)/heroic/heroism, 11, 15, 17, 22, 26, 35, 38, 50-51, 56, 59, 61-63, 67, 69, 75, 83-84, 86, 104, 107, 123-124, 129-130, 133, 141-144, 152, 160, 163-165, 169-170
Hillman, James: 29, 32, 40, 43-45, 49, 61, 141, 170, 174
  Archetypal Psychology, 119
  "Essay on Pan," 42
  "The Great Mother, Her Son, Her Hero, and the Puer," 22, 48

Hillman, James *(cont.)*
  on Jung's concept of *puer/senex,* 20-22
  Loose Ends, 153-154
  "On the Necessity of Abnormal
    Psychology," 23
  Pan and the Nightmare, 69, 95
  Revisioning Psychology, 33, 35
Hodgson, Mary, 124n, 149
Hodler, F.: *The Look Into Eternity, 162*
Hook, Captain, 15-16, *55,* 63, *79,* 85, 89, 93,
  102, 108-110, 115-116, 119-133, *134,*
  135, 136n, 145, 152n, 153, 168, 172-
  174, *179*
Huizinga, Johan: *Homo Ludens,* 150
Hyacinth, 58, 60-61

Icarus/Icarian, 15, 52-54, *55,* 124, 141, 174
identification, 15, 17, 61-62, 79, 91-92, 94,
  96-98, 109, 123, 142-143, 160, 170,
  173, 177-178
identity, 22, 24-25, 86, 94, 117-119, 135,
  138, 145, 171, 176
imaginal/imagination, 31-35, 57, 65-67, 86,
  101-102, 114, 117, 119, 121, 132, 147-
  148, 150-151, 164, 168, 170, 177
imago, 127-130. *See also* projection; symbol
incarnation, 49-50, 63, 65-68, 110, 178
incest, symbolic, 135
Indian(s), 85, 108, 129, 133, 140, 142. *See
  also* redskins
individuation, 19, 102, 112, 174, 177
inflation, 92, 94, 143
infirmitas, 23-24, 32, 45, 147
instinct/instinctive, 17, 19, 42-44, 48-49, 57-
  58, 60, 74-75, 89, 92-97, 101-102, 121,
  131, 135-136, 143. *See also* chthonic
  and archetype, 74
Internet, 175-176
I-Thou relationship, 58

Jacoby, Mario: *Individuation and
  Narcissism,* 26
Jesus, 64-68, 124. *See also* Christ
Joyce, James, 160
  A Portrait of the Artist as a Young Man,
    18, 54
  Ulysses, 34, 54, 161
Jung, C.G., 16, 19-21, 23, 26, 29, 32, 42, 43,
  57, 77n, 111, 129, 152n, 174, 176-177
  on divine child, 123

  on fantasy, 86-87
  model of the psyche, 103
  on snake(s), 135
  "Definitions," 32, 79
  Memories, Dreams, Reflections, 110n
  Mysterium Coniunctionis, 39, 45n, 112
  "On the Relation of Analytical
    Psychology to Poetry," 32, 76
  "Psychological Aspects of the Mother
    Complex," 97-98, 101, 130, 135n, 144
  "Psychology and Literature," 32, 88
  "The Psychology of the Child
    Archetype," 92-93, 114, 119-122, 125,
    140, 175
  *The Structure and Dynamics of the
    Psyche,* 78, 117-119, 127-128
  Symbols of Transformation, 48, 56-58,
    60-61, 74, 124n, 129, 130, 138, 139n,
    141-143
  "The Syzygy: Anima and Animus," 18
  "The Transcendent Function," 57
  "Two Kinds of Thinking," 75

Kafka, Franz: *The Castle,* 84
  The Trial, 84
Keats, John, 33
Kerényi, Karl: *Hermes:* 36, 38, 40, 50
Kiley, Dan: *The Peter Pan Syndrome,* 73n
king, 138
  old, 93, 137-138. See also *puer/senex;*
    senex
Kluger, Rivkah Scharf: *Psyche in Scripture,*
  132
Kohut, Heinz, 95

libido, 20, 28, 48, 50, 52, 57, 59, 128-130,
  136-137, 140-141, 143
Llewelyn Davies family, 89, 102, 150
  Arthur, 70, 79, 101, 149
  boys/children, 70, *71,* 79, 107, 147-150
  death of parents, 79, 149
  George, 70, 73n, 107, 149-150
  Jack, 107
  Michael, *10, 21, 27,* 63, 148, 149, 153-
    154, *159,*
  Morgue, 149
  Nico, 147, 149n, 150
  nurse, 124, 149
  Peter, 149
  Sylvia, 79, 99, 149

London, Edwardian, 62, 83, 129
lost boy(s), 12-13, 73, 85, 99, 101, 107-108, 110, 111, 115, 125-129, 131, 140, 173
love, 127
Lucifer, 48, 52, 54-58, 63
Lug, 137-138, 141. *See also* Tuatha De Danann

Mackay, Johnny, 148
Marlowe, Christopher: *Dr. Faustus,* 88
masculine/masculinity, 50, 53, 57, 92, 95-96, 116, 133, 140, 145, 152, 152n, 164-165
  development, 51-52, 112
matricide, 130, 143
matrix, 28, 135, 145
maturity, 16, 51, 58, 115, 131, 169
meaning, 66-68, 121n, 176, 178
Melville, Herman: *Moby Dick,* 136n
Mercurius, 39. *See also* Hermes
Mercury. *See* Hermes
mermaids, 102, 131-132, 169
Milton, John: *Paradise Lost,* 57, 76
Mithras, 61
Monick, Eugene: *Phallos,* 28
mother(s)/motherhood, 12, 17-21, 24-26, 28-29, 38, 48-49, 54, 57, 60-62, 96-99, 101-102, 111, 115-116, 120, 125-130, 132, 136-137, 140, 142--143, 149, 153, 164-165, 168-169. *See also* Darling, Mrs
  archetype 18-20, 24, 50, 97, 99, 111, 127, 129, 135-136
  -child relationship, 24, 101
  complex, negative, 26, 52, 60, 62, 98, 116, 120, 125, 127, 135-136
"mother's son," 17-18, 20, 51, 61, 89, 93, 111, 141
Mother Goddess, 50, 58, 60
myth(s)/mythology, 33, 68-80, 114, 117, 121-122, 123n, 124, 124n, 125, 129-130. *See also* story(ies)
  Celtic, 84, 103-104, *105,* 106-108, 114, 117, 123n, 132, 137
  classical, 117, 123n
  Egyptian, 124n, 133
  Norse/Northern, 112, 117
  old king motif, 93, 137-138
  psychological approach to, 43, 69, 75, 135
  trickster, 42, 117, 152-153, 173

Narcissus, 58-59, 61
narcissism, 26, 94-95, 125-126, 145
nature, 22, 40, 42, 46, 54, 60, 62, 69, 76, 115, 118-120, 124, 131-132, 138, 152
Neolithic, 122n
Neumann, Erich, 95, 176
  The Child, 24
neurosis, 129n, 140, 142, 144
Never-bird, 125
Never tree, 110-111
Neverland, 62-63, 79, 83-89, 92, 96, 101-120, 128-133, 137, 140-144, 152, 168, 170, 173. *See also* Otherworld
  cyberspace as, 176
  map of, 103
  as Purgatory, 107
Nietzsche, Friedrich, 77n
Norse/Northern mythology, 112, 117
Nuada, king, 137-138. *See also* Tuatha De Danann

Odysseus, 38, 59, 62
Ogilvy, Margaret, 72-73, 79, 149
Old Boy(s), 160, 168
old king, 93, 137. *See also* senex
opposites, 121, 153
  tension of, 57, 129n, 172
Otherworld, 103-104, 107-108, 114, 117, 141, 150. *See also* Neverland; Tir Nan' Og; Underworld
Ovid, 43-44
  Metamorphoses, 46, 52-54, 58-60
Owen, Wilfrid: "Anthem for Doomed Youth," 161

Pan, 40, *41,* 42-48, 50, 62, 95, 98, 124, 133. *See also* Hermes; Mercurius
panic, 40, 42, 95
parent(s)/parental, 19-20, 25, 51-52, 61-62, 81, 88-89, 91, 101, 163, 168. *See also* mother(s)/motherhood; father(s)
  complex, 19, 25, 62. *See also* father(s), archetype; mother(s), archetype
participation mystique, 122n
patrix, 28, 39. *See also* father(s); masculine
Peake, Mervyn: *Peake's Progress,* 31
Pentheus, 48-49, 92, 95
Persephone, 60
Perseus, 62
persona, 91, 95, 122, 133, 145

Peter Pan (character), 11, 15, 16, 26, 28, 32, 34, 36, 62-68, *68*, 70-71, 73, 77, 81-99, *100*, 101-145, *146*, 147-156, 163-165, *166*, 168-175, 177-178, *179*
  as Adam, 107
  as bird, 124
  as boy vs. youth, 152
  as boy who wouldn't grow up, 13, 15, 26, 63, 81-82, 110, 139, 144, 153
  as child hero, 124
  chthonic, 15
  as creative impulse, 63
  as divine child, 120
  as eternal youth, 15, 82, 170
  as fate, 102
  as father, 111, 131
  and Hook, 16, 63, 119-144. *See also* Hook, Captain; *puer/senex*
  lack of memory, 13, 67, 96, 122, 144-145
  as myth, 69-79, 120, 170
  mythological links, 15, 31-68
  popularization of, 34-35
  as puer, 120, 125, 144-145, 170-174, 177
  shadow aspects, 64, 172
  as spirit, 63-64, 67, 74, 142, 153, 176-177
  as tragic figure, 63-64, 67, 85, 110, 139
Peter Pan (novel/play). *See* Barrie, J.M.
Peter Pan syndrome, 73
Phaeton, 15, 52-53, 124
phallic energy/power, 48, 60, 141, 175
pirates, 81, 85, 102, 108-109, 116, 125-126, 129, 131-132, 140, 142. *See also* Hook, Captain; Smee
play/playfulness, 70-72, 114, 150-151, 171
Pluto/Hades, 96
poet(s)/poetic process, 32-33, 59n, 60, 116-117. *See also* creative/creativity
  Georgian, 161
  Romantic, 56-57, 165
  War, 161
Pop, 109, 168
Pothos, 153
Pre-Raphaelites, 160, 165
projection(s), 98-99, 127-128, 130, 138, 172, 174, 178. *See also* imago
Prometheus, 48, 52, 54-58, 64
Proteus, 45, 50
psyche/psychological, 51-52, 69, 74, 88-89, 102-103, 109, 114-123, 132, 140-145, 152n, 153, 170-171, 176, 178

psychomachia, 88
public school(s), 158-164, 167-168
puer aeternus, 16, 20, 26, 67, 74, 88, 102, 120, 125-126, 139, 141, 144-145, 153-154, 164, 170, 172, 174, 176-177. *See also* eternal boy
  as archetype of change, 29
  characteristics, 17-19, 24-25, 28-29, 51, 89, 93-94, 144-145
  early death of, 58, 59n, 61
  and father, 19, 49, 52, 58, 164
  as hero, 22, 51, 61, 141
  as "mother's son," 17, 18, 26, 51, 58, 61
  provisional life, 17
  and spirit, 20, 26, 49, 51, 61, 89
  in women's psychology, 29
puer/senex, puer-et-senex, 16, 20-23, 40, 45, 48-54, 57-58, 61, 63, 95, 137-138, 141, 144, 170

reason, and inspiration, 57
rebellion, against the father, 54-56, 139
redskins, 102, 108. *See also* Indians
religion(s)/religious, 16, 19, 32, 61, 66, 75, 103, 107, 117, 132
Rolleston, T.W.: *Celtic Myths and Legends,* 104, 106, 108
Romantic movement, 56-57, 86, 116, 160, 165. *See also* poet(s)/poetic process
Rutherford, J.: *Forever England,* 87n, 165

sacrifice, 65-68, 114, 117, 126, 140-144
Satan, 57. *See also* Lucifer
Satinover, Jeffrey, 94
  "Puer Aeternus," 24, 28-29, 145
Saturn, 153
Schumacher, Joel: *The Lost Boys,* 173-174
Schwartz-Salant, Nathan: 29
  Narcissism, 26
Scott, Robert Falcon, 165
self (ego), 176, 178
  development of, in infancy, 24-26
Self (archetype), 109, 123, 151, 152n, 178
senex, 93, 99, 101, 139, 141, 145, 153, 173, 176. *See also* old king; *puer/senex*
sex/sexual/sexuality, 16, 23-24, 29, 39, 87, 110-111, 115, 131-133, 147, 152, 163-164, 167-169, 171-172
shadow, 92, 95, 123, 132, 141-143, 157, 171-174, 176

Shakespeare, William, 32-33, 38n, 76
Shelley, Percy Bysshe: "Alastor," 59-60, 88
    Prometheus Unbound, 56, 88
shore(s), 116-117
sidh/Sidhe, 104, *105,* 106. *See also* burial
    mounds; Celtic mythology
Silenus, 20, 40, 42, 49, 138
Simon Peter, 64-68
Smee, 109, 125. *See also* pirates
soul, 115-119, 131, 172, 178
Spielberg, Steven: *Hook,* 172
spirit/spiritual, 16, 19-22, 34, 39-40, 48-56,
    60-68, 74, 84-93, 102-104, 118, 132-
    136, 141-143, 153, 164, 172-178
Stevens, Anthony: *On Jung,* 150-151
story(ies), 67-69, 101, 114, 117-120, 126,
    143, 167. *See also* myth(s)/mythology
sacred and secular, 69
stuckness, 129
symbol(s)/symbolic, 32-33, 50, 79, 84, 112-
    115, 120-121, 123n, 124, 127-132, 140-
    144, 170, 178. *See* also imago
child as, 50, 120, 125
crocodile, 133,135
dragon as, 133
egg as, 124n
golden ball as, 120
incest, 135
matricide, 130
pearl as, 120
snake, 135
syzygy, 174, 176

Tatham, Peter, 144
    The Makings of Maleness, 28n, 29, 174
thinking, directed vs. fantasy, 74-75
Tiger Lily, 108-109, 111, 131-132, 143-144
Tinker Bell, 12, *79,* 82, 99, 111, 115, 131,
    131n, 132, 139, 143-144, 167, *179. See
    also* fairy(ies)
Tir Nan' Og, 103-104
Tolkein, J.R.R., 85, 88, 167
    The Hobbit, 84
    Lord of the Rings, 84
    theory of fantasy, 84-85
Townsend, Peter Rowe: *Written for
    Children,* 81-82, 88
tragedy/tragic, 63, 85, 116
transcendent function, 78-79, 171
    divine child as, 123

transformation 29, 31, 39, 44-45, 51, 57, 60-
    61, 65, 68, 110, 115, 119, 126, 142,
    152-154, 155, 170, 172, 174-175, 177
tree, 61, 111, 112, *113,* 114, 120, 131, 136
    of Life, 112, 114
trickster, 42, 117, 152-153, 173
Tuatha De Danann, 104, 132, 137. *See also*
    Celtic mythology
Bres, king, 137
Nuada, king, 137-138
two worlds, 62, 83-86, 115, 117-118, 151,
    154, 174
two year old child, 126

unconscious, 19-20, 22, 28, 32-33, 36, 48-
    54, 60, 62, 65, 69, 71-74, 77-78, 83, 89,
    92-99, 102-103, 109-110, 114-115,
    119, 121, 127, 129-133, 136n, 138,
    140-145, 171, 177
collective, 76, 78, 103, 115, 151
Underworld, 103, 114. *See also* Neverland;
    Otherworld; Tir Nan' Og

Venus, 58, 60
von Franz, Marie-Louise, 29, 111
    *An Introduction to the Psychology of
    Fairy Tales,* 87
    Puer Aeternus, 17-18
    "The Religious Background of the Puer
    Aeternus Problem," 93

war/warfare, 157, 161, 163, 169, 172
poets, 161
water, 132-133, 135, 143
Winnicott, D.W., 125, 171
    Playing and Reality, 71-72, 74, 151
wise old man, 152, 152n. *See also* senex
Woodman, Marion, 39
    The Pregnant Virgin, 28n
    The Ravaged Bridegroom, 20
Wordsworth, William: "Ode: Intimations of
    Immortality," 116

Yeats, W.B., 160
    "The Hosting of the Sidhe," 106
    "The Stolen Child," 104, 106
    "The Wanderings of Oisin," 106
Yggdrasil, 112

Zeus, 46, 56

Studies in Jungian Psychology
by Jungian Analysts

Quality Paperbacks

Prices and payment in $US (except in Canada, and Visa orders, $Cdn)

Jung Uncorked: Rare Vintages from the Cellar of Analytical Psychology
Two vols.. *Daryl Sharp (Toronto)* ISBN 978-1-894574-21-1/22-8. 128 pp. $25 each

Jung and Yoga: The Psyche-Body Connection
Judith Harris (London, Ontario) ISBN 978-0-919123-95-3. 160 pp. $25

The Gambler: Romancing Lady Luck
Billye B. Currie (Jackson, MS) 978-1-894574-19-8. 128 pp. $25

Conscious Femininity: Interviews with Marion Woodman
Introduction by Marion Woodman (Toronto) ISBN 978-0-919123-59-5. 160 pp. $25

The Sacred Psyche: A Psychological Approach to the Psalms
Edward F. Edinger (Los Angeles) ISBN 978-1-894574-09-9. 160 pp. $25

Eros and Pathos: Shades of Love and Suffering
Aldo Carotenuto (Rome) ISBN 978- 0-919123-39-7. 144 pp. $25

Descent to the Goddess: A Way of Initiation for Women
Sylvia Brinton Perera (New York) ISBN 978-0-919123-05-2. 112 pp. $25

Addiction to Perfection: The Still Unravished Bride
Marion Woodman (Toronto) ISBNj 978-0-919123-11-3. Illustrated. 208 pp. $30/$35hc

The Illness That We Are: A Jungian Critique of Christianity
John P. Dourley (Ottawa) ISBN 978-0-919123-16-8. 128 pp. $25

Coming To Age: The Croning Years and Late-Life Transformation
Jane R. Prétat (Providence) ISBN 978-0-919123-63-2. 144 pp. $25

Jungian Dream Interpretation: A Handbook of Theory and Practice
James A. Hall, M.D. (Dallas) ISBN 978-0-919123-12-0. 128 pp. $25

Phallos: Sacred Image of the Masculine
Eugene Monick (Scranton) ISBN 978-0-919123-26-7. 30 illustrations. 144 pp. $25

The Sacred Prostitute: Eternal Aspect of the Feminine
Nancy Qualls-Corbett (Birmingham) ISBN 978-0-919123-31-1. Illustrated. 176 pp. $30

Longing for Paradise: Psychological Perspectives on an Archetype
Mario Jacoby (Zurich) ISBN 978-1-894574-17-4. 240 pp. $35

The Pregnant Virgin: A Process of Psychological Development
Marion Woodman (Toronto) ISBN 978-0-919123-20-5. Illustrated. 208 pp. $30pb/$35hc

Discounts: any 3-5 books, 10%; 6-9 books, 20%; 10-19, 25%; 20 or more, 40% .
Add Postage/Handling: 1-2 books, $6 surface ($10 air); 3-4 books, $8 surface
($12 air); 5-9 books, $15 surface ($20 air); 10 or more, $15 surface ($30 air)

Visa credit cards accepted. Toll-free: Tel. 1-888-927-0355; Fax 1-888=924-1814.

INNER CITY BOOKS
Box 1271, Station Q, Toronto, ON M4T 2P4, Canada

Tel. (416) 927-0355 / Fax (416) 924-1814 / booksales@innercitybooks.net